THE ROUTE 66 COOKBOOK

The Route 66 Cookbook

COMFORT FOOD FROM THE MOTHER ROAD

MARIAN CLARK

75th ANNIVERSARY EDITION 1926–2001

COUNCIL OAK BOOKS
SAN FRANCISCO/TULSA

Council Oak Books, LLC
1290 Chestnut Street, Ste. 2, San Francisco, CA 94109
1615 S. Baltimore, Tulsa, OK 74119
800-247-8850

The Route 66 Cookbook: *Comfort Food from the Mother Road*.

Book design by Carol Haralson. Cover and color insert design by Shannon Laskey.
Food photography by Don Wheeler.

Color photo insert credits:
Vintage postcards (p. 1); Rock Cafe, Caveman Bar-B-Q, Red Cedar Inn (p. 4);
Granny's Country Kitchen, Travis Dillon and Ted Drewes (p. 6); El Rancho Motel (p. 15);
Norma's Diamond Cafe (p. 16) courtesy of the author. All other insert photos copyright © Shellee Graham.

Recipe on page 142 from *The Pink Adobe Cookbook* by Rosalea Murphy, © 1988 by Rosalea Murphy.
Used by permission of Dell Books, a Division of Bantam Doubleday Dell Publishing Group, Inc.

Recipes on pages 2 and 3 from the *Taste of Chicago Cookbook,* © 1990 by The City of Chicago.
Used by permission of the Mayor's Office of Special Events.

Postcards on pages 163, 133, 146, 73, 75, 90, 91, 27, 55, 66 courtesy of Dorothy Earhart Marang and Pauline Earhart Davis.

Photo on page 125 courtesy of Lance Pollard.
Photos on pages 174, 182, 186, 187, and 200 by Donna Lea.
Photos of pages 172 and 190 by Liz Medley.
Photos on pages 211 and 224 by Mary Fair.

Postcards on page 118 from *Amarillo, Texas: The First Hundred Years, A Picture Postcard History,* © Ray Franks and Jay Ketelle.

Maps on endpapers and on page 19 © 1991 by R. Walkdmire. Used by permission of the artist Robert Waldmire.

Art on page 53 by Lowell David.

Graphics on page 51 © Lowell Davis Gazette. Used by permission.

Thanks to the Deli 2000 Diner, Tulsa, Oklahoma.

Library of Congress Cataloging-in-Publication Data

Clark, Marian, 1934–
        The Route 66 Cookbook / by Marian Clark
                272 p.
                Includes bibliographical references and index.
                ISBN 1-57178-095-5 (cloth)
                ISBN 1-57178-128-5 (paper)
                1. Cookery, American. 2. Restaurants—United States—Guidebooks.
        3. United States—Guidebooks. 4. United States Highway 66.
                I.Title.
                TX715.C5778   1993
                641.5'0973—dc20

Printed in South Korea.

03 04 05 06 07   5 4 3 2 1

For my husband, Ken,
and my son, Kevin,
who made this book possible.
Thank you!

CONTENTS

INTRODUCTION
TO THE 75TH ANNIVERSARY EDITION
MARIAN CLARK

Seventy-five years along, Route 66 continues to provide an eight-state culinary adventure. Menus change right along with the scenery. Highway cafes, diners, drive-ins, and occasional greasy spoons offer a patchwork quilt of all-American food that stretches for 2,400 miles and encompasses a rich tapestry of the old and the new.

As I have traveled the ribbon of eateries that makes up America's Main Street, I've discovered cuisine both fancy and simple. The amazing variety blends together to offer a dining experience like no other. One-of-a-kind eating places regularly dot the Mother Road. All eight Route 66 state organizations have maps and highway markers to direct travelers to the off ramps and a slower pace of life (see page XXIX). Route 66 is still there—it is just a little harder to find in some areas. A few segments of the old highway are gone, new construction has covered other links, but much of the historic road is available to drive. Illinois is especially well marked and has several wonderful short segments that include vintage highway signs.

The longest uninterrupted segment of Route 66 stretches through more than two dozen communities between Springfield, Missouri, and Oklahoma City. Another excellent long segment begins west of Ash Fork in Arizona and glides through high desert country to Seligman, Kingman, Oatman, and the California line.

Since I began this cookbook in the fall of 1990, many changes have taken place. There are more books and videos about the highway. Good maps are available. State groups have become more active and much more conscious of preservation. Restaurant owners, in particular, are more aware of Route 66 travelers coming through their communities.

Our foreign friends are traveling Route 66 in record numbers. They have seen television re-runs of Buzz and Todd and their Corvette on "Route 66," which aired here from 1960 to 1964. They have enjoyed Bobby Troop's music and absorbed the new documentaries and magazine articles about the highway's historical significance. Driving 66 is the perfect way to discover America. One recent visitor, Petra Brixel from Stuttgart, Germany, recorded her trip through fresh eyes and shared the experiences in an outstanding eight-part saga published in the *Route 66 Federation Newsletter*. Petra said *The Route 66 Cookbook* traveled with her as a guide to track down all the places she wanted to see—and food she wanted to eat. Petra heard firsthand stories from cafe owners and went home with her cookbook full of autographs and memories to last a lifetime.

Interest is growing in other nations, too. A crew from the United Kingdom traveled Route 66 between Chicago and Tulsa in the summer of 1999 to film fifteen episodes for their Discovery Channel. The series, "Cookabout with Greg and Max," is a regular show in the United Kingdom. The directors used both *The Route 66 Cookbook* and *The Main Street of America Cookbook* (published in 1997) to locate restaurants, food festivals, bed and breakfasts, and other favorite sights along Route 66. When Greg and Max arrived in Tulsa, they asked me to prepare a dish that had caused the most comment from all my readers—and so we made pinto bean fudge (see page 147).

To date, I have made the candy perhaps a hundred times. When the recipe was shared as the First Place Winner in the Moriarty, New Mexico, Pinto Bean Festival in 1991, I was sure that it would never work! Ann Arwood, a fellow home economist who tested many of the recipes for the book, prepared it first with certain misgivings. When she called to report success, Ann assured me the candy would be the most popular recipe in the book. She was right. Pinto bean fudge is quick, easy, and tasty. I love to serve the candy first, then tell guests about the ingredients later. Be sure to use a large capacity food processor or heavy-duty mixer for guaranteed success.

In order to collect all of the recipes and stories for this book, I traveled Route 66 many times. I have lived on or near Route 66 all my life, but the search for road food gave me a new aware-

ness and appreciation of our country. Route 66 became the destination, not just a means to go somewhere. After each excursion I would return home, record the new memories and recipes, then head out yet again with family or friends on a new voyage of discovery.

When I visited with restaurant owners, cooks, and waitresses, I always asked that they share a favorite dish. Their selections resulted in amazing variety and quality. No recipes were repeated and almost all came in family-sized portions. Eating at one-of-a kind food stops still provides the best way to experience regional cuisine. Cozy, comfortable cafes and restaurants best reflect our nation's cultural patterns. At every stop along Route 66 travelers will find real food and real people—people whose stories and lives unfold like a map. Their memories offer a giant serving of Americana that most historians have ignored.

In Illinois, age has improved the many variations from our German, Italian, and Greek heritage. Along the highway's mid-section, recipes focus on the meat-and-potatoes goodness of our no-nonsense prairie grandmothers. Throughout the Southwest, creatively seasoned Mexican and Indian flavors offer zest. Then comes California, home to twenty-first-century eclectic dishes.

Each trip down the road reminds me that nothing remains the same forever. The all-American quilt continues to change. Many of the early-day entrepreneurs and their cafes have disappeared, but their memories and recipes—many of which you will find in this book—remain. Their generation dates to a time before air conditioners and dishwashers. Their stories, landmark restaurants, and food offer a picture of what it was like to live through drought and depression, prohibition and war.

Norma and Bob (Mr. Norma) Hall have presided at *Norma's Diamond Cafe* in Sapulpa, Oklahoma, since 1950. They may hold the record for being original owners, continuously in business at the same location for the longest time.

NORMA'S CABBAGE PATCH STEW
Norma's Diamond Cafe
408 N. Mission, Sapulpa, Oklahoma

½ pound lean ground meat
1 tablespoon shortening
2 medium onions, thinly sliced
1 cup shredded cabbage
½ cup diced celery
2 cups water

1 can (15 ounces) red kidney beans, with juice
1 cup cooked tomatoes
1 teaspoon chili powder
Salt and pepper to taste
Hot mashed potatoes

In a large skillet, brown beef in shortening; drain. Add onions, cabbage, and celery and continue cooking until vegetables are golden. Add water and cook an additional 15 minutes. Add beans, tomatoes, and seasoning. Simmer 15 minutes. Serve in bowls topped with hot mashed potatoes. 6 servings.

NORMA'S HAM LOAF

2/3 pound ground smoked ham
1½ pounds ground pork
1 cup dry bread crumbs or croutons
¼ teaspoon pepper
2 eggs, well beaten
1 cup milk
¼ cup chopped bell pepper
¼ cup chopped onion
Honey and Catsup Topping

Combine all ingredients in a large mixing bowl and blend thoroughly. Form meat mixture into an oblong loaf and place in a 8½ x 11 baking dish. Bake in a preheated 325° oven for 1 hour.

HONEY AND CATSUP TOPPING:
½ cup honey
½ cup catsup
Combine honey and catsup and spread over hot ham loaf. 8 servings.

From 1926 to 1985, the Main Street of America was our nation's "road most traveled." It reflected the influence of Fred Harvey and Duncan Hines. It flourished during the days of etiquette experts like Emily Post and Amy Vanderbilt, who dictated twentieth-century manners and good taste. Fred Harvey expected all of his Harvey Houses to serve customers on linen tablecloths with matching napkins. Harvey Girls brought culture and refinement to food service all along the railroad and along Highway 66.

In the early part of the twentieth century, Emily Post's *Etiquette* dictated that fried chicken should be cut from the bone with a knife and eaten with a fork. When Route 66 businessman Beverly Osborne introduced *Chicken In The Rough,* (a 1936 Oklahoma City based franchise), he upset the fashionable standard—but Americans were ready for change. Half a fried chicken in a basket with shoestring potatoes, a roll, and honey—all for fifty cents—revolutionized our dining habits and became one of the catalysts that brought about a new and more relaxed lifestyle.

By the time I began researching this book in 1990, a spirit of nostalgia had already set in. A decade later, the Mother Road continues to draw fans new and old in search of another time. Like an old, worn quilt, Route 66 has become a warm and comfortable highway. Yet, as always, eateries remain as varied as the entrepreneurs who operate them.

For me, food continues to mark the trail. At every stop, a story unfolds. Barely north of Gardener, Illinois, the 1928 *Riviera* serves outstanding Italian food today. The first-floor barroom resembles a cave with stalactites hanging from the ceiling, a holdover from its origins as a Depression-era roadhouse. Known gangsters frequented the spot. Out back, an old, decaying dining car continues to hide other mysteries.

In Tulsa, a 1925 art deco Blue Dome Chastain Oil Filling Station is coming back to life as *Arnie's Irish Pub.* The station boasted the city's first compressed air pumps and restrooms with hot and cold running water. Tulsa entrepreneur Rick Bilby credits his great-grandfather, Oscar Weber Bilby, with serving the first burgers on buns in Indian Territory in 1891. This took place on Oscar's 640-acre ranch just north of the Route 66 community of Sapulpa. The family had a root beer stand on Route 66 in Tulsa from 1934 until 1960. Today there are three locations for Weber's Root Beer (and hamburgers). The most famous is at 3817 S. Peoria, where Oscar's original grill is still in use.

During the 90s, fire destroyed the historic *Spring River Inn* in Riverton, Kansas, and *Pop Hicks Restaurant* in Clinton, Oklahoma. Neither will be rebuilt. The long-empty *Satellite Cafe* near Lebanon, Missouri, also collapsed in ashes. An Oatman, Arizona, fire destroyed *The Mining Company,* which had replaced the *Silver Creek Saloon and Steak House.*

Other eateries have survived fire and returned. They include the *Route 66 Diners* in both Albuquerque and Tulsa, the *Range Cafe* in Bernalillo, *Clanton's Cafe* in Vinita, and *Ollie's Restaurant* in Tulsa.

Several other historic stops have come back to life. The beautifully restored *Will Rogers Hotel* in Claremore, Oklahoma, now houses a restaurant geared to healthy eating. Restaurant owner Teresa Collins says this popular recipe has only 5 grams of fat:

TORTILLA AND GREEN CHILI CASSEROLE

Café René, Located inside the Historic Will Rogers Hotel, Corner of Lynn Riggs Blvd. and Will Rogers Blvd., Claremore, Oklahoma

2 pounds ground turkey breast
1/2 cup onion, chopped
1/4 cup water
1 can (15 ounces) tomato sauce
1 envelope taco seasoning
1 1/2 tablespoons chili powder
1 can (8 ounces) green chilies
1/4 cup black olives, sliced
salt to taste (optional)
1 cup salsa, chunky style
12 corn tortillas
2 cans (10 3/4 ounces each) Campbell's Healthy Request cream of mushroom soup
1 soup can of skim milk
2 cups fat-free shredded cheddar cheese

Coat a 7 1/2 x 12 baking pan with cooking spray. Crumble and cook turkey and onion in water. Drain using a colander. Rinse with warm water to remove excess fat. Wash skillet used to cook turkey and replace turkey mixture, tomato sauce, taco seasoning, chili powder, green chilies, and black olives. Heat slowly until thick and bubbly. In a separate bowl whisk together the soup and skim milk. Pour salsa in bottom of prepared baking dish and spread evenly. Cover evenly with six tortillas. Spoon half the meat mixture and half the cheese over tortillas. Repeat layers except for salsa. Pour soup mixture over top. Bake in a preheated 350° oven for 30-35 minutes. Serve with extra salsa and nonfat sour cream. 6-8 servings.

In South Pasadena, *Fair Oaks Pharmacy* has been re-created as an authentic old-fashioned drug store. The pharmacy dates from 1915 when it was known as the South Pasadena Pharmacy. Just a stop at the antique fountain makes the trip worthwhile. Try the Route 66 Sundae, made with a giant scoop of chocolate ice cream and a giant scoop of vanilla, both topped with chocolate syrup and dusted with malt powder. The creator says the powder reminds him of dust from the road. The homemade chicken salad is one of the most popular offerings and has a faithful following.

New places have also made important marks along Route 66 during the 90s. Ideally, begin your trip at Navy Pier in Chicago and drive all the way to Santa Monica. Navy Pier took on new life in the 90s. The entertainment complex houses at least twenty eateries. Try the outstanding meatloaf at *Charlie's Ale House*. At the other end of the road, on Santa Monica Pier, *Rusty's Surf Ranch* makes for a vibrant stop. The Shrimp and Lobster Bisque always receives rave reviews.

FAIR OAKS CHICKEN SALAD SANDWICH

Fair Oaks Pharmacy, 1526 Mission Street, South Pasadena, California

2 cups coarsely chopped chicken breast
1/2 cup thinly sliced celery
1/2 cup chopped green peppers
1/2 cup chopped yellow peppers
1 teaspoon Mrs. Dash
1/2 teaspoon seasoning salt
1/2 cup mayonnaise

Combine all and mix thoroughly. Serve as salad or sandwich filling.
4-5 servings.

SHRIMP AND LOBSTER BISQUE

Rusty's Surf Ranch, Santa Monica Pier
Santa Monica, California

1 cup white wine
3 cups water
½ pound shrimp
1 ½ pounds Pacific Lobster
¼ pound butter
½ cup diced carrots
1 medium onion, diced
1 clove garlic, chopped
½ cup flour
1 tablespoon parsley

2 bay leaves
6 cups milk
3 tablespoons tomato paste
1 ounce sherry

Combine white wine and water and bring to a boil. Steam shrimp and lobster over wine broth for 7 to 8 minutes. Remove the shellfish and pull the meat from the shell.

Return the shells to the broth and reduce to 2 cups liquid. Strain the broth and chop lobster and shrimp. Hold separately. Melt butter in a soup pot. Add vegetables and sauté on medium heat for 4 to 5 minutes. Add the flour and herbs and mix well. Add milk and lobster broth and bring to a boil. Reduce heat and simmer for 30 minutes. Strain the soup into another pot and add the lobster and shrimp meat, tomato paste, and sherry. Heat over medium flame and serve. 8 servings.

Many other good eating places have arrived on the highway since the early 90s. *Caveman Bar B-Q and Steak House,* located a few miles north of Route 66 between Waynesville and Lebanon, Missouri, serves good food in a cave where locals drank and danced during prohibition. This amazing restaurant offers an eating experience that will never be forgotten.

Granny's Kitchen in Chandler, Oklahoma, serves authentic home cooking including great breakfasts. The *Yippie Yi Yo Cafe,* found inside the vintage 1910 *Kamp's Grocery* in Oklahoma City, is known for outstanding coffee, quality sandwiches, and Alfred Kamp's wonderful coconut cake.

The *Route 66 Brewery and Restaurant* can be found in historic Union Station in St. Louis, just a few blocks west of the old city alignment of Route 66, now called Tucker Boulevard. The restaurant serves this meatloaf with homemade garlic mashed potatoes, a red wine roasted garlic shallot sauce, and a medley of sautéed vegetables.

BEEF AND BISON MEATLOAF
Route 66 Brewery and Restaurant, St. Louis, Missouri

2½ pounds ground beef
1¼ pound ground bison
½ pound yellow onions, diced
6 ounces celery, diced
2 tablespoons tomato paste
1½ teaspoons salt and white pepper, mixed
3 large eggs
1½ quarts breadcrumbs

Mix all ingredients in a large bowl and form into one large or two small loaves. Bake in a preheated 350° oven for 30 minutes. Cool slightly before slicing into portions. 7-8 generous servings.

In Santa Rosa, New Mexico, the new *Lake City Diner* and *Joseph's* offer good Southwestern fare in the community made famous by the celebrated *Club Cafe* fat man.

Remember that change is inevitable. Expect new owners in new locations on every trip. In the early spring of 2000, when I made an appointment to interview fourth-generation owners of *Clanton's Cafe* in Vinita, Oklahoma, I learned that a Christmas morning fire in 1999 had destroyed much of the interior. Melissa Clanton Patrick's great-grandfather opened the hometown-friendly stop back in 1927. *Clanton's Cafe* is now remodeled and ready for customers again and Melissa and her husband, Dennis, are enthusiastically moving their treasured inheritance into the twenty-first century.

To feast on highway history today in Illinois, stop by *The Berghoff* on Adams Street where Route 66 begins. Photograph the giant Paul Bunyon at *Bunyon Drive-In* in Cicero. Meet Dell Rhea at *Dell Rhea's Chicken Basket* in Willowbrook and stop at historic *White Fence Farm* in Lemont where, among other things, brandy ice and corn fritters are world famous.

Have a sandwich at *Snuffy's* in McCook and photograph the Gemini Giant at the *Launching Pad Cafe* in Wilmington. Buy maple "sirup" at *Funk's Grove*. Visit the *Old Log Cabin Restaurant* north of Pontiac and the *Cozy Dog Drive In* in Springfield. Have a piece of butterscotch pie at *Art's Restaurant* in Farmersville or some wonderful baklava or this Pineapple Coconut Cake at *The Ariston* in Litchfield.

ARISTON PINEAPPLE COCONUT CAKE

Nick and Demi Adam
The Ariston, Litchfield, Illinois

2 cups flour
2 cups sugar
2 eggs
1 teaspoon baking powder
1 cup coconut, shredded
½ cup nuts, chopped
1 can (20 ounces) crushed pineapple, with liquid

Combine all ingredients and stir by hand. Place in a greased 9 x 13 pan. Bake at 350° for 40-45 minutes.

FROSTING:
1 (8 ounce) package cream cheese
¼ pound (1 stick) margarine, softened
1 cup powdered sugar
1 teaspoon vanilla
4 ounces whipped pie topping (Cool Whip)

Combine well with mixer. Spread frosting on cooled cake. 10-12 servings.

Regional flavors in Missouri begin at *Ted Drewes Frozen Custard* in St. Louis. Meet Ginger Gallagher at *Red Cedar Inn* in Pacific. In St. James, eat at a local favorite, *Douglas Company,* or try the wonderful pastries at *Hickory Tree Sausage Farm and Pastries.*

In Springfield, Missouri, sample Cashew Chicken, the city's signature dish, at *Leong's Tea House* or *Gee's East Wind.* Lowell Davis, near Carthage, has closed the nostalgic *Fox Fire Farm,* his re-created turn-of-the century hometown, but breakfast at *C.D.'s Pancake Hut* in Carthage remains a real treat. The *Bradbury Bishop Deli* in Webb City, Missouri, a few miles away, offers great decor from the 30s.

The *Buffalo Ranch* near Afton, Oklahoma, has also closed. But a stop at *Little Cabin Creek Pecan Company,* just east of Vinita, should be on every itinerary, to learn about and sample the abundant pecans grown along Route

66 in eastern Oklahoma. In Claremore, have a slice of prize-winning pie at the *Hammitt House* across the street from the *Will Rogers Museum* or feast on barbecue at *Cotton Eyed Joe's. Molly's*

Landing can be found in a "tastefully cluttered" barn-sized log cabin next to the twin bridges on the Verdigris River. The food is outstanding.

BLACK BEAN SALAD OR SALSA
Molly's Landing, Catoosa, Oklahoma

2 cans (15 ounces each) black beans, drained
2 cups chopped tomatoes, canned or fresh
1 can (15 ounces) white corn, drained
1 can (2½ ounces) chopped or sliced black olives
Cilantro or parsley to taste
1 can (14 ounces) chopped green chilies

¼ cup olive oil (or to taste)
Juice of 2 limes
Juice of 2 lemons
Garlic to taste
Jalapeno to taste

Combine all ingredients and adjust seasonings to taste. Serve on a fresh lettuce leaf with rings of sliced red onion or use as a salsa. 7-8 cups

Train lovers will find paradise at *Ollie's Restaurant* in west Tulsa.

BREAD PUDDING
Ollie's Restaurant, John and Lin Gray,
4070 Southwest Blvd., Tulsa, Oklahoma

1 can (29 ounces) sliced peaches, including juice
1 3/4 cups water
3 eggs
2 tablespoons vanilla extract
3/4 cup sugar (adjust to desired sweetness)
6 tablespoons margarine, melted
8 ounces non-dairy creamer
4 cups cinnamon rolls, torn in pieces (may use leftover bread, rolls, or biscuits, or a combination)

1 tablespoon cinnamon and sugar mix (1 part cinnamon to 2 parts sugar)
Raisins to taste, about 1/4 cup

Pour peaches, including juice, into a large container. Chop peaches into smaller pieces if desired. In a separate bowl, combine one cup of the water, eggs, vanilla, sugar, and margarine. Beat until creamy. Combine non-dairy creamer and remaining water and beat until smooth. Add to egg mixture. Pour egg mixture over peaches. Spread torn cinnamon rolls and/or bread evenly in a 9 x 12 buttered baking dish. Pour peach mixture over bread. Sprinkle with raisins and sugar mixture and bake in a preheated 350° oven for 35 minutes, or until lightly browned. 10-12 servings.

Try Onion Burgers in El Reno at *Johnnie's Grill, Robert's Grill,* or *Sid's Diner.* Onions are chopped and cooked into the meat in this town that has a festival to honor their unique burgers each year. The *Country Dove Gift Shop and Tea Room* in Elk City should also be on every travel itinerary for the spectacular French Silk Pie. Ruby Denton can be found at the *Golden Spread Grill* in Groom, Texas, where she has been serving her friends since 1951. This is the place to enjoy crookneck squash, fried okra, and black-eyed peas, all Southwestern summer favorites.

Get off Route 66 for a few miles for a "Cowboy Morning Breakfast" on the edge of Palo Duro Canyon south of Amarillo. An authentic outdoor experience and fantastic view awaits. Don't forget the *Big Texan Steak House, Golden Light Cafe,* and *The Blue Front Cafe* in Amarillo. They all have stories to tell.

In Adrian, Texas, meet Fran Houser at the *Adrian Cafe,* advertised as the mid-point along Route 66—1136 miles to Los Angeles, 1136 miles to Chicago. This is another cafe noted for good home cooking, and the pie—try Mel's Midpoint Coconut—is outstanding. Have a slice for me!

Tucumcari, New Mexico advertises twenty-six motels and seventeen restaurants. There were many more during Route 66 days. Don't miss the famous *Blue Swallow Motel* (under new management) and have dinner at *Del's Restaurant.*

Albuquerque has so many wonderful places to eat, it's hard to choose. Just stay awhile, you can hardly go wrong! *Lindy's* serves a mean bowl of

DEATH BY LEMON
Tom Fenton and Mat DiGregory,
Range Cafe, Bernalillo, New Mexico

CRUST AND TOPPING:
6 cups flour
3 ounces powdered sugar
1 stick cold butter, cut into small pieces
1 egg
Apricot preserves, melted and strained

Combine flour, powdered sugar, and butter in mixing bowl. Mix until it resembles oatmeal. Add egg and mix until combined. Let dough rest covered in plastic for 1 hour in the refrigerator. Spray a 9-inch cheesecake pan with cooking spray or butter. Press dough in pan bottom and up the sides approximately 2 inches. Place prepared pan

chili and remains the oldest restaurant on 66 doing business in the same location. It can be found across the street from the KiMo Theater. Be sure to have breakfast burritos at the thirty-year-old *Frontier Restaurant* across from the university. Dorothy Rainosek's staff dish out five hundred breakfast burritos each weekday and a thousand a day on weekends!

At The *Range Cafe* in Bernalillo, the food is so good that locals as well as travelers return again and again to feast on a wide variety of gourmet dishes. Their Mexican food isn't for the timid tongue, but it is the on-site bakery that first catches the eye. Death by Lemon is only one example of the pleasures that await.

La Posada Hotel in Winslow, Arizona, is open again and offers travelers an opportunity to experience Fred Harvey's last great hotel, a true piece of history. The town is also home to two remaining Valentine diners. The *Falcon Restaurant,* a must-stop location, has been presided over by the Kretsedemas family since 1955. In Flagstaff, *Miz Zip's Cafe's* wonderful old neon sign finally failed and could no longer be repaired but the longtime family owned cafe remains on the east side of town. *The Museum Club,* recognized as one of the best roadhouses in the country, should be on every itinerary.

Rod's Steak House and *Old Smokey's Pancake House and Restaurant* are longtime cornerstones in Williams, Arizona. The *House of Chan* and *4th Street Social Club* are gone in Kingman, but the Hotel Brunswick should be inspected as well as the excellent Route 66 Museum. Meet the unforgettable Juan Delgadillo at the *Snow Cap* in Seligman.

in refrigerator until filling is ready.
FILLING:
5 lemons, zest and juice
17 ounces of sugar
2 cups heavy cream
2 eggs

Combine all ingredients in mixing bowl and blend well. Pour into crust and bake in a preheated 325° oven until slightly golden brown and firm to the touch. Cool in refrigerator until set. Spread apricot preserves on top. 16 servings.

Juan and his brother, Angel, will always be associated with the rebirth of Route 66 because of their dedication to and love for the highway.

El Garces, Fred Harvey's Moorish castle, is Needles' miracle in the desert. The nearby hamlets of Goffs and Chambless Camp have faded further into the sand. In Amboy, Buster Burris has retired and leased *Roy's Motel and Cafe,* the famous stop he tried to sell for so many years.

The Summit Inn, on Cajon Pass, was established in 1952 and experienced a facelift in 1997. Hungry patrons can still talk with Hilda Fish about the day Elvis came in, discovered his recordings weren't on the juke box, and left without eating. Autographed copies of happier celebrities grace the walls. *Bono's Restaurant and Deli* is open again in Fontana. Joe Bono now runs this wonderful stop that began when his mother went into business on the road in 1936.

Sycamore Inn in Rancho Cucamonga remains the granddaddy of all eateries along 66. A hospitality house of some kind has been located in this old sycamore grove since the days of the Butterfield Stage. Reggie Sellas, the owner, doesn't share secret recipes but says the mashed potatoes are whipped with a combination of half butter and half cream cheese and are "to die for."

Pinnacle Peak in San Dimas, the *Trails Restaurant* in Duarte, the *Aztec Hotel* in Monrovia, and the *Derby* in Arcadia all have long and unique stories. Make a stop at *Barney's Beanery* on Santa Monica Boulevard then cruise on to the aforementioned *Rusty's Surf Ranch* on Santa Monica Pier for a grand finale meal.

Route 66 remains a living link to our recent past. With time, more and more of the eateries recorded in this book will disappear. There are many other good places to eat that I surely haven't discovered yet. Search for your own favorite places and flavors, and savor the people you meet and the food they serve. Ask them to autograph your cookbook. Start your own patchwork quilt of Route 66 memories.

I could not offer this expanded book without adding my own list of a dozen lasting flavors of the Mother Road. Some of these foods can be found in only one location. Other dishes are re-created in many places with many variations. For me, these foods will always reflect what Route 66 is all about.

Route 66 offers 2,400 miles of memorable food. Let your search begin!

A DOZEN UNFORGETTABLE FLAVORS OF ROUTE 66

★ Maple "sirup" from Funk's Grove, Illinois.

★ Cozy Dogs from the Cozy Dog Drive In in Springfield, Illinois.

★ Ted Drewes Frozen Custard in St. Louis—absolutely the best on the road!

★ Wine from St. James, Missouri. Try the St. James Winery or the Meramec Vineyards.

★ Six-ounce bottles of soda pop from an old-fashioned red cooler at Eisler Brothers' Old Riverton Store in Riverton, Kansas. Raise the lid, plunge your arm into icy water, and remember the days of five-cent Orange Nehi and Delaware Punch.

★ Chocolate malts, served in tall, old-fashioned glasses and poured from metal Hamilton Beach mixing cans that come right to the counter for refills. The real thing can be found at the Metro Diner in Tulsa and Fair Oaks Pharmacy in Pasadena.

★ Texas Caviar, made witblack-eyed peas spiced with jalapeño. Find it at the Big Texan Steak House in Amarillo.

★ Chicken fried steak, found anywhere real comfort food prevails. Try Clanton's in Vinita or Ollies Restaurant in Tulsa, or Rod's Steak House in Williams, Arizona.

★ Barbecue (the Southwestern favorite is beef) as it comes in no-frills locations like Johnny's Smoke Stack in Rolla, Missouri, Cotton Eyed Joe's, Dan's Barbecue Pit, or P.J.'s Bar-B-Cue in Oklahoma, or Beans and Things in Amarillo, Texas.

★ Black bean salsa, served in several locations but especially good at Idle Spurs in Barstow, Molly's Landing in Tulsa, and La Fonda Hotel in Santa Fe.

★ Indian tacos, especially good at the Ranch Kitchen or Earl's Family Restaurant in Gallup, New Mexico, or the Oatman Hotel in Oatman, Arizona.

★ Pie, frequently served by the person who baked it. Indulge in the real thing at good stops like the Adrian Cafe in Adrian, Texas, the Pink Adobe Restaurant in Santa Fe, or Art's Restaurant and Motel in Farmersville, Illinois.

ACKNOWLEDGMENTS

To the many valuable contributors who blazed the trails I have traveled, my heartfelt thanks and appreciation. Each of you has enriched this collection with your own piece of the Route 66 story!

I am especially indebted to my friend and fellow home economist, Ann Arwood, who did much of the recipe testing.

Her careful attention to detail and thoughtful comments made my job much easier. And my deep appreciation goes to her husband, J.P., for his interest, patience, and help as he sampled the wide variety of dishes Ann prepared.

Liz Medley was always available to help with research. Her skill in computer networking was invaluable in the search for accuracy.

Bob and Mary Fair made the trip from San Bernardino to the coast in California a memorable experience. They maneuvered the highways and located my stops with unbelievable ease and skill. Donna Lea was my traveling companion and photographer through Arizona and parts of New Mexico and California. Our time together became an enjoyable working vacation. Libby O'Donnell introduced me to the Carthage, Missouri, area. And Ethel Riggin traveled with me to Texas and tested some of the recipes we found there.

My husband has been a fantastic supporter from the first idea through the final manuscript. He traveled Route 66 with me, ate up the results of my recipe testing, and has been a sounding board for ideas. My son was the patient teacher who guided me through the basics of Word Perfect, calmed me down when I lost whole blocks of material, and gave me confidence to face the computer screen again. My daughter and son-in-law, Rebecca and Jason Barnes, added their creative suggestions and occasionally tested recipes.

Others have been most generous with their time and talents. Mary Gubser read my first proposal and encouraged me to begin this adventure. Michael Wallis graciously wrote the introduction for the cookbook and shared his support and enthusiasm. Dorothy Earhart Morang shared generously from her collection of Route 66 postcards. Clarence and Virginia Pleake gave me a wealth of information on restaurants I might otherwise have missed from St. Louis to Amarillo. Chuck Tegeler came to my aid with computer help.

To all the wonderful people I have met in diners, cafes, restaurants, and hotels all along Route 66, my sincere appreciation. If your story appears elsewhere in the cookbook, I have not included your name in this list. I have learned much from each of you!

I am especially appreciative of help from librarians, museum employees, and Chamber of Commerce members in communities all along Route 66 who went out of their way to be of help. I am also indebted to enthusiastic Route 66 Association members from Illinois to California.

This book would not have been possible without the help of hundreds of wonderful people who shared their stories and their recipes. Death has taken many of those friends I met along the Mother Road. I was enriched by knowing them and thankful to have begun my journey in time to record their stories. They are missed by all of us who have grown to love the road. I met Ken Sipe and Ed Waldmire in Illinois. In Missouri, I spent memorable time with Allyne Earls, Loren and Norma Alloway, Jim Sponseller, Julia Chaney, and Bob Gleeson. Howard Litch and Margaret Mary Reddy shared unforgettable stories in Kansas. Bebe Nunn, the original owner of the U Drop Inn, Grace Bruner of McLean, and Carlton Scales, Bob Dowell, and Mr. and Mrs. Homer Rice, all in Texas, enriched my life.

I spent an unforgettable evening with Lillian Redman in Tucumcari. Jerry Richard shared his love for Route 66 in Arizona. Mrs. Bono, (who never shared her first name) was one of my favorite highway queens. She was still presiding at Bono's Restaurant and Deli when I last stopped in Fontana, California.

Other road giants have retired but they have left their distinctive marks along the highway. Among them are Ernie Edwards, Lowell Davis, Cleo Noe Lamson, Linda Kelly, Howard and Mary Nichols, Cal Rogers, Ron Chavez, Lucia Kreutzer, Peggy Putnam, and Buster Burris.

These people also deserve special thanks:

ARIZONA

Angel and Vilma Delgadillo, Seligman; Janice Griffith, Winslow; Edith Hester, Holbrook; Rose Hilgedick, Flagstaff; Lynda Moore, Kingman; Carol Naille, Flagstaff; Jerry Richard, Kingman; Tommy Thompson, Winslow; Peter Werdermann, El Tovar, Grand Canyon; Flagstaff Chamber of Commerce staff.

ILLINOIS

Mark Abrahams, Chicago; Charlotte Beeler, McLean; Peter Berghoff, Chicago; Paul Fine, Springfield; Glaida Funk, Funks Grove; Anthony Lauck, Springfield; Susan Lock, Office of the Mayor, Chicago; Jeff and Laura Meyer, Illinois Rt. 66 Association; Ken Price and Kaarin Anderson, Chicago; Tom Teague, Illinois Rt. 66 Association; Robert Waldmire, Rochester; Edwardsville Chamber of Commerce.

MISSOURI

Wayne and Pat Boles, Rolla; Lowell and Charlotte Davis, Carthage; Sandy Dunn, Springfield Chamber of Commerce; Robert Elgin, St. James; Alberta Fisher, Waynesville; Danny Hensley, Carthage; John Hensley, Waynesville; Ramona Leaman, Lebanon; Barbara Letterman, Marshfield; Bob and Ada Moore, Lebanon; Ida Painter, Halltown; Mr. and Mrs. Tommy Pike, Springfield; James Powell, St. Louis, Missouri Route 66 Association; Jerry and Thelma White, Halltown.

KANSAS

Mary "Tiny" Finley, Riverton; Howard Litch, Galena; Scott Nelson, Riverton; Carolyn Nichols, Baxter Springs; Margaret Mary Reddy, Baxter Springs; Dorothy Spencer Waddell, Baxter Springs; Baxter Springs Museum staff.

OKLAHOMA

Ruth Sigler Avery, Tulsa; Jack Collins, Verdigris; Debi Durham, Miami Chamber of Commerce; Chief Eaton, Sapulpa; Jeanette Haley and Pauline Boos, Lincoln County Historical Museum, Chandler; Melvena Heisch, Oklahoma Historical Society, Oklahoma City; Mike Higgs, Tulsa; Suzanne Holloway, Tulsa; Miriam Horn, Stroud; Louise Johnson, Edmond; Mira Kemp, Bristow; Mary Martinkewiz, Tulsa; Marjorie Meggs, Edmond Historical Society Museum; Susan Phelps, Elk City; Lynnda Sooter, Ex. Dir., Vinita Chamber of Commerce; Annabell Southern, Vinita; Debbie St. John, OKC Chili Hoochpod; Tulsa City/County Library staff members; Francis Webb, Miami; Rosilyn Warren, Tahlequah.

TEXAS

Katherine Byler, Amarillo; June Ehresman, Glenrio; Bertha Lea Faulkner, Amarillo; Helen Hutcheon, Amarillo; Robert and Priscilla Jacobson, Adrian; Bobby Lee, Amarillo; Rue Nell Marshall, Tacoma, WA; Bebe Nunn, Shamrock; Wayne Smith, Amarillo; Delbert Trew, McLean.

NEW MEXICO

Karen Armijo, Moriarty; Paty Ayre, Moriarty; Lisa Bertelli, Santa Fe; Amelia Crowther, Gallup; Lenore Diaz, Gallup Tourist Bureau; Howard Hill, Albuquerque; Eskie Mazon, Grants; Moriarty Museum staff; Dave Nidel, Route 66 Association of New Mexico, Albuquerque; Joshua Peino, Bernalillo; Santa Fe Convention and Visitors Bureau; Winnie Steele, Albuquerque; David and Becky Steele, Albuquerque; Tucumcari Chamber of Commerce.

CALIFORNIA

Robert Balestra, Monrovia; Dennis Casebier, Goffs; Vivian Davies, California Route 66 Association, LaVerne; Bill Delaney, Barstow; Sara Faulds, Santa Monica; Ann Flower, Santa Monica; JoAnn Robuck, Rancho Cucamonga; San Bernardino Chamber of Commerce; Tom Snyder, Oxnard. Route 66 Association of Illinois: 2743 Veterans Parkway, Suite 166, Springfield, IL 62704.

ROUTE 66 ASSOCIATIONS

STATE ORGANIZATIONS

ARIZONA
Historic Route 66 Assn. Of AZ
PO Box 66
Kingman, AZ 86402
(520) 753-5001

CALIFORNIA
California Historic Route 66 Assn.
2117 Foothill Blvd. #66
La Verne, CA 91750
(310) 997-9817

ILLINOIS
Route 66 Assn. Of Illinois
2743 Veterans Pkwy, Room 166
Springfield, IL 62704
(815) 998-2300

KANSAS
Kansas Route 66 Assn.
PO Box 169
Riverton, KS 66770
(316) 848-3330

MISSOURI
Missouri Route 66 Assn.
PO Box 8117
St. Louis, MO 63156
(417) 358-7742

NEW MEXICO
New Mexico Route 66 Assn.
1415 Central NE
Albuquerque, NM 87106
(505) 298-2809

OKLAHOMA
Oklahoma Route 66 Assn.
PO Box 21382
Oklahoma City, OK 73156
(405) 258-0008

TEXAS
Old Route 66 Assn. of Texas
PO Box 66
McLean, TX 79057
(806) 267-2719

NATIONAL ORGANIZATIONS

National Route 66 Federation
PO Box 423
Tujunga, CA 91043
(818) 352-7232

FOREIGN ORGANIZATIONS

BELGIUM
Route 66 Assn. of Belgium
Georges Moreau St 172
1070 Brussels
BELGIUM
32-2-6402635

CANADA
Canadian route 66 Assn.
PO Box 31061
Port Moody, BC
V3H 4T4 CANADA
(604) 341-6634

FRANCE
French Route 66
30 Rue de Cerisiers
91160 Longiumeau
FRANCE

Assn. Francaise Route 66
88 Rue de Chateau
F. 92600 Asnieres
FRANCE

JAPAN
The U.S. Route 66 Club
c.o Itochu Fasion System Co.
4-1-3, Kyutaro-machi
Chuo-ku, Osaka City
JAPAN 541

THE NETHERLANDS
The Dutch Route 66 Assn.
PO Box 2013
1620 EA Hoorn
NETHERLANDS

Route 66
Post Bus 28
7730 AA Ommen
NETHERLANDS

INTRODUCTION

MICHAEL WALLIS

Route 66 and everything it stands for remains one of my passions. As I sit at my desk in Tulsa, Oklahoma, the old highway is only a few miles away. Chunks of the original pavement from various locations are in my collection of cherished totems. Memories of the people and places from the road are indelibly stamped in my mind. One of the nation's first continuous spans of paved highway coupling east and west, Route 66 is not just another American highway. For millions of travelers, this artery has forever meant "going somewhere."

Many of my best remembrances come from the Mother Road—as John Steinbeck called the highway in his novel, *The Grapes of Wrath*. Known as "America's Main Street," the famous Route 66 name alone invokes a spectrum of images.

To truly comprehend the attraction of Route 66 it is helpful to understand the old road has endured several eras of history. Each one has left an unalterable impression on the people who live and work along the highway and those travelers who still prefer its well-worn lanes. I urge everyone to revisit one of the fabled highway's incarnations. The trip is made easier because of the literature, film, and music that deals with the fabled highway. Simply allow your imagination and mind to take you back in time.

You could return to the bittersweet 1930s, when migrants and refugees fled the Depression and Dust Bowl. They headed west on Route 66 to the land of milk and honey in California. Perhaps you should experience the years of World War II. Civilians had little or no gasoline and tires, auto manufacturing ceased, and the highway was filled with troop convoys. You may be better served by revisiting the period after the war's end—during the decades that make up the glory years of Route 66.

Come back with me to June 1952.

It was another time, another place. I was six years old. I recall people in their backyards searching the night sky for flying saucers. Newspapers offered the latest reports on labor strife and atomic tests. The Korean Conflict raged. Threat of a polio epidemic gripped the land. Out of Wisconsin Senator Joe McCarthy, blinded by rancor and fear, prepared for his insidious Communist witch hunt.

Despite the discord and apprehension, all was right with the world if you happened to be like me—a kid growing up in Missouri within easy striking distance of Route 66.

Although Harry Truman was not running for another term, our family was proud that the Show-Me State's favorite son was still President of the United States. Down at the neighborhood theater, my small band of friends felt that Gary Cooper was worth every penny of admission, portraying the stoic lawman in "High Noon." Our television favorites included "I Love Lucy," "The Ernie Kovacs Show," and "The Adventures of Ozzie and Harriet." I also never missed "Dragnet," starring Jack Webb as the poker-faced Sergeant Joe Friday.

Much to my delight, plastic vinylite swimming pools and "Mad" comics made their debut that summer. So did the mechanical lawn mower. Most of my attention, however, was turned to "The Man" Musical. The St. Louis Cardinal slugger was on his way to winning the National League batting crown with a hefty .335 average. I can still see the blimps and skywriting airplanes flying above my neighborhood. I remember uniformed service station attendants pumping gas and washing windshields without having to be asked.

Best of all, June meant it was summertime. School was out for three whole months. Everyone went on vacation. If you were a kid of summer back then, like I was, you only worried about capturing more lightning bugs than your pal, explaining grass stains on your good pants to Mom, and trying to collect enough pop bottles for refunds in order to buy baseball cards as well as firecrackers for the Fourth of July.

On most June days just after dawn the air remained cool. But as the sun climbed higher, the dreaded St. Louis humidity was already sneaking out of the damp lawn and off the hillside covered with honeysuckle. Thank God for attic fans and sun-brewed tea.

Out in the garage, my Dad packed and repacked suitcases, thermos bottles, road maps, ball gloves, fishing gear, and the other essentials needed to keep a family going for two whole weeks. His pride and joy—the shiny green Plymouth—finally was loaded. Every item was checked off the list. Our dog was in the kennel and the parakeet was temporarily residing with friends. The milkman was alerted. Neighbors vowed to water the tomatoes and take in the mail and papers. My mom got every bill paid and birthday card off. It was time for us to take to the open road.

Just the act of "getting there" was an important part of our vacation experience. We didn't want to be gypped out of a single moment so we made the drive an indispensable component of the overall trip. There was an assortment of manmade and natural attractions to visit, tourist traps to survive, detours to avoid, and truck stop meals to consume. Less than thirty years later people would be more interested in their final destination than in the process of traveling. American families would be flying off to tennis resorts and dude ranches or taking impersonal interstate highways that might as well be airport runways to one of countless look-alike theme parks crowding the country. "Getting there" would not matter any more. That was not the case in 1952.

No way.

In 1952 and throughout the heyday of Route 66 windows were cranked down. Black-eyed Susans and Queen-Anne's lace lining the road flashed by as Dad mashed the gas pedal. Everyone else tried to figure out when the first pit stop would occur. I stuck my stocking feet out the back window into the summer breeze. The voices of Peggy Lee, Eddie Fisher, Teresa Brewer, and Hank Williams poured from the radio. The Mother Road beckoned. I dreamed of all the reptile farms, Indian artifacts, and outlaw hideouts that waited for me further down the highway. My mouth watered for cheeseburger platters and thick chocolate malts. The fantasy had begun. My hunger for the road and all that lay ahead grew with each passing mile.

The excitement of traveling was certain whether our family headed east, across the Mississippi River into Illinois and inched up Route 66 through the "Land of Lincoln" to Springfield or Chicago, or drove west out of St. Louis. Route 66 ambled down the Ozark Plateau, and pushed onward to Kansas, Oklahoma, Texas, New Mexico, Arizona, all the way to the California shore. In either direction there was plenty of pure adventure. Nothing was predictable. The potential for an escapade lurked around every curve and bend.

There was excitement just in the dining experience. Food has never taken a back seat on Route 66. It never will.

In those glory years on Route 66, if my family had not stopped at a particular cafe or truck stop before, there was no way to know what waited inside. A person could wind up with a case of ptomaine poisoning or else find the ultimate feast—a burger or a piece of freshly fried chicken so juicy it was necessary to use a dozen napkins to sop off hands and chin.

Along the many surviving stretches of Route 66 through eight states remain greasy spoons and pie palaces where folks have been serving up generous helpings of hospitality for generations.

Authentic oases, many of them family-owned, still turn out home cooking. These meals are made on the premises, not bland turnpike food or franchise fare that has been processed and shipped from a factory thousands of miles away. Diners anxious to rid themselves of hunger pangs can actually sit at a lunch counter and watch their meal prepared right before their eyes. Biscuits are piping hot, there are lumps in the mashed potatoes. As the Puritan poet Edward Taylor would have put it if he had been able to sit down to a Route 66 blue plate special: "It's food too fine for angels."

At genuine Route 66 eateries, the cooks rely on the gifts of summer—ripe peaches and berries for cobblers and pie, as well as tomatoes, cantaloupe, and sweet corn. As travelers of the old road move through hundreds of small towns and villages, they find the cuisine changes right along with the scenery. The journey on Route 66 features a variety of dishes, ranging from ethnic to the gamut of purely American vittles.

Standard road chow along the way usually means bumper crops of chili, omelettes, biscuits and gravy, pancakes, meat loaf, enchiladas, chicken fried steak, barbecue, pork chops, catfish, fried chicken, tacos, spare ribs, stew, hamburgers, hash browns, coleslaw, baked beans, grilled red onions, ice cream, short cake, and pie. There is enough iced tea, coffee, and soda pop to drench the Mojave. Or else tie into a slab of watermelon so cold it makes your teeth ache.

There are many others like me who have never lost their appetite for traveling Route 66, or for the basic honest-to-goodness road food that has fueled us all. Thankfully, the recipes for the best dishes from the old highway have been collected and are presented in The Route 66 Cookbook.

In this superb book, Marian Wilson Clark has captured the sizzle and spice from the most venerable kitchens on Route 66. She truly shares with her readers all the flavor and spirit—both past and present—of the "movable feast" that is the Mother Road.

Like other excellent books dealing with the art of turning raw ingredients into palatable feasts, it is actually a misnomer to label this fine effort as just a cookbook, even though, in truth, that is exactly what it is—a volume chock full of directions for cooking and recipes for hundreds of time-tested dishes. Yet, the author goes far beyond the traditional information found in most cookbooks, to provide essential road wisdom and insight that helps keep the road alive. You can smell the fresh-cut hay and hear the change in dialect as your car glides down the pavement.

If you fancy yourself to be a true "road warrior" and savor hot food and cold drink, you will understand that meal stops are still the best way to mark your trail when traveling this country's most famous highway. You will also be sure to break out your bib and tucker when pouring through the pages that follow. Relish each and every morsel. Remember that these are the treasured recipes of men and women who help preserve a key length of Americana.

"Big time" food critics might not recognize the Mother Road's cafes, truck stops, and diners as depositories for the nation's most revered gastronomic delights. It's true, there's certainly nothing fancy about the people or the food of Route 66. Don't look for too much fancy cooking on the Mother Road. Be that as it may, the fact remains that by reading this book and taking to the open road you will come away with a better notion of what this nation was like before we allowed our culture and our collective palate to become homogenized.

Enjoy the cruise. And don't forget—save room for the pie.

ILLINOIS

I

Illinois. **What better place to begin an exploration of good food and good places to eat along Route 66 than at the premier food event of the summer in Chicago, a festival that is celebrated right where Route 66 began its 2,400-mile journey across America.**

Grant Park on Lake Michigan at Jackson Boulevard offers a cool oasis in sweltering mid-summer Chicago heat. The city has capitalized on this wonderful waterfront asset by offering its citizens eight days of fabulous food and nonstop family entertainment billed as "America's City Picnic," the Taste Of Chicago Festival.

The Festival reflects mid-America in all its variety. Each year, an estimated 2.5 million people wander through the park seeking best sellers like veal porcini, toasted ravioli, white chocolate brownies, crab cakes, fried ice cream, potato skins, and a whole world of unbelievable cheesecakes. Restaurant, hotel, and tavern vendors are prepared to satisfy every gourmet whim and each year the list of participants grows longer. Currently, over seventy Chicago area restaurants offer ethnic specialties and all-American favorites. Cooking experts from around the world share culinary secrets and a chili championship is up for grabs.

In 1926, when the dream for a cross-country road was fulfilled and Route 66 was certified, Chicago was already a city with a rich cultural heritage. Route 66 became the artery along which our history would merge. In Grant Park, where Route 66 began, the blending takes place anew each summer.

These three recipes make noteworthy additions to the festival and typify the diverse cultures that make up Chicago. Like the Taste of Chicago festival, the cuisine reflects the city at its best!

POLKA SAUSAGE AND DELI POTATO PANCAKES

3 LARGE POTATOES, GRATED (ABOUT 3 CUPS)
1½ TO 2 TABLESPOONS FLOUR
2 EGGS
1 TEASPOON MILK
1 TEASPOON SALT
DASH PEPPER
CORN OIL
SOUR CREAM AND/OR APPLESAUCE

DRAIN POTATOES WELL. Add flour, stirring lightly. Beat eggs with milk and stir into potatoes with salt and pepper. Add more flour if mixture appears too loose. Heat 2-3 tablespoons oil in a large skillet. Drop potato mixture by spoonfuls into hot oil. Flatten slightly with back of spoon. Cook, turning once, until golden brown on both sides, about 2-3 minutes. Add more oil to the skillet as needed. Serve hot with sour cream and/or applesauce. *4 to 6 servings.*

TASTE OF CHICAGO MARINATED SEAFOOD SALAD

SEAFOOD

½ CUP WHITE WINE
½ CUP BOTTLED CLAM JUICE
2 BAY LEAVES
½ POUND SWORDFISH, CUT INTO ½-INCH CUBES
½ POUND BAY SCALLOPS
½ POUND MEDIUM SHRIMP, PEELED AND DEVEINED
½ POUND SQUID, CLEANED, IN RINGS (OPTIONAL)
12 CHERRYSTONE CLAMS, RINSED
24 MUSSELS, BEARD REMOVED, RINSED

MARINADE

JUICE OF 2 LEMONS
2 CLOVES GARLIC, MINCED
JUICE OF 2 LIMES
SALT AND PEPPER TO TASTE
¾ CUP OLIVE OIL
½ EACH RED, YELLOW AND GREEN PEPPER, DICED SMALL
10 SPRIGS CILANTRO, CHOPPED
10 SPRIGS FLAT-LEAF PARSLEY

6-8 LARGE RED LEAF LETTUCE LEAVES, CHOPPED

In large saucepan combine wine, clam juice, and bay leaves. Add swordfish, scallops, shrimp, and squid (if desired). Bring to simmer. Simmer, covered, over medium heat 5 minutes. Remove cooked fish with slotted spoon to large bowl; allow to cool. Add clams to simmering liquid; cover and cook until clams open. Discard shells and add clam meat to other fish. Add mussels to simmering liquid and repeat process, but discard only half of each mussel shell, leaving the meat clinging to one side. Reduce liquid to 1/4 cup and strain over fish.

FOR THE MARINADE, combine marinade ingredients, mix with cooked seafood, and allow to marinate in refrigerator at least 2 hours, or overnight if possible. To serve, place lettuce leaves on each plate as a bed. Spoon seafood onto each plate, arranging 3 or 4 mussels attractively around it. Garnish with peppers.

This salad also makes a beautiful presentation arranged on one large platter. It is great for parties and buffets. *8 servings.*

ELI'S CHICAGO'S FINEST, INC. WHITE CHOCOLATE MACADAMIA CHEESECAKE

CHOCOLATE COOKIE CRUST

1 PACKAGE (9 OUNCES) CHOCOLATE COOKIE WAFERS
½ CUP PLUS 1 TABLESPOON UNSALTED BUTTER

CHEESECAKE

1½ POUNDS CREAM CHEESE, AT ROOM TEMPERATURE
¾ CUP PLUS 2 TABLESPOONS SUGAR
2½ TABLESPOONS SIFTED COCOA
1 TABLESPOON SIFTED FLOUR
¼ TEASPOON SALT
2 TEASPOONS VANILLA
2 WHOLE EGGS
1 EGG YOLK
3 OUNCES SEMI-SWEET CHOCOLATE, MELTED
¾ CUP WHIPPING CREAM
2 OUNCES TOASTED MACADAMIA NUTS
2 OUNCES CHOPPED WHITE CHOCOLATE

WHIPPED CHOCOLATE GANACHE

1 CUP WHIPPING CREAM
3 OUNCES BITTERSWEET CHOCOLATE CHIPS

FOR CRUST, butter bottom and sides of a 9- or 10-inch springform pan with about 1 tablespoon butter. Grind the cookie wafers and put cookie crumbs in pan; add ½ cup melted butter. Toss until butter is absorbed. Press crumb mixture onto bottom and sides of pan. Refrigerate until firm, approximately 10 minutes.

FOR CHEESECAKE, BEAT CREAM CHEESE AND SUGAR in large mixing bowl until smooth. Beat in cocoa, flour, salt, and vanilla. Add eggs and egg yolk, one at a time, beating after each addition until very smooth. Add melted semi-sweet chocolate and beat until chocolate is well incorporated. Beat in whipping cream. Chop macadamia nuts coarsely. Fold in chopped nuts and white chocolate by hand.

Pour into prepared chocolate crust. Bake at 350° for 5 minutes. Reduce oven temperature to 325° and bake 35 to 40 minutes more. Cool on wire rack 2 hours. Refrigerate several hours or overnight before unmolding.

FOR GANACHE, HEAT WHIPPING CREAM TO SIMMERING in a saucepan. Remove from heat and whisk in bittersweet chocolate chips. Whisk until chocolate is completely melted and mixture is smooth. Refrigerate until thoroughly chilled, preferably overnight. Whip chilled mixture gently until soft peaks form. Do not overmix. Smooth whipped ganache evenly on top of cheesecake. (Extra ganache may be frozen for later uses or enjoyed as an ice cream topping). Decorate cake with toasted macadamia nuts or chocolate shavings, if desired. *One 9- or 10-inch cake.*

The Palmer House Hilton

Near Lakeshore Drive and Jackson Boulevard, two premier hotels provide customers with the same quality service and gourmet food they were famous for in 1926. The Palmer House Hilton and The Blackstone are Route 66 anchors. Their tradition of excellence has made them landmark hotels where the historic road began.

The Palmer House Hilton, at 17 East Monroe, is one of Chicago's grand hotels. The ground floor, with antique lighting fixtures and a patterned marble floor, houses an arcade with gleaming shops, restaurants, and service establishments. But it's the lobby, one flight up, that commands attention. Richly carpeted and opulently furnished, The Palmer House Hilton remains the ultimate emblem of a bygone era. It was built by Potter Palmer, a merchant and real estate promoter who revolutionized sales techniques in the late nineteenth century. About 1865 Levi Leiter and Marshall Field became Palmer's partners. In 1881, their unique enterprise became Marshall Field and Company.

The hotel restaurants continue to be highly acclaimed, offering mid-continent cuisine in world-class surroundings. At The Palmer House Hilton, the convenience and comfort of the present combines perfectly with the elegance and history of the past. Here is the Palmer House Hilton's excellent gumbo. For another delicious gumbo recipe that produces a smaller yield, try Route 66 Fish Gumbo.

PALMER HOUSE HILTON FRENCH QUARTER SEAFOOD GUMBO

2 QUARTS OIL
¾ POUND FLOUR
2 POUNDS FRESH SLICED OKRA
3 POUNDS DICED ONIONS
1 POUND DICED CELERY
2 POUNDS DICED GREEN PEPPERS
2½ OUNCES CHOPPED GARLIC
1 BAY LEAF
3 GALLONS SHRIMP OR SEAFOOD STOCK
2 OUNCES GUMBO FILÉ
3¾ OUNCES LOBSTER BASE
3 OUNCES SALT
1 OUNCE BLACK PEPPER
1 TABLESPOON WHITE PEPPER
¾ TEASPOON CAYENNE PEPPER
¾ OUNCE GRANULATED ONIONS
1 OUNCE GRANULATED GARLIC
1 TEASPOON THYME
1 TEASPOON OREGANO
¾ OUNCE PAPRIKA

GARNISH

4 OUNCES CRAB
6 OUNCES CHICKEN
6 OUNCES ANDOUILLE SAUSAGE
4 OUNCES OYSTERS
8 OUNCES BUTTERED, COOKED RICE

IN A LARGE STOCK POT, heat oil until it begins to smoke. Add flour. Cook until medium brown in color. Add okra. Cook until it breaks up. Add onions, celery, and green pepper. Cook for 20 minutes. Add garlic. Cook 5 minutes.

Add bay leaf, stock, lobster base and spices. Simmer for ½ hour and add garnish.

Check crab for shells. Sauté chicken breast and dice. Cube sausage. Poach oysters in vermouth. Add to soup. *3 gallons.*

ROUTE 66 FISH GUMBO

½ POUND FRESH OKRA, SLICED

2 TABLESPOONS OIL

¼ CUP DICED HAM

1 MEDIUM ONION, CHOPPED

1½ TEASPOONS FLOUR

¼ CUP BELL PEPPER, DICED

¼ CUP DICED CELERY

1½ TEASPOONS FRESH AND CLEANED PARSLEY, CHOPPED

1 BAY LEAF

1 CLOVE GARLIC, MINCED

¾ TEASPOONS THYME

4 OUNCES TOMATO SAUCE

1 MEDIUM TOMATO, CHOPPED

3 CUPS BOILING WATER

¼ POUND CRABMEAT

½ POUND SHRIMP, PEELED

½ PINT OYSTERS WITH LIQUOR

SALT AND PEPPER TO TASTE

1 TO 2 TEASPOONS GUMBO FILÉ

COMBINE OKRA AND OIL IN A HEAVY POT WITH LID. Cook slowly for 25 minutes. Add ham and onions and cook 10 minutes. Sprinkle flour over mixture and stir until browned. Add just enough water to prevent sticking. Add bell pepper, celery, parsley, bay leaf, garlic and thyme, stirring constantly. Add tomato sauce and simmer 5 minutes. Add chopped tomato, then slowly add boiling water. Simmer slowly for 2 1/2 hours, adding extra water if necessary.

During the last 20 minutes, add crabmeat and shrimp. Salt and pepper to taste. About 10 minutes before serving, add the oysters and liquor. Stir and taste. Finally, add 1 to 2 teaspoons gumbo file. Serve hot. *8 cups.*

The Blackstone Hotel, at 636 South Michigan Avenue, offers vintage elegance and old-fashioned hospitality. The hotel opened amidst a great deal of fanfare on April 16, 1910, with Enrico Caruso as guest of honor. It was built in the French Renaissance style by Tracy and John B. Drake at a cost of three million dollars.

The Drakes named their hostelry in honor of the late Timothy Blackstone whose home had been located on the site. The Blackstone family crest still embellishes silverware, china, and linen at the hotel.

The celebrated twenty-two-story hotel has been the scene of numerous events that have helped shape our nation's history. The term "smoked-filled room" was coined at the Blackstone after Harding's nomination was secured behind the closed doors of Room 408 in 1920.

Many political figures, among them Presidents Truman and Eisenhower, have been guests of the Blackstone, and Will Rogers called it home when he stayed in Chicago. In 1985 a group of investors purchased the old hotel and began restoring it. It is now on the National Register of Historic Places.

Chequers Restaurant is the Blackstone's cozy 1940s-style grille. The Burnham Park Tap offers an intimate setting where guests can relax.

BLACKSTONE HOTEL TOM COLLINS

JUICE OF ½ LEMON
I TABLESPOON BAR SUGAR
2 OUNCES GIN
I SPLIT SODA

STIR TOGETHER THE LEMON JUICE AND SUGAR. Add the gin and pour into a tall glass with a couple of ice cubes. Add soda. Stir well and relax. *1 serving.*

Leaving Grant Park, Route 66 travelers will find The Berghoff restaurant at 17 West Adams Street. Established in 1898, this family-owned institution serves its many customers amid the skyscrapers of Chicago's Loop.

The extensive menu at Berghoffs changes seasonally. It includes classic German fare as well as lighter contemporary entrees. A variety of fresh seafood is always available.

An on-premise bakery produces tempting desserts as well as an outstanding brewer's loaf and robust traditional rye bread. At the Berghoff Cafe, sandwiches are available at an informal old-time stand-up bar. The Bergoff also brews its own all-malt beers.

The atmosphere is turn-of-the-century with large dining rooms surrounded by ornate woodwork and stained glass. The rush of city life is forgotten in a visit to this fine restaurant where Route 66 begins.

The Berghoff

BERGHOFF'S ALPEN RAGOUT

2½ POUNDS VEAL, SLICED IN 2 INCH STRIPS
¼ POUND BUTTER
¼ POUND FRESH MUSHROOMS, THINLY SLICED
½ POUND ONIONS, THINLY SLICED
I½ CUPS BROWN GRAVY
3 OUNCES WHITE WINE
SALT AND PEPPER TO TASTE
3 DASHES TABASCO SAUCE
4 OUNCES SOUR CREAM

BROWN VEAL IN BUTTER. Sauté mushrooms and onions in butter and add to meat. Add the gravy and wine and cook for 20 minutes. Season to taste with salt, pepper, and Tabasco sauce. Add sour cream just before serving. *5 generous servings.*

Until the mid-1940s, a premier Fred Harvey Restaurant was located at the Union Station next to the Chicago River.

A few blocks further, where Halsted crosses Jackson and Adams, the Greek Town Festival offers a weekend of delectable food each August. Over fifteen Greek restaurants participate in a kaleidoscope of festivities that include dancing, music, games, and plenty of traditional food.

Panagiotis Liakouras, president of the Greek Town Association and owner of the nearby Parthenon and Courtyards of Plaka restaurants, shares these Greek favorites.

1½ POUNDS KEFALOTIRI OR PARMESAN CHEESE, GRATED

SAUCE

1 CUP (2 STICKS) MARGARINE OR BUTTER
¾ CUP CORNSTARCH
2¼ CUPS MILK, HEATED
4 LARGE EGGS
½ CUP CHOPPED PARSLEY
SALT AND PEPPER, TO TASTE

STEAM POTATOES UNTIL JUST TENDER; PAT DRY. Slice and fry eggplant, potatoes, and zucchini in batches in olive oil until lightly browned. Remove and drain. Drain most of oil from cooking pan and add garlic. Cook gently until soft, about 4 minutes. Drain.

Preheat oven to 325°. Place half of grated cheese in greased 9 x 13 baking dish. Arrange sliced potatoes, then zucchini and eggplant over cheese. Sprinkle with garlic, then add salt and pepper to taste.

FOR SAUCE, melt margarine or butter in medium saucepan. Add cornstarch and stir until smooth. Add the milk and stir constantly for several minutes, until sauce is almost as thick as mashed potatoes. Add additional milk if necessary. Remove from heat. Beat eggs in a bowl; add to the sauce along with the parsley. Salt and pepper to taste.

Pour sauce over layered vegetables so that all are covered. Top with remaining cheese. Bake until top begins to brown, about 50 minutes. *8 to 10 generous servings.*

PARTHENON VEGETARIAN MOUSSAKA

2 IDAHO POTATOES, SLICED ½ INCH THICK (1 POUND)
2 SMALL EGGPLANT, SLICED ½ INCH THICK (2 POUNDS)
2 SMALL ZUCCHINI, SLICED ½ INCH THICK (1 POUND)
4 CLOVES GARLIC, CHOPPED
OLIVE OIL FOR FRYING

PARTHENON SAGANAKI

½ CUP MILK
I EGG
¼ POUND KASSERI CHEESE, CUT IN ½-INCH SLICES
FLOUR
VEGETABLE OIL
BRANDY, HEATED
LEMON HALVES

BEAT MILK AND EGG TOGETHER. Dip each slice of cheese in milk mixture, then in flour to coat. Refrigerate I to 3 hours. Heat about ¼ inch oil in skillet. Brown cheese slices on each side. Remove and place on heated metal steak plates or individual skillets. Pour about I tablespoon of brandy over each slice of cheese. Carefully flame by touching a lighted match to the surface of the brandy. Serve, dousing flames with squeezes of lemon juice. *2 appetizer servings.*

Route 66 angles onto Ogden near Ashland and heads for the suburbs through some of the worst of Chicago's inner city blight. Once a center for blue-collar employees, the area began collapsing during the early years of the depression. Route 66 became an escape route for displaced employees and the first seeds of abandoned hope stayed behind to fester.

Even in this depressed area, ghosted Coke signs like the one near Ogden and Homan remain on the crumbling walls as reminders of more prosperous days. Just past the quarry district is Cicero, a community that has overcome its early reputation as a center for organized crime. The Old Prague and Wishing Well are long time Route 66 eating places in Cicero.

Past Cicero, where Ogden jogs onto Harlem, a White Castle hamburger outlet once served miniature meat and buns by the bagful to Chicago's West Side residents. It was at this popular location that Ray Kroc first became aware of the power of the hamburger patty. He was past fifty, however, before the full potential of the hamburger blossomed into his first McDonald outlet in nearby Des Plaines.

In 1937, Ray Abbot's Cafe in Berwyn became one of the first "Chicken in the Rough" franchise restaurants in the country. Beverly Osborne began his chicken business in Oklahoma City in 1936 and the popular finger food spread quickly across the country.

Follow Joliett Road today into Countryside, where the story of Route 66 is being preserved at the Route 66 Cafe-Grill, part of the William Tell/Holiday Inn complex.

The attractive buffet and grill offers a fresh atmosphere, combining natural wood and brick decor with split-level design and generous skylights two floors above the tables.

Abundant plants accent a variety of Route 66 road signs, photographs, and old maps. The atmosphere is comfortable and relaxed. Barbara Mayer, hostess, says the Route 66 theme has been a popular drawing card. The chef, who specializes in buffet dinners, has found a large following for his distinctive food.

ROUTE 66 GRILL
BRAISED LAMB SHANKS

5 POUNDS WELL-TRIMMED LAMB SHANKS
½ CUP OIL
4 CELERY STALKS, COARSELY CHOPPED
4 LARGE CARROTS, COARSELY CHOPPED
1 LARGE ONION, COARSELY CHOPPED
2 GARLIC CLOVES, MINCED
1 OUNCE TOMATO PASTE
4 OUNCES DRY RED WINE
4 CUPS COMMERCIAL BROWN SAUCE
A SACHET FILLED WITH 8 WHOLE CRACKED PEPPER-
CORNS, 2 BAY LEAVES, CHOPPED PARSLEY, AND PINCHES
OF THYME, ROSEMARY, AND MARJORAM
SALT AND PEPPER TO TASTE

SEASON LAMB WITH SALT AND PEPPER. Sear in hot oil on all sides and remove from pan. Add celery, carrots and onion to oil and lightly brown. Stir in garlic, tomato paste, and red wine. Add brown sauce and a sachet wrapped in cheese cloth of peppercorns, bay leaves, parsley, thyme, rosemary, and marjoram. Add the lamb. Cover and braise until lamb is tender, about 1½ hours. Remove the lamb shank and the sachet and adjust seasonings with salt and pepper. Skim all fat from sauce and strain. Slice lamb and serve with sauce accompanied with browned potatoes or white rice pilaf. *6 to 8 servings.*

Turning right at the Route 83 exit off I-55 in Willowbrook, you'll find Dell Rhea's Chicken Basket on a section of original old Route 66. The Chicken Basket has been a fixture on the historic road since 1947. When Dell and Grace Rhea bought the business in 1962, they relied on local farmers to provide top-quality chickens and eggs. In true Route 66 tradition, Dell tended bar and handled advertising while Grace supervised the kitchen and did the hiring. The Rheas' son Pat operates the business today. The popular restaurant is open for lunch and dinner and Pat Rhea has added a thriving catering business, serving "The Best Dressed Chicken in Town" in addition to Grace Rhea's old family recipes for homemade chili and baked beans.

The restaurant was once a Blue Bird Bus Stop. Pat Huff, the hostess and a twenty-eight-year employee at the Chicken Basket, pointed to the

spot behind the cash register where the bus light switch used to be. "We would turn on the light when we had a customer, so the driver would know to stop," she said. "That was when Route 66 went right in front of our door and we were open day and night."

When the White Fence Farm opened in Lemont in the 1930s, dinner there meant a twenty-eight-mile drive from Chicago. Stuyvesant Peabody wanted his guests to enjoy a good dinner away from the rush of city life. His theory worked. First offering a variety of sandwiches, whole milk, homemade ice cream, and pies, the restaurant has maintained a quality menu throughout the years with a minimum of change. When the restaurant first opened, those waiting for tables could play shuffleboard, croquet, ping-pong, or quoits. Reservations were requested and Sunday meals by 1940 ranged from thirty cents to $1.25.

Many traces of small-town America remain along this stretch of Route 66. In McCook, Snuffy's makes a memorable stop. Bullock's Fine Foods in Wilmington is only a memory, but the Wellco Truck Stop serves folks who get off the interstate. Braidwood is all but gone. The tiny community was once home to the Rossi Macaroni Plant. Godley and Gardner are aging hamlets that hide secrets of a more prosperous past.

In Dwight, Historic 66 signs mark the access road next to the highway. The 1930 vintage Carefree Motel still offers no-frills comfort and the friendly young owners enthusiastically share Route 66 stories with their customers and across the street Fedderson's Pizza Garage is decorated with highway hype.

Phil Corrigan runs Phil's Harvest Table for locals and those who exit the interstate. Corrigan has been in the restaurant business for over twenty years, getting his start at the old N&J Truck Stop on Route 66. Several waitresses at the Harvest Table have worked there since the cafe began. Plain, no-frills decor and good home cooking add up to a full house every day. Down the street, Starks Family Restaurant does business in a comfortable family setting.

Pontiac, named for a famous Indian chief, is a lovely old city that was established in 1838. The city is home to the Fiesta Motel on Old

Highway 66, but the cafe that was once busy next door was closed. While in Pontiac, stop by the town square, whose courthouse has been placed on the National Registry. The Vermilion River is the focal point for Pontiac's lovely park system. The city is filled with beautiful homes, antique shops, and people who are proud of their heritage.

Pontiac is also home to The Old and New Log Cabin Restaurants and thereby lies a story.

The Old Log Cabin Cafe was built in the mid-1920s north of town on the original old, old Highway 66. When a new alignment of Route 66 moved the highway behind the little cafe, manager Paul Johnson took action. He located some of the highway crew, borrowed equipment, and had the little building jacked up, turned around, and plopped down again with its front entrance on new Route 66.

Brad Trainor runs the Old Log Cabin today. He is off the beaten path but serves a hardy group of regulars who keep their own mugs hanging on pegs behind the coffee pot.

Paul Johnson was lured away from his original location by developers who wanted his thriving restaurant as an anchor for a new shopping area closer into Pontiac, but still on Route 66. Johnson made the move in 1955, calling his new cafe Paul's New Log Cabin Restaurant. He brought with him his large following loyal to his famous homemade soups and great pies. The location was perfect for Highway 66 traffic between Chicago and the state capital in Springfield.

After Paul Johnson died, several owners operated from the location before Jerry and Sarah Hillyer bought it in 1973. Jerry had been in the restaurant business all his life and was the son of the owner of another Route 66 favorite, the Palamar.

The Hillyers built the New Log Cabin into a prosperous business, serving 300,000 customers a year. Good food in a comfortable setting is a priority.

Hillyer features several of the recipes his father made famous at the Palamar, including marinated pork chops and corn relish. Beef and chicken are also big sellers at the New Log Cabin.

Three of the Hillyers' five children work in the restaurant. "I hope they will have the interest and dedication to continue," he says. "There's a low profit margin in my business and it gets harder all the time, but I thrive on the challenge."

Hillyer retired recently after years of working from 4:30 in the morning until bedtime.

"I love the people and I love the work," he says. "It's been my life."

New Log Cabin Marinated Pork Chops

Marinade and Chops

1 CUP SOY SAUCE
¼ CUP SUGAR
½ CUP WATER
1½ TEASPOONS MOLASSES
1½ TEASPOONS SALT
6-8 THICK-CUT PORK CHOPS

Barbecue Sauce

¼ CUP BROWN SUGAR
1½ TEASPOONS DRY HOT MUSTARD
3 TABLESPOONS WATER
7 OUNCES KETCHUP
6 OUNCES CHILI SAUCE

COMBINE ALL INGREDIENTS FOR MARINADE and bring to a boil. Let cool. Place 6-8 thick-cut chops in pan and pour marinating sauce over chops. Cover and let stand overnight in refrigerator. The next day, take pork chops out of marinade, place in a single layer in a baking pan and cover tightly with foil. Bake in a preheated 375° oven until tender, about 2 hours.

FOR BARBECUE SAUCE, combine sugar and mustard with water. Blend until smooth. Combine with ketchup and chili sauce in saucepan and bring to boil. When chops are tender, remove from oven and dip in barbecue sauce. Return to uncovered baking pan and continue cooking in a 350° oven until lightly glazed, about 30 minutes. Serve hot. *6 to 8 marinated pork chops.*

In Chenoa, Steve's Cafe is a Route 66 original that shouldn't be missed. Its owners and operators, Ken and Peg Sipe, bought the cafe in 1975 because they liked the idea of running a "local institution." Steve's is located in an original 1918 battenboard building that has undergone at least four major renovations and additions. The original owners called it the Zirkle Brothers Cafe. They ran it through the depression years, finally leasing it to the Whal brothers.

Steve's came to be known for Steve Wilcox, chef at the little cafe when the Whal brothers ran it. The name has never changed. Many older residents of Chenoa worked at Steve's during their high school years. Sports great Stan Alback took his turn as a waiter. Cotton McNabrey, a former employee, remembers waiters who could carry four dinners, complete, on their arms in one trip to the table. "The most I could do was two cups of coffee," he said.

For years, the cafe was "the" Route 66 stopping place on the road from Chicago to Springfield and it was open twenty-four hours a day. Politicians ate with Steve as they traveled to and from the capital, and it is said that Al Capone was also a customer.

When Steve left in the 1950s, the cafe closed for a while. Ken Sipe says Steve was as memorable a character as he was a cook. People flocked to the cafe because of his personality as much as for his food.

Ken and Peg have reinstated Steve's most popular dinner—cube steak with hash browns, a lettuce wedge, and toast. It originally sold for fifty cents but is on the menu today as "Steve's Original" for $2.95.

Lexington is a quiet farming community until the last weekend of July each year when local folks host the "Taste of Country Fair." An old car parade always kicks off the festivities and there are plenty of booths featuring antiques, arts, crafts, and food. The fair offers a good taste of wholesome mid-American life and is the oldest annual Route 66 celebration in Illinois.

ROUTE 66 POTATO DOUGHNUTS

6 CUPS FLOUR
1⅓ TABLESPOONS BAKING POWDER
1 TEASPOON SALT
1 TEASPOON NUTMEG
3 EGGS
2 CUPS SUGAR
1½ CUPS WARM MASHED POTATOES
6 TABLESPOONS MELTED SHORTENING
¾ CUP MILK
OIL FOR FRYING

Sift flour with baking powder, salt, and nutmeg. Beat eggs and add sugar, potatoes, and shortening. While continuing to stir, add dry ingredients and milk, mixing only until flour disappears. Chill dough for at least 1 hour.

Place about half the dough on a lightly floured pastry cloth. Roll to ½-inch thickness. Cut with doughnut cutter and fry doughnuts in hot oil (360°) until lightly browned; turn and fry other side. Drain on paper towels and sprinkle with powdered sugar if desired. *4 dozen doughnuts.*

The Filling Station Cafe in Lexington is the place to eat. Obe and Gari Riisburg, who run the cafe, serve up a fine cup of coffee. Toby's Place used to be a Route 66 stop but is only a memory today.

Towanda is the last Route 66 community before travelers hit the Normal-Bloomington complex. Almost hidden by fields of corn, its elevators are all that can be seen from the interstate.

With two universities, the twin cities of Normal and Bloomington are youthful and lively communities. A great majority of their combined population is made up of young people. Perhaps this is the justification for the cities' claim to fame as the largest grab bag of fast-food joints in middle America. The area is home to the Steak'n'Shake chain, Beer Nuts, and the Nestle Beich Candy Company located next to the railroad tracks on old Route 66.

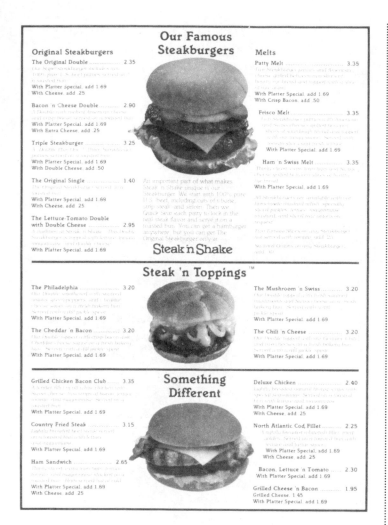

Our Famous Steakburgers

Original Steakburgers

The Original Double 2.35
The Original Steakburger includes two 100% pure U.S. beef patties served on a toasted bun.
With Platter Special, add 1.69
With Cheese, add .25

Bacon 'n Cheese Double 2.90
With Platter Special, add 1.69
With Extra Cheese, add .25

Triple Steakburger 3.25
With Platter Special, add 1.69
With Double Cheese, add .50

The Original Single 1.40
With Platter Special, add 1.69
With Cheese, add .25

The Lettuce-Tomato Double with Double Cheese 2.95
With Platter Special, add 1.69

Melts

Patty Melt 3.35
With Platter Special, add 1.69
With Crisp Bacon, add .50

Frisco Melt 3.35
With Platter Special, add 1.69

Ham 'n Swiss Melt 3.35
With Platter Special, add 1.69

An important part of what makes Steak 'n Shake unique is our Steakburger. We start with 100% pure U.S. beef, including cuts of t-bone, strip steak and sirloin. Then we Quick-Sear each patty to lock in the real steak flavor and serve it on a toasted bun. You can get a hamburger anywhere, but you can get The Original Steakburger only at

Steak 'n Shake

Steak 'n Toppings™

The Philadelphia 3.20
With Platter Special, add 1.69

The Cheddar 'n Bacon 3.20
With Platter Special, add 1.69

The Mushroom 'n Swiss 3.20
With Platter Special, add 1.69

The Chili 'n Cheese 3.20
With Platter Special, add 1.69

Something Different

Grilled Chicken Bacon Club 3.35
With Platter Special, add 1.69

Country Fried Steak 3.15
With Platter Special, add 1.69

Ham Sandwich 2.65
With Platter Special, add 1.69
With Cheese, add .25

Deluxe Chicken 2.40
With Platter Special, add 1.69
With Cheese, add .25

North Atlantic Cod Fillet 2.25
With Platter Special, add 1.69
With Cheese, add .25

Bacon, Lettuce 'n Tomato 2.30
With Platter Special, add 1.69

Grilled Cheese 'n Bacon 1.95
Grilled Cheese, 1.45
With Platter Special, add 1.69

Nestle Beich is the largest chocolate and confection manufacturer in the country dedicated primarily to the fund-raising market. The company has long Route 66 ties. In 1854, Paul F. Beich, a young Prussian immigrant, began selling candy for the J.L. Green Confectionary Company in Bloomington. He prospered and in 1892, his father-in-law helped him buy The Lancaster Caramel Company from Milton Hershey.

The sale enabled the Hershey company to consolidate in Pennsylvania.

The Lancaster Caramel Company occupied the red brick building that now forms the central part of the Nestle Beich office. In 1912, Beich added The Hageley Chocolate Company from Chicago. By the 1930s, all manufacturing was concentrated in Bloomington where sales of the Whiz Bar, Pecan Pete, and survival rations continued through World War II.

In 1984, Nestle Fund Raising purchased the Paul F. Beich Company. Nestle Beich continues to provide high-quality chocolates and confections for fund-raising.

Gus Belt became a pioneer in the fast-food industry when he opened his first Steak'n'Shake in 1934. That early Normal restaurant offered curb service complete with carhops — a revolutionary idea at the time. Steak'n'Shake was one of the first chains with standardized facilities to be readily recognizable, to control portions, and to limit the menu size. The chain has become an institution along Route 66 in Illinois and Missouri, serving thousands of customers in other midwestern states as well. Steak'n'Shake still promotes "Steakburgers" instead of hamburgers and their milk shakes are made the old-fashioned way — with hand-dipped ice cream. Chili is another popular item on the menu. The motto is still "So don't just plan a meal out — Plan a meal outstanding at Steak'n'Shake."

Recently an Asian influence has become apparent in this heavily Caucasian Farm Belt area due to the Chrysler Mitsubishi plant. Sushi bars are moving in where only burgers had dared to go before.

Those who drove Historic 66 through the 1970s will remember Bob Johnson's Brantville Cafe as the place to go for some of the best broasted chicken anywhere along Route 66. Today, the Double Nickel Drive-In in Bloomington has become a modern-day classic, bringing back memories of the 1950s.

South of Bloomington, turn off I-55 at the Shirley exit and continue a few miles south through lush cornfields into Funk's Grove. This unique spot didn't rate its own exit when the interstate bypassed one of the few sites in Illinois where maple syrup is still produced.

The ridge is home to a grove of giant sugar and black maples where "sirup" has been harvested commercially since 1891. Elms, ash trees, black walnuts, sycamores, and burr oaks also help to provide New England-style charm to this lovely grove in the heart of the midwest. The old Funk's Grove railroad station and the general store give travelers a chance to absorb area history.

Isaac Funk homesteaded the grove some seven generations ago. Today, Mike and Debbie Funk and Mike's parents, Steve and Glaida, operate the only commercial maple syrup business on Route 66. By the terms of Hazel Funk Holmes' will, the grove can never be used for anything except producing maple "sirup." Mrs. Holmes was a stickler for the spelling, insisting that "sirup" was Webster's preference. The spelling is a tradition that continues.

When Steve took over management of the grove, he began applying new, more scientific methods of collecting sap. Today, the Funks hang some 4,000 buckets a year. Mike and Debbie direct most of the operation so Steve and Glaida have time to relax and enjoy their customers and grandchildren.

FUNK'S GROVE MAPLE SIRUP BARS

½ CUP BUTTER
¼ CUP SUGAR
1 CUP FLOUR
¾ CUP BROWN SUGAR
⅓ CUP MAPLE SYRUP
1 TABLESPOON BUTTER
1 EGG
½ TEASPOON VANILLA
⅓ CUP CHOPPED PECANS

CREAM BUTTER AND SUGAR IN FOOD PROCESSOR. Add flour and process until just blended. Dough does not form ball. Pat into bottom of greased 9-inch square pan. Bake at 350° for 15 minutes or until lightly browned. Beat brown sugar, syrup, and butter to blend. Beat in egg and vanilla. Pour over shortbread. Sprinkle with nuts. Bake 25 minutes or until set. Cool and cut into bars. *2 dozen bars.*

FUNK'S GROVE PEACH COBBLER

1 STICK MARGARINE
1 CUP FLOUR
3 TEASPOONS BAKING POWDER
½ CUP MAPLE SYRUP
½ CUP SUGAR
1 CUP MILK
1 CAN (29 OUNCES) SLICED PEACHES, DRAINED

MELT MARGARINE IN 9 x 13 INCH BAKING PAN. Stir flour, baking powder, syrup, sugar, and milk into margarine. Place drained peaches on top of batter. Bake in preheated 350° oven for 45 minutes. *6 to 8 servings.*

FUNK'S GROVE
ROUTE 66 SUGAR COOKIES

1 CUP MARGARINE
1 CUP GRANULATED SUGAR
½ CUP POWDERED SUGAR
¾ CUP CORN OIL
½ CUP MAPLE SYRUP
2 EGGS
1 TEASPOON SODA
1 TEASPOON CREAM OF TARTAR
½ TEASPOON SALT
4 CUPS FLOUR

CREAM MARGARINE AND SUGARS TOGETHER, add corn oil, maple syrup and eggs and cream well. Sift together the soda, cream of tartar, salt and flour. Knead dry ingredients into creamed mixture to form dough. Chill dough for 1 hour.

Drop dough by teaspoonsful on cookie sheet and press with glass dipped in sugar to flatten. Bake in preheated 350° oven for 12 minutes or until browned. *7 dozen cookies.*

A few miles south of Funk's Grove is McLean and the Dixie Trucker's Home, "offering comfort on the plains since 1928." The huge truck stop was founded on Route 66 just before the depression by J.P. Walters along with his daughter and son-in-law, Vi and John Geske.

Today, Vi and John's daughter and son-in-law, Charles and Charlotte Beeler, and their two sons, Mark and David, own and manage the Dixie Trucker's Home. Their motto continues to be, "You can't

operate successfully by remote control." To prove their point, the truck stop has closed only one day since 1928, and that was due to a 1965 fire that burned the original building. At the truck stop, you'll find a good, clean atmosphere and enough cars and trucks in the parking lots to actually believe all America is still traveling down Route 66. Just count the license tags!

The Illinois Route 66 Hall of Fame can be found at Dixie Trucker's Home. Exhibits featured in a prominent hallway tell the story of Route 66 in Illinois. Stop by for a look!

Entering Lincoln from the north, you can't miss the Tropics. It stands behind a big, glitzy sign and the parking lot is always full of cars. Lew and Beverly Johnson and their family have operated this palm tree-embellished restaurant on Route 66 since 1955. It was much smaller then, but the building has burned twice, and each time has reopened with more space. Route 66 is an important part of the Johnsons' lives. Kimball Johnson remembers traffic stacked up bumper to bumper for miles as Highway 66 drivers headed for the state fairgrounds just down the road. The Tropics sports a coffee shop, dining room, cocktail lounge, and space for private parties. Unlike many Route 66 eating places that no longer maintain long hours, it is open from six-thirty a.m. until midnight daily. Try the Old Route 66 Hamburger, a house specialty. Or choose your meal from the regular buffet that always includes succulent Illinois pork and prime rib.

The Mill was a fixture on Route 66 from 1945 until it was torn down in 1993. It was located on Washington Street in Lincoln, across from the railroad tracks. The building, once named the Blue Mill was vintage 1929 architecture with its tower and windmill.

Schnitzel was the house specialty. It could be ordered with a dinner, a la carte, as a sandwich, or to take home in any quantity. The pork and veal cutlets came with a special sauce that was a Mill secret, sure to draw customers back for another visit.

Decor at the Mill was worth a visit, even without the house specialty. Life-size Indian mannequins greeted guests at a table by the door, antique toys and household goods adorned the walls, and a man's foot and lower leg hung from the ceiling, as if he had just stepped through the rafters. The bar was a taxidermist's paradise. In the midst of numerous game mounts like deer and antelope was a sure-enough horse. The prey of an ambitious hunter or maybe a family pet? You could get the story when you stopped by. Eleanor and Randal

Pig-Hip
RESTAURANT

"They Made Their Way By The Way They're Made"

PIG-HIP
Reg. U.S. Pat
SANDWICHES

ROUTE U.S. 66, BROADWELL, ILLINOIS

Huffman, owners of the Mill, were happy to answer questions.

During the 1930s and 1940s, the Spinning Wheel in Lincoln was considered a lifesaver after the long slow stretches through Illinois cornfields. The menu was simple but very good—soup, fried chicken, broiled steak or chops, salads and desserts. The homemade cinnamon rolls were some of the best along the highway.

Broadwell is home to the Pig Hip Restaurant, one of the truly unique eating places along Route 66 in Illinois. (Owners Ernie and Francis Edwards have closed the restaurant and retired but still live "within hollerin' distance" of the classic cafe.) Ernie was one of the first people to be inducted into the Illinois Route 66 Hall of Fame and continues to be a member of the association board.

Ernie began his restaurant career back in the post-depression days of 1937 when his father urged him to take out a $100 loan and go into business. With the money, Ernie says he bought three tables, sixteen chairs, a gas pressure grill, and a refrigerator. Then he signed twelve promissory notes. Before long, he bought another cafe seven miles north, and began to fulfill his dream of owning a chain.

"The name of our place was Harbor Inn at that time," he said. "We just picked that name by accident. When we got the place we went down to the paint store. We didn't have much money, but we found some paper with ships on it for a nickel a roll. So we bought it, then we went to the dime store and found glasses with ships on them. So that's how the name came about."

The Pig Hip name originated in 1938. "There was an old man down here; he was mad 'cause his wife had left him right in the middle of harvest. He came in here and wanted a sandwich. I was eager to please and asked him what kind he wanted. He said to just give him a slice of that pig hip back there."

The pig hip sandwich caught on. Edwards had the name copyrighted and changed his cafe name. Then he began to franchise. "Gus Belt, at Steak'nShake, he got mad at me one time 'cause I was using black and white and Gus said those were his colors," Edwards reflected. "And Colonel Sanders would come by and would want to sell me a franchise, way before he was famous, and I would want to sell him one. Once he said he would go out and get his pot and secret herbs if I would supply the

chicken — so he fixed our dinner. He was really hungry! Now that's a true story."

"Now Duncan Hines, he did a little book with recipes and a tour guide. I never would give him a recipe. But he would stop by and write me up," he said.

Ernie says the sauce he used on his pig hip sandwiches was originally developed in Pittsfield, Illinois, by two Dinsmore brothers who were on his franchise sales force. "We sold some distant cousins in Amarillo a franchise years ago. They claimed they had developed the pig hip sauce but it was my recipe they used," he said. "Those folks in Amarillo were about three branches off the family tree."

Ernie doesn't give out any of his recipes, but says he baked his good twenty-pound hams for four and a half hours, then sliced the meat paper thin and piled it on the buns, all topped with his pig hip sauce in just the right amount. It brought folks back for years!

This recipe for Pig Hip Sauce didn't come from Ernie, but is guaranteed to be the next best thing.

ROUTE 66 PIG HIP SAUCE

Chill a stainless steel mixing bowl until very cold. Take 1 large egg from refrigerator and using an electric mixer, beat egg thoroughly. While continuing to beat, slowly add 3 cups of good quality vegetable oil and 7 ounces of Heinz catsup. To this, add 2 ounces of Worcestershire sauce, ½ cup of sugar, and a pinch of salt. Serve over thinly sliced ham. *1 quart.*

The Fleetwood Restaurant in Springfield served Route 66 customers daily from 1957 until 1993. When Tony and Opal Lauck opened the restaurant's doors, they determined the combination of quality food, good service, and low prices would bring customers back again and again. Their recipe for success, "homestyle meals at modest prices," was carried on by the Lauck's daughter Linda, her husband John, and the couple's three sons.

In its thirty-five year history, seating capacity increased to over 300, while staffing averaged seventy employees. Tourists from across the country would return each year to eat the house specialties of Broasted Chicken and homemade desserts. Broasted Chicken is said to have been a favorite of the governor of Illinois, Jim Edgar, one of the Fleetwood's most notable patrons.

The Fleetwood was located on a small stretch of Route 66 which was renamed Dirksen Parkway in the early 1970s.

On the other side of town, Ed Waldmire found success in his search for the perfect wiener wrap. The results of his work are for sale today at the Cozy Dog Drive In on City 66 South in Springfield. It's a Route 66 business that is a must for everyone searching for the perfect all-American story.

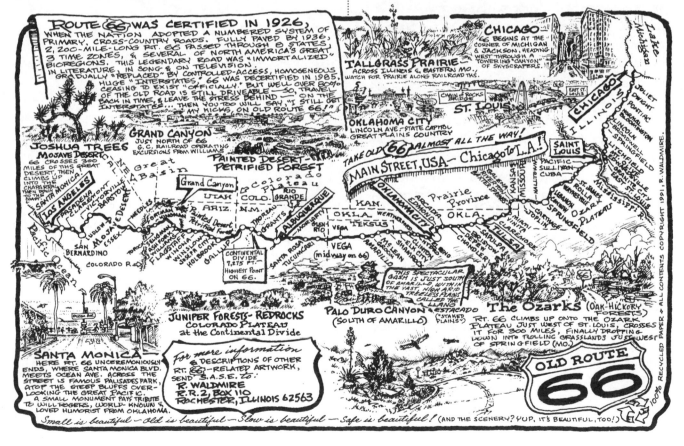

Ed remembers visiting a brother in Muskogee, Oklahoma, in 1941 where he ate his first corn dog in a local greasy spoon. "They were made in a contraption like a waffle iron. The batter was poured in a trough, then three wieners were added and the whole thing baked fifteen minutes," he said.

While Ed was stationed at Amarillo Air Base during World War II, he had time on his hands and began wondering how he could make the corn dogs faster and better. He finally called Don Strand, who ran a bakery in Galesburg, Illinois, and asked him to make some batter that he could dip a wiener in and deep fry like a doughnut.

Ed prepared his first corn dogs at the base PX in Amarillo. They were an immediate success. Soon he was ordering hundreds of pounds of the mix at a time and began selling his batter fried wieners as "crusty curs."

His wife, Virginia, convinced him that another name would sell better and after a number of suggestions, they finally settled on "Cozy Dogs" with a logo of two hot dogs in love.

Waldmire registered the "Cozy Dog" trademark and set about marketing. Cozy Dogs were an instant success at the 1946 Illinois State Fair. The business was off and running.

One patent Waldmire holds is for a special machine to fry Cozy Dogs. It immerses the dogs while frying since a floating dog is prone to absorb more oil. Today's Cozy Dog batter is the result of experimenting, too. Waldmire and Don Strand, his supplier, finally settled on a mixture that includes garlic, mustard and ground popcorn.

Ed's son Buz and daughter-in-law Sue run the Cozy Dog Drive In today, serving cozy dogs and good home-cooked food. Ed and his wife moved just a few miles off Route 66 to Rochester where Ed continued to franchise his Cozy Dog mix and Old Route 66 Chili Mix until his death in 1993.

A second son, Bob, is an artist who often travels Route 66 in search of living history for his unique postcards and maps of the old road. Bob is in the process of moving to Hackberry, Arizona, where he is establishing an "International, Bioregional Old Route 66 Visitor Center." The Chili Mix called for in the recipe that follows is the famous Cozy Dog Chili Mix, which lends a mild flavor. To heat the chili up, add extra chili powder, ground cayenne pepper, Tabasco sauce, or other hot red chili sauce.

ROUTE 66 VEGETARIAN CHILI

1 POUND DRY RED BEANS, SORTED AND RINSED
2 QUARTS WATER
1 MEDIUM ONION, DICED
1 CUP VEGETABLE OIL
5 TABLESPOONS 66 CHILI MIX
1 SMALL CAN TOMATO PUREE
EXTRA WATER AS NEEDED

COMBINE BEANS WITH WATER and 2 tablespoons of the chili mix. Simmer in covered pan for 2-3 hours or until beans are soft. Add water as needed. Saute diced onion in vegetable oil. Stir in remaining 3 tablespoons of the chili mix and a small can of tomato puree. Stir and let simmer for 5 minutes. Add mixture to beans, stir well, then ring the dinner bell for hungry chili lovers. *12 servings.*

Springfield's Georgian Restaurant, a Route 66 stop for years, is only a memory now. And Maldaner's, open through the 1930s and into the 1940s, is also a memory. Maldaner's, always retained a slightly old-fashioned, restful atmosphere. The owners boasted that their lemon cream sherbet was made from the same recipe as that which was served at Abe Lincoln's wedding reception.

Springfield resident Joe DeFrates was the originator of Chili Man Chili and produced it in Litchfield for years. DeFrates began peddling his chili mix along Route 66 years ago. The business grew with the popularity of his chili and when Joe retired, he sold out to Milnot Milk. Milnot is now a part of Beatrice Foods in Litchfield.

Drive south through the hamlet of Glenarm where Mort's Roadhouse draws a loyal following. The building dates from 1893 and for most of its life was a garage. The atmosphere at Mort's is worth the stop. The logo, "Be a Sport, Stop at Mort's," leaves just enough question to have appeal.

There is a lot of Route 66 history at Art's Restaurant and Motel in Farmersville. Built as Hendricks Brothers Service Station by Harry and Fred Hendricks before the days of Route 66, it was bought by Cecil and Dorothy Hampton in 1926. "We did a little bit of everything — pump gas, serve food, sell beer. We even had six tourist cabins," Dorothy said.

Dorothy Hampton remembers living in the two-room apartment above the cafe. There was no air conditioning and the thermometer in the kitchen would sometimes hit 120°. When the Chicago World's Fair drew cross-country traffic in 1932 and 1933, business boomed, and the Hamptons stayed open twenty-four hours a day. After prohibition ended in 1933 they began selling beer, but many shipments didn't arrive because of hijackings along the way. The station had a legal slot machine, but a robber took it one day.

The Hampton's ran Hendricks Brothers until 1937 when they sold to Art McAnarney and Martin Gorman, who renamed the restaurant Art's Fine Foods.

Art McAnarney's sons joined him in the business after World War II. In November of 1952, Art's Fine Foods burned to the ground. Art rebuilt and, disregarding unlucky numbers, added thirteen motel units.

Roger and Grace Brown and their daughter and son-in-law, Darry and Debra Lucas, bought Art's in 1978. The restaurant continues to be a family-operated business with grandchildren helping out.

Art's is a popular stop for Cub and Cardinal fans and has been host to such notables as George Gobel and Marlin Perkins. The large parking lot is always filled, a sure-fire testimonial for Grace's cooking. Her coconut cream pie is a work of art.

ART'S BARBECUE

1 PORK BUTT (4 POUNDS)
¾ CUP BROWN SUGAR
2 TEASPOONS SEXTON BARBECUE SPICE, OR TO TASTE
1½ TABLESPOONS VINEGAR
1½ CUPS HEINZ KETCHUP

BOIL THE PORK BUTT UNTIL WELL DONE. When cool, strip into small pieces. Combine remaining ingredients and pour over pork. Serve hot.

ART'S COCONUT CREAM PIE

PIE FILLING AND CRUST

1½ CUPS SUGAR
½ TEASPOON SALT
1 TABLESPOON FLOUR
4 TABLESPOONS CORNSTARCH
3 CUPS MILK
3 EGG YOLKS, SLIGHTLY BEATEN
1 TABLESPOON BUTTER
2 TEASPOONS VANILLA
½ CUP COCONUT
1 TEN-INCH PIE CRUST, BAKED

MERINGUE

5 TO 6 EGG WHITES, BEATEN
½ TEASPOON CREAM OF TARTAR
1 TABLESPOON POWDERED SUGAR
5 TABLESPOONS SUGAR

FOR THE PIE FILLING, combine sugar, salt, flour, and cornstarch in saucepan. Carefully stir in milk and heat slowly until slightly thickened. Beat together the egg yolks, butter, and vanilla and stir into milk mixture, continuing to cook for about 3 minutes. Add coconut and pour into pie crust.

FOR THE MERINGUE, add cream of tartar and sugars to beaten egg whites and continue beating until glossy. Spoon on top of filling and bake for 10 to 12 minutes in a preheated 400° oven. *7 to 8 slices.*

The Ariston in Litchfield is a Route 66 classic. It was opened originally in Carlinville by Pete Adam in 1924. Carlinville was on old, old 66. In 1931, Adam moved the restaurant to Litchfield, then into its present location in 1935. Nick Adam, son of the founder, runs The Ariston today. He has served thousands of travelers along the historic route, among them, Hubert Humphrey and Jimmy Dorsey.

The Ariston, "The St. Louis-Springfield" Restaurant, is a masterpiece on Historic 66, and one of the few that has survived with original owners. There is a real sense of history about the place and the food continues to please customers as it has for years.

The Ariston has outlasted numerous Litchfield Route 66 eateries, including Skinny's Truck Stop, The Annex Cafe, The Blue Danube, The Overhead, and The Saratoga Club.

The Hut has been a Litchfield fixture since the "good ol' days" when lunch was dinner and dinner was supper. R Place in Litchfield was once known as the Belvedere Cafe. Clara Bow is said to have spent the night at the Belvedere Motel next door.

In the 1930s, Scherer's Cafe served the traveling public in Mount Olive. In Staunton, the Hi Cafe and Kendon's are gone, but the Mill Cafe is still south of town. Harold's Place on South Hackman looks like it came right off a movie set from the 1940s.

In Hamel, travelers who stop at Ernie's Bar can get the real stories about the number of times the front door has been moved to attract new patrons.

Edwardsville is a lovely old river-bottom community, proud of its rich heritage and beautifully preserved historic homes. Many Civil War vintage buildings are a part of the city's walking tour program. Maps are available at the Chamber of Commerce.

Route 66 follows Highway 157 through Edwardsville where Musso's Restaurant and Tap Room was once located opposite the courthouse. The restaurant was run by George Musso, a former captain of the Chicago Bears. Today, good eating places along the old road in Edwardsville include Chez Seamus, PK'S, and Rusty's Restaurant. If you are hungry for great pie, stop at the Yum Yum Shoppe.

Leave Edwardsville on the interstate and jump the mighty Mississippi into the heart of St. Louis. The only floating McDonald's in the country sits on the river near the Gateway Arch.

MISSOURI

MISSOURI. **Route 66 plunges diagonally across Missouri from the Mississippi River to the southeastern corner of Kansas. The historic road offers a roller-coaster ride, a breathtakingly beautiful and often dangerous drive through the state's ridges and valleys. The historic road that begins in St. Louis passes through the main street of nearly a hundred Missouri communities.**

Bits and pieces of a hybrid alignment wind through St. Louis. Don't be a purist along here. Take time to explore the Jefferson National Expansion Memorial and Gateway Arch, Forest Park, the National Museum of Transport, and the many other cultural and recreational offerings this vibrant city has to offer.

St. Louis was host to the 1904 Louisiana Purchase Centennial Exposition and World's Fair where ice cream cones and hot dogs were introduced to the American public. Iced tea and Dr. Pepper also gained popularity at this great fair. Take advantage of the fine eating places around Laclede's Landing in the heart of historic St. Louis. At Jake's Steaks, hungry patrons will find an enticing twin filet, prepared with garlic and mustard beer sauce. Tony's, only a few blocks away, is considered one of the best Italian restaurants in the country.

Pope's Cafeteria was located next to the Greyhound Bus Station for years and can be found in several other locations around the city today. At one time, cross-country bus travelers rated Pope's as a favorite Route 66 stop. Today, Sandwich Shops, Big Boy, and Steak'n'Shake line the city route.

But Ted Drewes Frozen Custard is the name most synonymous with Route 66 and good eating in St. Louis. The Chippewa Street stand is right out of Norman Rockwell. In fact, a whole series of home-town Americana scenes come to life every day around this white frame building with the icicle eves.

A kaleidoscope of hungry customers stand continually in front of the service windows. At any given time there will be teens in shorts or jeans, dignified couples who have just left the comfort of their Jaguars, whole families with children in tow, grandmotherly friends deep in conversation about what to order, and several young yuppie business types. Inside, the service is as smooth as the custard. Efficient young people in bright yellow shirts never miss a beat in preparing orders. The atmosphere radiates enthusiasm.

Plain custards, sundaes, sodas, floats, splits, malts, and extra-thick "concretes" pour through the windows as fast as hands permit. Names on the menu wall come from Drewes' vivid imagination and a love for his product and for people: Cindermint, Riverboat Blues, Dutchman Delight, Terramizzou, and Crater Copernicus.

"Crater Copernicus is our specialty alone," grins Travis Dillon, Drewes' son-in-law and one of the managers. "When the new St. Louis Science Center near Forest Park opened in the summer of 1991, they asked us to create a custard in celebration. We came up with this and it's been a real hit."

Crater Copernicus begins in a large bowl with chocolate cake topped with a giant dipper of custard. The custard is hollowed out in the center to make a crater that is filled with hot fudge, surrounded with whipped cream and topped with a cherry.

Ted Drewes Frozen Custard began when Ted, Sr., decided to take a used custard machine on the carnival circuit in 1929. When his wife finally persuaded him to quit traveling, he bought his first St. Louis custard stand and soon added the Route 66 Chippewa Street spot. The custard recipe he perfected is dispensed in unbelievable quantity without the benefits of inside seating, drive-in windows, or curb service.

The business has always been family operated. "Ted went to work here when he was ten and I was twelve," says Margie Aussicker, Drewes' sister, who takes her turn on the line with other employees and radiates her own enthusiasm and pride in the business.

Frozen custard flows from the immaculate stand every day from eleven a.m. to eleven p.m. The custard stand closes for a few weeks after Christmas each year if the weather is bad.

Meanwhile, custard enthusiasts who have found the real thing on Route 66 keep Ted Drewes Frozen Custard happily in business.

Phil's Bar-B-Cue is another long-time St. Louis enterprise located on Gravois Road and in Eureka on West 5th Street. Both are city aliases for Route 66. Phil's father began barbecuing in north St. Louis back in 1942 and the Gravois location opened in 1962. Phil's Quonset hut home in Eureka is much newer.

Phil, who does most of the cooking in the Eureka location, says he measures by hand and relies on experience. His succulent barbecue sauce is a family secret he sells to addicts by the quart. The restaurants have won numerous awards for barbecue and have a regular following.

"For each ten-pound can of baked beans, I add honey, brown sugar, mustard, bacon, barbecue sauce and a little cinnamon," Phil says. "I don't measure; it just comes naturally."

In the late 1940s, Kirkwood was shown on Missouri maps as 18 miles southwest of St. Louis. At the Green Parrot Inn, discriminating people returned again and again to eat fried chicken and steak dinners that cost as much as $2.75. The restaurant was considered one of the best in the St. Louis area.

Further west, in Pacific, the Red Cedar Inn has been serving Route 66 customers with only one break since it opened in 1934. Built by James Smith and his brother, Bill, the red cedar logs were cut on the family farm in Villa Ridge on St. Louis Rock Road.

The historic old building tells a story all its own. The logs were chinked by two brothers, George and Otto Manetzke. The original chinking is still in place after all these years and remains in good condition. In the center of the main dining room, a cedar tree trunk stands as part of the frame. Clients through the years have carved their initials on the old tree and occasionally return to see if they can find their "mark."

Ginger Smith Gallagher, proprietress and granddaughter of founder James Smith, serves guests at an old oak table that is a family heirloom. Several other pieces of treasured family furniture can be found at the inn. Ginger says she and her mother discovered the original meat slicer and food grinder that her grandfather used in 1934 when they were cleaning in preparation for reopening the inn in 1987. "I even found some of my dad's old records that he always kept in cigar boxes," she said.

In 1944, James Smith II and his wife, Katherine, bought the business from his father and continued to run the inn until Smith retired in 1972. For many years, the inn was the only restaurant serving mixed drinks in a 190-mile radius.

When Ginger and James III reopened the Red Cedar Inn, they determined to follow the family tradition of good food and good service. Katherine still helps her daughter with favorite recipes and a younger generation of family members, including Robert Myers and Michael Gallagher, work part time at the inn.

Katherine developed this carrot recipe some thirty years ago and picked up the recipe for French Dressing somewhere in the Ozarks on her honeymoon in 1940. Both have become family favorites.

RED CEDAR INN COUNTRY CARROTS

4 CUPS SLICED CARROTS
1½ TEASPOONS MINCED ONIONS
1 TEASPOON SUGAR
2 SLICES BACON
1½ TEASPOONS BACON DRIPPINGS
½ CUP GROUND ONION
½ CUP WATER FROM PARBOILED CARROTS
½ TEASPOON CHICKEN BASE
1½ TEASPOONS SEASONING SALT*

CLEAN AND SLICE CARROTS. Parboil carrots with minced onion and sugar in barely enough water to cover. Meanwhile, fry bacon until crisp. Drain on absorbent paper and crumble. Sauté ground onion in bacon drippings, then add water, chicken base, and seasoning salt. Continue cooking carrots until tender. To serve, top carrots with crumbled bacon.
* A good mixed seasoning like Vandzant's or Lowery's.
6 to 8 servings.

RED CEDAR INN FRENCH DRESSING

1 CAN (51 OUNCES) TOMATO SOUP
3¾ CUPS SUGAR
5 CUPS WHITE VINEGAR
3¾ CUPS CORN OIL
5 TEASPOONS SALT
¼ TEASPOON PEPPER
5 TEASPOONS PAPRIKA

BLEND FIRST SIX INGREDIENTS WELL, then add corn oil very slowly and mix well again. *1 gallon.*

Another classic on old Route 66 in Pacific is DJ's Cafe, standing for Delisa and Joye. The little cafe can be found in a corrugated metal Quonset hut on Osage Street.

Thirty-five miles west of St. Louis and ten minutes from Six Flags Over Mid-America is The Diamonds, the "world's largest roadside restaurant." The business was founded in 1918 by Spencer Groff when he opened a Villa Ridge banana stand next to the road. As business grew, he expanded to serve food and drinks. Lewis Eckelkamp, a dishwasher at the eating place, bought Groff's business.

The Diamonds has been located in three buildings, survived a disastrous fire, and moved down the road to accommodate the expanding highway. Years ago, Eckelkamp installed one of the first public swimming pools in the country. Actually, there were two pools, one to be used while the other was drained, cleaned, and refilled with well water.

THE DIAMOND'S CHEESE BALL

2 CUPS GRATED CHEDDAR CHEESE
16 OUNCES CREAM CHEESE, SOFTENED
1 CUP BLUE CHEESE, CRUMBLED
½ CUP FINELY CHOPPED ONION
2 TABLESPOONS WORCESTERSHIRE SAUCE
1 TEASPOON SALT
CHOPPED PECANS

COMBINE cheeses with onion, Worcestershire, and salt. Mold into ball then roll in chopped pecans.

BREAD PUDDING, DIAMOND STYLE

6 EGGS, BEATEN
6 CUPS MILK
2 TABLESPOONS VANILLA
1 TABLESPOON MELTED MARGARINE
1 CUP SUGAR
½ TEASPOON SALT
½ CUP RAISINS
3 CUPS DRY BREAD CUBES
1 TEASPOON CINNAMON

COMBINE eggs, milk, vanilla, margarine, sugar, and salt. Blend to dissolve sugar. Butter a 9- x 11-inch baking pan and fill with raisins and bread cubes. Pour egg mixture over bread and sprinkle with cinnamon. Place baking dish in larger pan containing water. Bake in preheated 350° oven for 45 minutes or until a knife inserted near the center comes out clean. *10 to 12 generous servings.*

During the 1940s and 1950s, St. Claire was home to the New England Pantry, set down in the wildwoods of the Ozarks. The restaurant was located in a Cape Cod cottage where Mrs. Conant, a transplanted New Englander, did all the cooking. Her specialties included clam chowder, beans, brown bread, and baked Indian pudding. The price for a 1947 meal averaged sixty-five cents.

Everyone who has ever driven Route 66 knows the name Meramec Caverns. Located in an oak forest near Stanton, the cave is billed as Missouri's 400-million-year-old buried treasure. Lester Dill, who developed the cave, grew up in the Stanton area. He had explored most of the caves along the Meramec River valley by the time his father became the first superintendent of the 7,000-acre Meramec State Park in 1928. Dill launched a cave guiding business in the park, complete with food and souvenirs.

When his contract ran out, Dill leased Salt Peter Caves, a few miles from the park. He eventually bought the property and put every penny he had into development. The name was changed to Meramec Caverns.

Lester Dill was an advertising genius. He began by applying large white letters to the highway side of every suitable barn he could find from Ohio to Texas. He did the work himself and the signs he lettered always carried the same message: "See Meramec Caverns, Route 66 Mo." Dill and his partner, Lyman Riley, are also credited with inventing the bumper sticker, another nationwide phenomenon. Dill's grandson and his wife, Les and Judy Turilli, manage the five-story-tall underground mansion today. The cave makes a spectacular visit for those seeking variety and adventure along Historic 66.

Ruth Ann Lambing has been the restaurant manager at the caverns since 1968. She shares this clam chowder recipe she developed for the Meramec Restaurant.

LES DILL   MERAMEC CAVERNS
ON HY. 66 STANTON, MO.

MERAMEC CAVERN'S CLAM CHOWDER

3 LARGE BAKING POTATOES, PEELED AND CHOPPED
½ CUP ONION, CHOPPED
1½ STRIPS BACON, CUT INTO SMALL PIECES
½ POUND BUTTER
½ CUP FLOUR
4-6 CUPS MILK
12 OUNCES CHOPPED CLAMS, UNDRAINED
SALT AND PEPPER TO TASTE

ORANGE	TOMATO	KELLOGG CEREALS	.90
PRUNE	GRAPE	HOT OATMEAL	.90
GRAPEFRUIT	.45 .75	HASH BROWN POTATOES	.70
		BISCUITS & GRAVY	$1.10

Ho-made Donuts & Pastry

FRESH DONUTS	.30
APPLE or CHERRY TURNOVERS	.90
TOAST & JELLY	.80
CINNAMON TOAST	.90

Beverages

FRESH COFFEE	.50
HOT TEA	.50
HOT CHOCOLATE	.60
MILK	.75 95

Our Grill

1 EGG $1.50
with Sausage, Bacon or Ham.
$2.75

2 EGGS $1.75
with Sausage, Bacon or Ham.
$3.00

SIDE ORDER
Sausage, Bacon or Ham.
$1.50

SHORT STACK [2] $1.75
with Sausage, Bacon or Ham.
$3.00

HOT CAKES [3] $1.95
with Sausage, Bacon or Ham.
$3.25

FRENCH TOAST $1.95
with Sausage, Bacon or Ham.
$3.25

Above orders include Toast and Jelly, Biscuits and Gravy Additional.

Biscuit Substitute - 45

Caveman Special $4.40
Choice of Juice, 2 Eggs, Hash Brown Potatoes with Ham, Bacon or Sausage; Toast and Jelly or Hot Biscuits and Gravy; Coffee, Tea or Milk.

Jesse James Special $3.95
2 Eggs, Hash Brown Potatoes, Toast and Jelly with Ham, Bacon or Sausage, and Coffee, Tea or Milk.

Big Cave Special $3.75
Choice of Juice, 2 Pancakes with Ham, Bacon or Sausage, and Coffee, Tea or Milk.

Loot Rock Wake Up Breakfast $3.50
Choice of Juice, 1 Egg with Ham, Bacon or Sausage, Toast and Jelly, and Coffee, Tea or Milk.

Meramec Low Calorie $2.95
Choice of Juice, Cereal, 1 Egg with 1 Slice Toast, and Coffee or Tea.

Little Jesse James Specials
1. $2.60   2. $2.25   3. $3.10
Juice, 2 Pancakes.   Juice, Cereal, 1 Slice Toast.   1 Egg with Bacon or Sausage, Toast.

All orders include Milk or Hot Chocolate.

BISCUITS & GRAVY ARE AVAILABLE JUNE THROUGH AUGUST.

COMBINE POTATOES WITH ¼ CUP ONION. Barely cover with water and simmer until potatoes are soft. Meanwhile combine chopped bacon with remaining onion in small skillet and cook until onions are golden. In a third saucepan, melt the butter and add flour, stirring to a smooth paste. Add milk slowly to make a thick sauce. Add clams to the potato and onion mixture and stir in the sauteed bacon and onion. Slowly add the thickened white sauce, stirring constantly.

Salt and pepper to taste. Simmer mixture at least 10 minutes, adjusting thickness with more milk if necessary. *12 to 14 servings.*

For years, Wurzburger's, in Stanton, was considered to have the best food in the area. The restaurant was located in a home with two dining rooms supplemented by a porch used by guests in the summertime. Steak and chicken were the specialties and travelers always returned.

Down the road in Sullivan today, McDonald's has been remodeled as a memorial to Route 66 and includes several good Route 66 photographs and murals. On the north access road, the Du Cum Inn welcomes those who exit the interstate.

Sweeney's Steak House, on Pine Street, was the most popular eating place in Bourbon for years. As with so many Missouri cafes, when I-44 replaced Route 66, business dwindled and the restaurant closed.

The landscape between Bourbon and Cuba is scenic. Take time to enjoy the natural beauty.

Cuba is an old railroad town where several turn-of-the-century buildings still front on the tracks. The two-story Cuba Hotel can be identified by its ghosted sign but most of the business district moved a few blocks north when Route 66 came through town.

The Wagon Wheel Cafe served hungry travelers for years on the east side of town, but now it is gone. The motel next door still operates in vintage giraffe-rock cottages.

The Midway Cafe on the corner of Franklin and Route 66 is also closed. In the early 1930s, this location was home to a garage and car showroom with a small restaurant out front.

Times were hard when Allyne Earls leased the place from Bill Mullen. But she was determined to succeed and it wasn't long before she owned the cafe. "I stayed there thirty-eight and one-half years and when I sold the place in 1972, we had to have a key made. I never locked it up in all that time," says Allyne.

Allyne had good help and business boomed. Fort Leonard Wood soldiers and Route 66 travelers kept the place going twenty-four hours a day. The Midway began with four booths, six tables and a bar that seated eight. Allyne expanded several times and business grew to 500 customers a day.

"When I decided to add the second floor for sleeping rooms, things were really a mess," she said. "We swung beams over folks' heads and moved tables from one side to the next to accommodate folks, but I never closed."

Allyne remembers that construction blocked the front entrance for several months so her customers had to enter through one of the big front windows. One couple traveling Route 66 saw all the cars around The Midway and decided to stop. When they realized people were climbing in and out through a window, they almost turned away. But curiosity got the best of them and they decided to give the place a try. They had such a good time they returned on every trip they made through Cuba. Allyne says she got Christmas cards from them for years.

Allyne's regular customers came from Fort Leonard Wood. One night a liquor inspector came in and demanded she immediately move some soldiers who had passed out. Allyne got friends to carry the men out the back door and deposit them on the lawn of the Mullens' house next door. When Mrs. Mullens saw what was going on, she climbed down her back porch steps carrying a load of pillows and blankets to make every soldier comfortable. When asked what she was doing, she replied that she had sons in the service someplace and she hoped someone would do the same for them.

Allyne is retired now and has a home behind the abandoned Midway. "I had thirty-six people working for me during those busy years," she says, "And I loved every minute of it." The enthusiasm in her voice is real— Route 66 years were good to Allyne Earls.

Here is a pudding cake Allyne served soon after cake mixes became popular in the 1940s.

MIDWAY CAFE
CHOCOLATE PUDDING CAKE

1 CUP BROWN SUGAR
½ CUP COCOA
2 CUPS WATER
12 MARSHMALLOWS, CUT IN QUARTERS
BATTER OF 1 DEVIL'S FOOD CAKE MIX
1 CUP PECANS, CHOPPED

COMBINE BROWN SUGAR, COCOA, AND WATER. Spread in greased 9- x 13-inch baking pan. Dot with marshmallows. Spoon devil's food cake batter over sugar and cocoa mixture. Top with chopped pecans and bake for 45 minutes in preheated 350° oven.

If baking in Pyrex dish, reduce heat to 325°. Serve in bowls with whipped cream on top. *10 to 12 servings.*

The Old Route 66 Cafe is located on Washington Street in an old building that still has original tiles around the windows and doors. Gary and Terry Hughes have operated the cafe since 1986. For thirty-five years, the location housed Ross and Ruby's Diner, then it became The Doughnut Hole before the Hughes changed its name and image.

Gary says he serves the best biscuits and gravy in the state. This may well be true because folks are waiting when he opens each morning at six a.m. and he doesn't even try to count the number of $1.99 breakfast specials and twenty-five-cent cups of coffee that he serves up.

Terry has Route 66 memorabilia for sale, including her own Route 66 Cafe button. The menu cover features an old Route 66 Missouri map showing all the ghost towns along the old road. Stop by; it's a warm and friendly place.

Out west of town, the Route 66 Lounge is another Cuba enterprise that makes the most of the old road. You'll find it across the street from the cemetery.

From Cuba, continue on County 66 and KK into Rosati and St. James. This is a rich grape production area and is often referred to as "Little Italy of the Ozarks." Grape stands line the access roads on the interstate during harvest season.

Serious settlement began around Rosati and St. James around 1895 when nearly a thousand natives of Bologna, Italy, moved to nearby northwestern Arkansas. Hard times made the original families scatter and many came to the St. James and Rosati area to buy three-dollar-an-acre railroad land. By the time of the great depression in 1929, over a thousand acres of grapes were being harvested each year by Italian farmers in the area. A grape growers association had formed and wine production began. In 1943, Welch Grape Juice Company bought facilities in the area.

Today there are several wineries in the Ozark Highland viticultural region.

Most offer tours so that visitors have an opportunity to see production and sample the wide variety of wines produced in the area.

The award-winning St. James Winery is on Highway 66, the north access road of I-44, at the Highway 68 exit. Owners and operators James and Patricia Hofherr and their sons, John and Andrew, offer tours year round.

Wines from the St. James Winery have been recognized at the Missouri State Fair with the Best of Show, gold, silver, and bronze awards; silver and bronze awards at the International Eastern Wine competition; and gold, silver, and bronze at the San Francisco, Florida, and Indiana State Fairs.

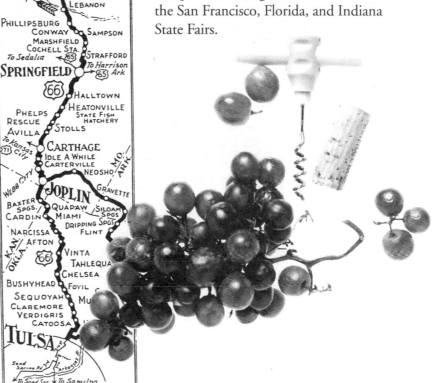

ST. JAMES WINERY SANGRIA

1 750 ML BOTTLE RED WINE
1 ORANGE, THINLY SLICED
1 LEMON, THINLY SLICED
½ CUP SUGAR
1 BOTTLE (28 OUNCES) CLUB SODA

COMBINE THE WINE, ORANGE, LEMON, AND SUGAR. Let sit one hour at room temperature. When ready to serve, add the club soda and serve over crushed ice. *6 eight-ounce servings.*

ST. JAMES WINERY GOURMET POTATO SALAD

12 TO 14 SMALL NEW POTATOES UNPEELED
(ABOUT 1 ½ POUNDS)
3 TABLESPOONS ST. JAMES COUNTRY WHITE WINE
¼ CUP OLIVE OIL
2 TABLESPOONS WINE VINEGAR
¼ TEASPOON DRIED WHOLE TARRAGON
¼ TEASPOON SALT
¼ TEASPOON WHITE PEPPER
1 TO 2 TABLESPOONS DIJON MUSTARD
¼ CUP THINLY SLICED GREEN ONIONS
¼ CUP MINCED FRESH PARSLEY

WASH POTATOES and cook in boiling water until tender. Cut into ¼-inch slices, add wine and let stand for 10 minutes. Combine olive oil and next five ingredients and stir well. Pour over potato mixture. Add green onions and parsley and stir gently. *8 servings.*

ST. JAMES WINERY LOGANBERRY WINE CAKE

½ CUP CHOPPED PECANS
1 BOX (18½ OUNCES) WHITE CAKE MIX
1 BOX (3 OUNCES) RASPBERRY GELATIN
4 EGGS
½ CUP VEGETABLE OIL
1 CUP ST. JAMES LOGANBERRY WINE

WINE CAKE GLAZE

1 CUP POWDERED SUGAR
½ CUP ST. JAMES LOGANBERRY WINE
½ CUP BUTTER

GREASE AND FLOUR BUNDT PAN and sprinkle nuts in bottom. In a large bowl, stir together the cake mix and gelatin. Add eggs, oil, and wine. Pour into bundt pan and bake one hour at 350°.

For the glaze combine and bring mixture to boil. Pour half over warm cake. Let cake sit 30 minutes, then pour remaining glaze over cake.

St. James, population 3,500, is a community filled with antique shops, turn-of-the-century homes, small businesses, and lovely green parks. Interesting activities are available for tourists almost all year.

In early May, local wineries have a festival featuring Missouri wines and food. In late May, the city of St. James sponsors a Strawberry Craft Festival highlighting the first fruits of the year. Over a hundred booths of good food and handmade crafts can be found.

Late August is the time for St. James Annual Grape Festival. Participants can take part in the grape stomp and enjoy a wide variety of related activities.

In late September, the wineries have a fall festival to celebrate the completion of harvest. A stop in St. James offers a memorable experience. Don't miss the fun.

ST. JAMES STRAWBERRIES IN WINE

Slice one quart of fresh strawberries and lightly sugar, using about ¼ cup sugar. Let berries sit to draw the juices. Stir in ¾ cup dry white wine before serving. *4 one-cup servings.*

ST. JAMES APPLES IN WINE

Pare and slice 2 to 4 apples. Place the following in microwave dish with a cover: ⅔ cup red dry or semi-dry wine, ⅔ cup sugar, 1 stick cinnamon, 4 cloves, ½ teaspoon salt (optional) and ½ thinly sliced lemon.

Heat mixture of wine and seasonings for 2 minutes on high with the lid on the dish. Pour sauce into measuring cup. Place apples in the same microwave dish and pour the sauce over the apples. Replace lid and cook on high 4-6 minutes, basting apples every minute until done. *3 to 4 servings.*

Tokey's Barbecue is a classic stop for Highway 66 road food. Originally on old 66 in Rolla, it is now located at the Junction of V and 66 near St. James. Just before entering Rolla, look for the Route 66 Motors and General Store on a piece of the old highway alignment. Formerly Strawhun Grocery and Filling Station, the old building dates from the 1880s and became a gas station in 1927. Wayne and Patricia Bales operate the store and are enthusiastic Route 66 Association members.

For years, Reg and Andy's was the downtown bus stop and a favorite with locals who enjoyed the coffee and good food. Andy Watterman, the popular owner, never met a stranger.

The Pierce Pennant Hotel dominated a bluff on the east side of Rolla during the 1930s and was the most elegant stop in the area. The hotel's restaurant was located away from the main building and parking service was offered in the basement. When Sinclair Oil bought into the business, it became the Sinclair Pennant Hotel.

"The oil companies that built the hotel designed amenities way before their time," says George Carney, who eventually bought the hotel and remodeled it in the popular tourist court mode. His Carney Manor served travelers for nearly fifteen years before he sold it in the 1960s. New owners leveled the historic structure and built a generic chain motel on the site.

Today George Carney owns and operates nearby Memoryville U.S.A., a lavish vintage car museum, sure to please Route 66 travel enthusiasts.

Zeno's Steak House and Motel has offered travelers in Rolla a superior stop since Zeno and Loretta Scheffer opened their business in 1955. The Scheffers' highest priorities were good service, quality, and a friendly atmosphere. Their vision and hard work has paid off.

"Zeno's is the place to go in Rolla for good steaks and good food," says Pat Bales, whose husband is a

Zeno's

Experience the Elegance

Missouri Route 66 Association director. Today, the Scheffer's sons carry on the outstanding tradition set by their parents. Tom and Janet Scheffer manage the business and Mike is the restaurant manager.

The lovely motel and steak house is on a piece of original Route 66, an access road for the interstate, and offers fine, casual dining of the highest quality. Zeno's has recently expanded and now has a steak house in the Route 66 community of Sullivan.

ZENO'S ITALIAN BROILED CHICKEN

½ CHICKEN, CUT UP (1 BREAST, 1 THIGH, 1 LEG, 1 WING)
1 STICK BUTTER
¼ CUP LEMON JUICE
SALT AND PEPPER TO TASTE
1 TEASPOON SWEET BASIL
2 TEASPOONS CHOPPED PARSLEY
1 TABLESPOON FRESHLY MINCED GARLIC

PLACE CHICKEN, SKIN SIDE UP, IN A SHALLOW BAKING DISH. Pour melted butter and lemon juice over chicken and season with salt pepper. Place chicken under broiler and cook approximately 10-12 minutes. Watch carefully to avoid burning. Turn chicken over and season with basil, parsley and garlic. Continue broiling and basting, turning chicken several times until done.

Remove chicken to hot platter. Discard most of the liquid in pan but pour a little of the seasoning over chicken. Garnish with lemon wedges to serve. *2 to 4 servings.*

Two miles west of Rolla city limits is the Old Homestead, opened in 1925 as one of the first truck stops in the country.

Vernelle's Cafe and Motel, eight miles west of Rolla, was built in 1952 by Fred and Vernelle Gasser. "We served a lot of barbecue and chicken," said Vernelle. "Soldiers from Fort Leonard Wood were some of our best customers." The Gassers had a fenced plot next to their business for horses, goats, and burros, which made a perfect drawing card for people traveling the highway with children.

Fred and Vernelle always had a New Year's Eve party for customers who stopped by. "We had a lot of fun and good times on Route 66," she said.

VERNELLE'S CAFE FRENCH DRESSING

1¾ CUPS SUGAR
2½ TABLESPOONS CURRY POWDER
⅓ TEASPOON GARLIC POWDER
1 TABLESPOON SALT
⅓ TEASPOON BLACK PEPPER
1 CAN (51 OUNCES) TOMATO SOUP
3 TABLESPOONS WORCESTERSHIRE SAUCE
1 TABLESPOON HEINZ 57 SAUCE
1 BOTTLE (17 OUNCES) OIL
½ TABLESPOON PREPARED MUSTARD
⅓ TEASPOON TABASCO SAUCE
17 OUNCES VINEGAR

COMBINE SUGAR WITH CURRY POWDER, garlic, salt and pepper.

Add remaining ingredients and beat with an electric mixer until well blended. Store in refrigerator until ready to use. *12 cups.*

The old highway along here was designed with half curbs meant to keep cars on the road by forcing them back into the travel lanes; instead, many cars tipped over. The road was also crooked and winding—lovely to look at, but deadly for unwary motorists. Small resort settlements built up in the area because Route 66 passed through good fishing and camping locations on the north edge of what is now the Mark Twain National Forest. Doolittle, Arlington, Stoney Dell, Powellville, Clementine, Hooker, and Devil's Elbow were within twenty miles.

Surprisingly, a five-mile stretch of highway along here became the first divided roadway between St. Louis and Tulsa. Built to accommodate Fort Leonard Wood troop movement during World War II, the improved highway bypassed some cafes and offered others an opportunity to thrive.

In Doolittle, the T&T Cafe was a popular stop. Near Powellville, east of the Fort Leonard Wood turnoff, Dink Denny's Cafe became a Greyhound Bus Stop on the new stretch of highway. Hamburgers were available for twenty-nine cents at Sterling's Hillbilly Store in Devil's Elbow. Near the Stoney Dell Resort, built by Vernon Prewitt, Bennett's Catfish did a thriving business when the fish were biting.

Waynesville is a picturesque community with a unique old Court House built in 1903. The community was the chief recreational center for Fort Leonard Wood soldiers during World War II and has settled into a quiet resort area today. The Hungry House Cafe and Tinkle Bar still operate on old Highway 66. The Bell Hotel, now the Waynesville Funeral Home, was advertised in a Highway Publicity Bureau's "Main Street of America" vintage map as: "Bell Hotel and Resort - West end of Waynesville - Good Meals - Hotel, Cottages, Tents, Camp Ground - Kitchen - Clean - Reasonable Rates."

Witmor Farms is on the north service road at the Buckhorn I-44 exit. Roy Moorman helped build the original steep-roofed, red-topped barn that became the first of the Nickerson Farms chain. He and his wife Norma bought the restaurant and have been serving their good food to hungry travelers since 1963. When Missouri Governor Ashcroft proclaimed Route 66 an official state historic highway, the Moormans provided the ceremonial trappings from Witmor Farms.

Roy remembers the time his wife prepared for a busload of English tourists. She knew they liked tea and took special pains to have teapots ready to serve them just as they were used to back home. One lady politely told Mrs. Moorman they were a little disappointed since they really wanted to try those "cute little teabags."

Roy serves his popular chili every day but says he can't make less than the four-gallon recipe without changing its flavor. Equally popular are these two regulars.

WITMOR FARMS PEACHES AND CREAM MOLD

1 CAN (29 OUNCES) SLICED PEACHES (2 CUPS, DRAINED)
1 CUP SYRUP FROM PEACHES
1 PACKAGE (3 OUNCES) LEMON GELATIN
⅔ CUP CREAM STYLE COTTAGE CHEESE
½ CUP CHOPPED PECANS
½ CUP WHIPPING CREAM

DRAIN PEACHES AND HEAT SYRUP TO BOILING. Add gelatin and cool until mixture is slightly thicker than unbeaten egg white. Stir in peaches, cottage cheese and pecans. Whip cream and fold into gelatin mixture. Pour into a 1-quart mold and allow to chill. Turn out to serve on buffet. *8 servings.*

WITMOR FARMS MACARONI SALAD

2 CUPS MACARONI
WATER TO COOK MACARONI
¾ TEASPOON SALT
½ TEASPOON WORCESTERSHIRE SAUCE
1 TABLESPOON SALAD OIL
¼ CUP CHOPPED ONION
1 CUP CHOPPED CELERY
½ CUP SWEET PICKLE RELISH
2 TABLESPOONS CHOPPED PIMENTO
1 CUP MAYONNAISE
1 TABLESPOON TARRAGON VINEGAR
¾ TEASPOON SUGAR
DASH WHITE PEPPER
½ CUP SHREDDED AMERICAN CHEESE

COOK MACARONI in boiling water until done, about 7 minutes.

Drain and add salt, Worcestershire and salad oil. Stir in onion, celery, relish and pimento. In a separate container, combine mayonnaise, vinegar, sugar, and pepper. Stir into salad and add shredded cheese. Chill before serving. *8 to 10 servings.*

This portion of Missouri 66 is especially lovely. Take time to enjoy the countryside, then drive into Sleeper to savor small-town America. The community is vintage Norman Rockwell.

For nearly fifty years, Loren and Norma Alloway operated Alloway's General Store in Sleeper. Norma remembered that her first customers bartered eggs and milk for gas that cost fifteen cents a gallon. At their rural version of a Quik Trip, they sold everything from cold cuts and cabbage to kerosene and chewing tobacco.

In 1965, the Alloways built the Satellite Cafe on Route 66. It stands abandoned on the north access road of I-44 today. Loren and Norma ran the cafe and service station next door for fourteen years, staying open twenty-four hours a day. Norma said she always hired older women who were good cooks since she had to divide her time between the cafe and the store.

The Alloway children have kept the General Store open. The store is Americana at its best—a must-stop on Missouri 66.

NORMA ALLOWAY'S SATELLITE CAFE ROLLS

1 CUP MILK
1 PACKAGE YEAST
3 TABLESPOONS SUGAR
3 EGGS, BEATEN WELL
¼ CUP MARGARINE, MELTED
½ TEASPOON SALT
4½ CUPS FLOUR

WARM MILK AND ADD YEAST AND SUGAR. Let stand a few minutes to proof. Stir in eggs, margarine, salt, and flour. Let rise, shape into buns and let rise again. Bake at 375° for 18 to 20 minutes. *30 rolls.*

NORMA ALLOWAY'S SATELLITE CAFE OATMEAL CAKE

1 CUP OLD-FASHIONED OATMEAL
1¼ CUPS BOILING WATER
1 STICK MARGARINE
¾ CUP SUGAR
1 CUP BROWN SUGAR
2 EGGS
1 TEASPOON VANILLA
1½ CUPS FLOUR
¼ TEASPOON SALT
1 TEASPOON CINNAMON
1 TEASPOON SODA
1½ TEASPOONS BAKING POWDER

FROSTING

1/4 CUP MARGARINE
4 TABLESPOONS MILK
½ CUP BROWN SUGAR
¾ CUP FLAKED COCONUT
½ CUP CHOPPED PECANS

IN A LARGE BOWL, combine oatmeal with boiling water and set aside for 20 minutes. Cream margarine; add sugar and blend. Stir in eggs and vanilla. Add dry ingredients to the oatmeal mixture, then stir into the shortening, sugar and eggs. Bake in a greased 8 x 12 inch pan in a preheated 350° oven for 35 minutes.

For the frosting, bring the margarine, milk, and sugar to a boil. Add remaining ingredients and cool slightly before spreading over cake. Place under broiler just long enough to toast coconut if desired. *12 servings*

Lebanon, the largest community between Rolla and Springfield, has almost overcome the dubious reputation of being the used car capital of the nation. In this town of 10,000, there were once over 150 used car dealers. Elm Street is Route 66 through town.

Lebanon's Munger Moss Cafe and Motel has a long history on Route 66. It all began when Jessie and Pete Hudson bought the Chicken Shanty Cafe and some land next to it in 1947. They changed the name to Munger Moss Cafe, put in a barbecue, and built a motel. The name had appeal. They had used it in their first barbecue cafe at Devil's Elbow where a Mrs. Munger had married a Mr. Moss and had run the original restaurant. Munger Moss at Devil's Elbow closed when that dangerous stretch of Highway 66 was straightened, leaving the tiny cafe high and dry, without customers.

Jim Sponseller bought the Munger Moss Cafe in 1952 and ran it until he retired in 1979. His mother, Iva, joined the business and was noted for her outstanding food, particularly her Cherry Cream Pie. Ada Moore, who worked as a waitress at the Munger Moss, says Mrs. Sponseller's pies were more than good, they were works of art. At the Munger Moss, hot rolls were big and mouthwatering and barbecue was considered the best in the Ozarks.

Sponseller remembers feeding people who were hungry and loaning money to those in need. One man remembered the loan. His son returned ten years later and repaid Sponseller the $20 that his father had accepted as he struggled to get his family to California. The Munger Moss Cafe now stands empty but the historic Munger Moss Motel still operates next door.

Here is Iva Sponseller's popular pie recipe.

MUNGER MOSS CHERRY CREAM PIE

1 PACKAGE (3 OUNCES) CREAM CHEESE
½ CUP POWDERED SUGAR
1 CUP DREAM WHIP
1 CAN (16 OUNCES) SOUR CHERRIES
2 TABLESPOONS CORNSTARCH
PINCH OF SALT
1 DROP OF RED FOOD COLORING
2 CUPS DREAM WHIP
1 TEN-INCH PIE CRUST, BAKED

SOFTEN CREAM CHEESE and blend with powdered sugar until smooth. Fold in 1 cup of Dream Whip and blend well. Spoon mixture into pie shell and place in freezer for 20 minutes. Drain cherries. Heat cherry juice and thicken with cornstarch. Add salt and a drop of food coloring. Add cherries to juice and allow mixture to cool. Spread over cream cheese mixture. Cover with Dream Whip. Store in refrigerator until served. *8 servings.*

Andy's Street Car Grill operated in Lebanon from 1946 through 1960. Rabbit and chicken were the specialties and the big sign out front proclaimed, "The finest foods in the Ozarks." Andy Lierl, the owner, said folks had never eaten good chicken unless they had eaten at his grill. The old streetcar was a classic diner where patrons lined the stools, bantered with the waitresses, and sipped coffee as black as the early morning sky.

Camp Joy, another early tourist mecca in Lebanon, became the Joy Motel and is now an efficiency apartment complex.

West of Lebanon, Gail and Izola Henson served good food at the Bungalow Inn from 1936 to 1946. Izola remembers serving plate lunches for thirty-five cents each and renting cabins out back from $1.00 to $3.00 per night. By 1946, they had made enough to buy a farm so they sold out and moved away. Soon, the new highway alignment took the location.

Izola remembers the day she served dinner for Tom Mix and his wife. Mrs. Mix had stopped by to fill up with gas at the Henson's Mobil pump. While she was in the Inn, her car caught fire. Despite efforts to save it, the car, and the fur coat, watch, and diamond ring she had left inside it were destroyed.

"She told us to just leave the ashes alone until an insurance man get could out there. We watched the car but someone stole the fancy TM logos from its doors," Izola said. "When the insurance people went over what was left of the car, they sifted the ashes and found her diamond and a coat hanger so they paid the insurance." Tom Mix gave Izola and her husband tickets to his performance in Lebanon when he and his group ate at the cafe a few nights later.

BUNGALOW INN'S BREADED PORK CHOPS

2 EGGS
½ CUP MILK
4 TO 6 PORK CHOPS
I CUP FINE CRACKER CRUMBS
SALT AND PEPPER TO TASTE
SHORTENING

BEAT EGGS AND MILK UNTIL BLENDED WELL. Dip chops into mixture, then into cracker crumbs to coat. Salt and pepper to taste and place in skillet with small amount of hot shortening. Brown on both sides. Reduce heat and cook until well done. *4 to 6 servings.*

Back in 1929, Marie and Barney Harris opened the Harris Cafe in Conway. The cafe's reputation spread all along Route 66 as "The Home of the Little Round Pie." Marie had seen small meat pies on a trip to California and decided she could copy the idea with fruit. She made meringue-topped cream pies with equal success. The pies sold for ten cents each and Marie made her name on the highway.

All kinds of travelers stopped at the Harris Cafe. There were repeat customers who had gone to California, then come back again after an earthquake in 1933. Unemployed men who rode the nearby railroad stopped in search of food, and during World War II, soldiers who were being bussed across the country ate at the cafe.

David McShane, a neighbor who owned three service stations in Conway, remembers the gypsy customers with their colorful clothes and jewelry who used to stop in Conway. Two just as colorful, and certainly more famous, customers were Bonnie and Clyde, who stopped at the Harris Cafe several times. Marie remembers they always ate near the window and Bonnie had such bowed legs that she wore long dresses to hide them.

McShane's Cafe is now located at the Conway exit of the interstate and sure enough, they still sell little round pies! Larry McShane and his wife operate the restaurant that makes a nostalgic stop.

Heading toward Marshfield, Route 66 is the north access road for the interstate. At Exit 107, another Route 66 classic stands abandoned with no indication that it was once The Garbage Can Cafe.

When Kermit and Letha Lowery decided to build a cafe on Route 66 in 1952, a friend told them no one would ever remember a name like Lowery's Cafe. So they began brainstorming and that same friend suggested, almost in jest, that people wouldn't forget them if the cafe was called The Garbage Can. The idea stuck and paid off. Letha inherited the little round pie dough recipe and The Garbage Can became the second home of the famous pies.

Barbara Letterman worked for the Lowerys at The Garbage Can when she was in high school and says she will always remember watching Letha pinch off the pie dough she made in quantity, roll it deftly into shape, add the filling, and pop a whole tray in the oven almost as fast as others could bake conventional pies.

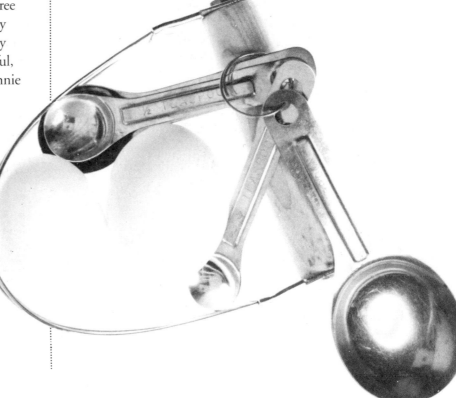

"We baked three to four hundred pies a day," Letha remembers. "And we always made the dough up a day ahead. It made a crisper crust after standing." Letha's recipe was simple. For each gallon of flour, a half gallon of shortening and half that amount of water was used. A little salt was added then the dough was stored in a tightly covered container until the next day. Through experience, Letha and her cooks learned exactly how much dough to use for each little pie. Letha still has several of the individual pie tins she used so often. She says each pie was just the right size to satisfy a hungry appetite.

LITTLE ROUND PIE DOUGH

2 CUPS FLOUR
1 CUP SHORTENING
¼ TEASPOON SALT
½ CUP COLD WATER

COMBINE FLOUR WITH SHORTENING until mixture resembles small peas. Add salt and water and blend only until dough holds together. Cover tightly with plastic wrap and store in refrigerator until next day. Roll out to make a double crust 9-inch pie or six little round pies.

Strafford is home to the Exotic Animal Farm. For those who remember the snake farms, coyote dens, and prairie dog towns that beckoned during the Route 66 heyday, this is the place to stop.

Stratford Confectionery and Highway Inn - Cold Drinks - Good Eats - Your Wants Satisfied."

(Highway Publicity Bureau's "Main Street of America" vintage map.)

During the 1930s and 1940s, Strafford's Ranch Hotel made a comfortable stop for travelers between St. Louis and Oklahoma City. Located sixteen miles east of Springfield, it dominated a country site along the highest elevation in the Missouri Ozarks. Practically everything served at their table came from their own farms and the hotel had one of the first electric dishwashers in the country.

Springfield, the "Queen City of the Ozarks," is a lovely college community that becomes a fairyland of lights each Christmas. Springfield is the Ozark gateway to Branson and the Missouri and Arkansas tourist region. Route 66 enters Springfield from the east on Kearney, turns south on Glenstone, takes St. Louis through the old town square, and continues west on College and Chestnut.

Pearl and Vern's Cafe has been a Route 66 stop on Kearney for years, but Pearl retired after Christmas in 1991. The cafe, built originally in the 1940s as Carl's Truck Stop, was first operated by Carl Appleby and his wife.

Route 66 travelers today will find good food at Trotters Barbecue and Grill on the corner of Glenstone and Chestnut. This award-winning restaurant was spawned back in 1976 when Steve Trotter graduated from college and joined his dad in the food business. Their first endeavor was a tiny barbecue stop with a walk-up counter where food was dished out on paper plates and there were only a few seats for the customers. Behind the scenes, good barbecue recipes were being tested and developed.

The Glenstone, Route 66, site opened in 1979. Today there are seven Trotter locations, including one on Historic 66 in St. Louis.

Unfortunately, many vintage Route 66 eating places in Springfield are gone. But memories die hard in Ozark country, and one of the best was Gabriel's Waffle House where hungry customers found good food even before Route 66 came through town. Harry Gabriel, Sr., opened his first restaurant in 1918 and had three locations on Route 66 before closing for good in 1966. For many years, Gabriel's was the only eating place open twenty-four hours a day between St. Louis and Tulsa. "My father came to the United States as a stowaway from Greece when he was nine years old," said Harry "Bud" Gabriel, Jr. "He found work with the railroad and when he got to the Ozarks, knew he had found a home."

GABRIEL'S WAFFLE HOUSE SPAGHETTI

3 TABLESPOONS OLIVE OIL
2 CLOVE GARLIC, CHOPPED
3 MEDIUM ONIONS, CHOPPED
1 CAN (6 OUNCES) TOMATO PASTE
1 POUND LEAN HAMBURGER MEAT
1 CAN (16 OUNCES) TOMATOES
1 CAN (10½ OUNCES) TOMATO SOUP
1 TEASPOON CINNAMON
2 TEASPOONS CHILI POWDER
SALT AND PEPPER TO TASTE

HEAT OLIVE OIL IN LARGE SKILLET. Add garlic and onions and cook until onions are golden brown. Add tomato paste and mix well. Add hamburger and cook until meat is well done. Add tomatoes, soup, cinnamon, chili powder, salt and pepper. Cover and simmer 1½ hours. Cook spaghetti and drain well. Cover each serving of spaghetti with sauce and sprinkle with grated Parmesan cheese. *6 servings.*

GABRIEL'S BLUE CHEESE DRESSING

1 BOTTLE (8 OUNCES) CATSUP
½ TEASPOON SUGAR SAUCE
½ TEASPOON CIDER VINEGAR
½ TEASPOON GARLIC POWDER
½ TEASPOON WORCESTERSHIRE
½ CUP VEGETABLE OIL
4 OUNCES BLUE CHEESE

COMBINE CATSUP, SUGAR, VINEGAR, GARLIC POWDER, AND WORCESTERSHIRE SAUCE. Blend with mixer, blender, or food processor. Add vegetable oil slowly, beating until smooth. Crumble blue cheese and stir into dressing. *1 ½ cups.*

Gabriel, Sr. opened Gabriel's Waffle House on the town square where Boatmen's Bank is located today. He moved to St. Louis Street in 1935, then back to the square in 1948. His son Bud worked in the restaurant. "My dad always said an idle kid is no good," he remembers. When Harry Truman began testing the political waters in southwestern Missouri, he would stop in Springfield at Gabriel's Waffle House to measure the barometer of local politics.

Bud Gabriel says his father maintained a large herd of dairy cattle and was one of the first persons in the area to pasteurize milk. Springfield has grown to be one of the country's largest dairy production centers.

Many other Route 66 Springfield eating places have disappeared with time. Among them are the Fred Harvey House at the Frisco Station, the Hotel Moran Coffee Shop, the St. Louis Street Cafe, the Cortez Coffee Shop, the Corn Crib Cafe, and K and K Hamburgers and Chili. At K and K, the cook had only to open a window above his grill when business was slow. The aroma of great hamburgers floated across the Southern Missouri State University campus and the place filled immediately with hungry students.

In the 1940s, Davidson's Cafeteria at 412 St. Louis was a popular stop. Noted for fine roast beef, baked ham, and chicken pie, the cafeteria also had a wide variety of desserts, including a memorable pecan pie.

The Kentwood Arms Hotel, three blocks from the square, was located on three and one-half acres of shaded lawn. Ozark rainbow trout and braised guinea hen were often featured on the menu.

The Colonial Hotel, in downtown Springfield, was built at a cost of $300,000 and opened to the public in 1907. For many years, the Colonial Dining Room was one of Springfield's most popular eating places. Mr. and Mrs. Charles Sansone owned and operated the hotel from 1926 to 1945.

The hotel is now owned by the Southern Missouri State University Foundation and has fallen into disrepair. It stands as an abandoned downtown relic, a souvenir of the past with a questionable future.

*"Springfield Boston Coffee Shop
Clean - Reasonable Good Coffee."*

(Highway Publicity Bureau's "Main Street of America" vintage map.)

Red Chaney purchased Wayne Lillard's old gas station on Chestnut Expressway just after World War II. He turned the station into "Red Chaney's Giant Hamburg," and advertised as the world's first hamburger stand with a drive-through window. Chaney opened his business at the peak of highway traffic on U.S. 66 and it was an immediate success. He stayed open evenings as long as there was traffic, often spending the weekend at the cafe.

Red and his wife, Julia, were entrepreneurs who took delight in being different. "Red put two-gallon water jugs on each table and two on the counter so his time wasn't spent on drawing water. It gave the customers something to do during the short wait for food," said Julia.

Customers made their own change from a shoebox on the counter. During business hours, Red served customers and turned the kitchen over to Julia.

Root beer, giant hamburgs, fish, chili, and shakes were each prepared using Red's own unique recipes. He ground his own hamburger meat, using the best grade of beef to ensure flavor, and made root beer from licorice. The root beer was stored next to magnets to "take nitrogen out of the water." Pinto beans were soaking by five a.m. each morning. He cooked the beans in crock pots scattered around the kitchen. By today's standards, Red might be labeled a food faddist, but whatever he did worked. For almost forty years folks flocked to his hamburger stand to eat his food and tell others of the experience.

His famous "Hamburg" sign was an accident that paid off. Space ran out before his painter had completed the sign out front. The idea of being unique appealed to Red, so the sign was never corrected. "We always had an old car parked in front of that sign so cars couldn't come close and break the neon letters," Julia said. After they retired, the city asked them to take the sign down. A local band group took pieces of the sign for souvenirs and by the time they had finished, there wasn't much to dispose of, she recalled. Decor inside was one-of-a-kind, too. The ceiling was a blue tint that Red declared flies wouldn't touch. Seats were outdoor green and the floor was dirt brown. He felt the picnic atmosphere he created would stimulate appetites. Red and Julia retired in the mid-1980s and Springfield lost a never-to-be-forgotten piece of history.

Red perfected his own sweet garlic dressing to go with lettuce salad. For many years he sold the dressing for $1.00 a pint but the last few years, he raised the price to $1.25.

RED CHANEY'S FAMOUS SALAD DRESSING

IN A LARGE SAUCEPAN COMBINE: 6¾ tablespoons paprika, 1½ teaspoons Accent, 1 scant teaspoon salt, 1 teaspoon ground pepper, 2⅓ tablespoons powdered garlic, and 2 tablespoons marjoram.

Blend these together well, then stir in: ¼ cup fresh lemon juice, 2½ tablespoons A-1 Steak Sauce, 5 tablespoons El Paso brand canned tomatoes and green chilies (can use another brand but tomatoes will have to be chopped fine).

Stir ingredients to a thick paste. Slowly add 6 ounces of vegetable oil, stirring constantly.

After adding the oil, stir in 3 cups Karo brand white corn syrup, one cup at a time. Mix well after each addition. Transfer dressing to wide mouth jar since the dressing should be stirred before using. Store in refrigerator. *1 quart.*

Red and Julia made this recipe four gallons at a time and never "cut" it in size. "Lots of people told me it was really great!" she said.

Farther west on Chestnut is the 7 Gables Restaurant, the oldest Route 66 eating place still in business on the historic road in Springfield. Built in the 1930s, the restaurant was a two-story affair with seven imposing gables. The cafe has had several owners and a roller-coaster existence. Today, Perry Lin and his wife own the historic location. Carl Hayden, Jr., remembers his family operating the 7 Gables in the late 1940s. Carl said his dad put up the biggest neon sign in the Springfield area.

The Hayden family had a direct hookup with Radio Station KWTO and broadcast from the restaurant with Uncle Carl and the Hayden family singing folk music. They were an important part of the famous Ozark Jamboree Music that originated in Springfield. The Hayden family had an apartment on the second floor above the restaurant. When a kitchen fire destroyed the place in 1949, they sold out and moved to Nebraska.

The old eating place was rebuilt, minus the gables and second floor, and for several years, Bud McCoy ran it with the help of his mother, Maude, who was an excellent cook. Ida Painter remembers taking her first job as a waitress at the 7 Gables. She was fifteen years old when McCoy hired her. Ida says it was a rude awakening for her when many out-of-state customers expected Ozark waitresses to be barefoot hillbillies, right out of Lil' Abner.

Interstate truckers, bus loads of students headed for football games, and thousands of tourists have kept employees at the 7 Gables busy during the years.

SCENIC HI-WAY

INTERSTATE 40

INTERSTATE 44

US 66

INTERSTATE 55

Jesse James Bank Robbery Sullivan, Mo.

Lake Lou Yeager Litchfield, Ill.

Longs Historical Museum Claremore, Okla.

Buena Vista's Exotic Animal Paradise Strafford, Mo.

CHICAGO

163

LINCOLN

88

LITCHFIELD

HERITAGE INN RESTAURANT, ANTIQUE COCKTAIL LOUNGE

LINCOLN MOTEL

ILLINOIS

68

51

THE ANNEX MOTEL & RESTAURANT

41 **STE. GENEVIEVE**

STANTON

OLD BRICK HOUSE RESTAURANT

3

7

SULLIVAN

MERAMEC CAVERNS

MISSOURI

8

BOURBON

DU-KUM-INN

3

CROSSROADS RESTAURANT

CUBA

7

11

12 (19)

ST. JAMES

ONONDAGA CAVE

34

9

ROLLA

SALEM

(72)

28

AKERS FERRY RESORT

CHAMPLIN RESTAURANT & TRUCK STOP

19

LEBANON

MUNGER MOSS MOTEL

STRAFFORD 37

132

DEWARD & PAULINE'S MOTEL & RESTAURANT

BUENA VISTA'S EXOTIC ANIMAL PARADISE

MISSOURI

CLAREMORE

FRIENDSHIP INN - HOLIDAY MOTEL & RESTAURANT

124

OKLAHOMA CITY

THE WILSON HOUSE MOTEL & RESTAURANT

7 GABLES STUFFED PEPPERS

STUFFED PEPPERS

1 POUND LEAN GROUND BEEF

1½ TEASPOONS BEEF BASE

2 TABLESPOONS DICED ONION

1 EGG

¾ CUP COOKED RICE

¼ TEASPOON GARLIC POWDER

¼ CUP BREAD CRUMBS

¼ TEASPOON SEASONING SALT

½ TEASPOON SALT

¼ TEASPOON PEPPER

4 LARGE PEPPERS, CUT IN HALF

CREOLE SAUCE

1 CAN (20 OUNCES) TOMATOES

1 CAN (10 OUNCES) TOMATO PUREE

2 TABLESPOONS MINCED ONION

2 TABLESPOONS MINCED GREEN PEPPER

1 TEASPOON MINCED GARLIC

¼ TEASPOON BASIL

1 TABLESPOON SUGAR

PREHEAT OVEN TO 350°. Combine meat with all ingredients except peppers. Stuff peppers with mixture and place in baking dish. Cover and bake for 15 minutes. Uncover peppers and continue cooking until done, about 30 minutes. Meanwhile combine all ingredients for Creole Sauce and heat in saucepan. Pour sauce over peppers and return to oven to keep hot until served. *8 servings.*

In Halltown, population 160, visitors will find more antique shops per capita than in any other community along Route 66. Halltown is also remembered for good food. Sylvia Rogers opened a cafe on Route 66 in the early 1930s. She served thousands of customers before Sylvia's Cafe was reduced to ashes in the mid-1950s.

Sylvia and her daughter-in-law, Wilma Rogers, were known as excellent cooks and were particularly famous for their pies. Sandy Dunn, who works at the Springfield Chamber of Commerce, remembers driving to Halltown to eat pie when she was still in high school. She says that after the fire, Wilma went to work next door at the Las Vegas Hotel and Cafe where she continued to cook for several years.

Sylvia's daughter, Inez Bullard, has lived in Halltown all her life and shares this chili recipe that was prepared in quantity at the cafe.

SYLVIA'S HALLTOWN CAFE CHILI AND BEANS

3 TABLESPOONS CHOPPED ONION
2 TABLESPOONS CHOPPED GREEN PEPPER
3 CLOVES GARLIC, MINCED
2 TABLESPOONS VEGETABLE OIL
1 POUND COARSELY GROUND LEAN BEEF
2 TABLESPOONS CHILI POWDER
1 CAN (16 OUNCES) TOMATOES
1 CAN (16 OUNCES) PINTO BEANS

SAUTÉ ONIONS, GREEN PEPPER, AND GARLIC in vegetable oil until tender. Add ground beef and brown thoroughly. Add chili powder, tomatoes, and beans. Heat thoroughly, adding water if needed. *4 to 5 servings.*

The Las Vegas Hotel and Cafe was built after Charlie Dameron, the Halltown barber, took a trip west one year and returned with his winnings. "When he got off the Greyhound bus out there, he had a suitcase so heavy that he had to get his wife to help carry it home," said Jerry White, a lifetime resident of Halltown. "I was just a kid when I watched them put a hoe through the handle so they could carry it across the street and up the block to their house." Charlie built the hotel and cafe and named it the Las Vegas. It had six rooms upstairs and a ground floor cafe with a big circular counter.

Whitehall Mercantile is the oldest surviving building in Halltown. It was built in 1900 as a general store, and Jerry and his wife, Thelma, run it today. Both are enthusiastic Route 66 Association supporters in Missouri.

Down the street, at The Flea Market and Post Office, Ida Painter can serve you a quick lunch from her tiny kitchen. Ida owns the antique and collectable business today, but she has lived and worked in eating places on Route 66 from Baxter Springs, Kansas, to Springfield, Missouri. She's a good cook.

"Halltown Mason's Cafe, Service Station and Hotel
Regular meals - Drinks - Cigars - Candies - Free Camp Tourist Supplies."
(Highway Publicity Bureau's "Main Street of America" vintage map.)

If you take a short stretch of old, old 66, called Highway N, off Highway 96 beyond Halltown, Betty's Country Inn immediately comes into view. This unexpected stop has been an eating place on the old road since the 1930s. Betty says some of the timbers in the original building were hand cut. The restaurant today is plain vanilla white stucco but it's what's inside that counts. Betty's is always filled.

The hardworking waitresses are friendly and helpful, and most of the customers are regulars who have known each other all their lives. Truckers make a point to eat with Betty and go out of their way to be there at mealtime.

Tea at Betty's is clear and perfectly brewed, hamburger plates come out hot and flawlessly prepared, and her plate-lunch specials can't be beaten.

Bob Gleason recalls, "I owned the place up there before Betty. I called it the Cowboy Inn Cafe and opened it in 1963 after I had renovated the place. All it had was running water back then— right through the roof." Bob sold the restaurant to Betty and "Cotten" Hopper in July of 1974.

BETTY'S COUNTRY INN HASH BROWNS SUPREME

IN SEPARATE SKILLETS OR ON THE GRILL, fry 2 cups hash brown potatoes and 4 ounces sausage. Scramble together. Add 2 tablespoons each of finely chopped onions and bell peppers. Stir and turn until done. Shape potato mixture like an omelet and sprinkle grated cheddar cheese on top. Allow cheese to melt then turn out on two platters and add freshly chopped tomatoes on top. *2 servings.*

BETTY'S COUNTRY INN SALAD DRESSING CAKE

2 CUPS SUGAR
4 TABLESPOONS COCOA
4 CUPS FLOUR
4 TEASPOONS SODA
¼ TEASPOON SALT
2 CUPS SALAD DRESSING
2 CUPS LUKEWARM WATER
2 TEASPOONS VANILLA

SIFT TOGETHER THE SUGAR, cocoa, flour, soda and salt. Add salad dressing, water and vanilla. Stir well. Do not beat!

Grease and flour three 9-inch layer cake pans. Pour batter in pans and bake in preheated 350° oven for 30 to 35 minutes. Frost with your favorite frosting. *3 layers, 20 generous servings.*

Today Bob Gleason can be found in his office next to the Crossroads Cafe where Missouri 39 and 96 intersect. The tiny community of Albatross nestles along the highway here. Bob says old-timers named the village for the bird because early Route 66 cars flew through town without stopping. His Crossroads Cafe is located where a filling station, cafe and dance hall have served highway customers since 1929. Ten years ago, Ida Painter worked at the Crossroads Cafe. She shares the favorite French Coconut Pie that she makes occasionally at the Flea Market in Halltown.

IDA PAINTER'S FRENCH COCONUT PIE

3 EGGS, BEATEN
1½ CUPS SUGAR
½ CUP MARGARINE, MELTED
1 TABLESPOON VINEGAR
1 TEASPOON VANILLA
1 CUP COCONUT
1 UNBAKED 9-INCH PIE SHELL

COMBINE INGREDIENTS in order given and pour into pie shell.

Bake in preheated 350° oven for 40 to 45 minutes or until set. *6 to 8 servings.*

Tiny communities grew up on Route 66 as the need arose. When residents moved on, empty buildings were left behind to harbor ghosts from the past. Along here were Plano, Spencer, Heatonville, Albatross, Phelps, Rescue, Plew, Log City, and Stone City. Travelers can only imagine what life must have been like when Highway 66 reached its heyday and traffic kept them all alive.

Avila is a small survivor. A sign at the edge of town says "Population 100." Years ago, Floyd Melugin operated the Friendly Cafe and Tavern in Avila and there was a choice of filling stations and eating places.

> *"Avila Dew Drop Inn*
> *Sandwiches - Cold Drinks - Ice Cream -*
> *Smokes - Candies - Coffee - Home Made*
> *Pies. 6:30 a.m. to 10:00 p.m."*

(Highway Publicity Bureau's "Main Street of America" vintage map.)

Ozark artist Lowell Davis maintains a forty-acre farm just outside Carthage where he is resurrecting memories of his own Route 66 childhood at Foxfire Farm, Red Oak II. The expanding complex is open for all those who love to reminisce.

Davis grew up in the minuscule Missouri Route 66 community of Red Oak. He was seven or eight when he took his first trip west on Highway 66. It was on that trip that he ate in a cafe for the first time. On a recent trip west, he rediscovered in Santa Rosa, New Mexico, the same cafe that he remembered from childhood.

To recognize and honor Route 66, in 1991 Davis introduced three figurines inspired by the old road. "I want to preserve vanishing America in my art, and Route 66 is certainly a big part of it. I just want to make sure its memory stays alive for future generations," he says.

Davis puts out a quarterly newsletter for his fan club members called the Lowell Davis Farm Gazette and in each issue, his wife, "Miss Charlotte," shares a recipe. Here is the recipe from the inaugural issue of the paper, along with other summertime favorites.

She begins, "I can get more honey-do's done in one day than I can in a month, if Mr. Lowell knows he's getting Poulet and Dumplings for supper. I feel it only fitting that I share his most favorite down-home meal. Most people call it Chicken and Dumplings, but here on the farm it's called Poulet and Dumplings, due to the fact that Big Jack or one of the hens might be within hearing distance. (They don't understand French.)"

CHARLOTTE'S POULET AND DUMPLINGS

BOIL WHOLE CHICKEN IN BIG KETTLE TILL TENDER. Remove from broth and pick meat off bones when cool. Strain broth. To the broth, add 6 to 8 chicken bouillon cubes, 6 grated carrots, 4 stalks chopped celery, 2 chopped onions, 2 tablespoons chopped parsley, 2 leeks, chopped (if used, omit one onion), and salt and pepper to taste. Boil until tender and add diced chicken and bring to a boil. Add dumpling dough by small spoonful onto hot vegetables, not directly into liquid. Cook uncovered 10 minutes. Cover and cook another 10 minutes. Check to see when dumplings are fluffy.

DUMPLINGS

Mix 1½ cups flour, 2 teaspoons baking powder, and ¾ teaspoon salt. Then thoroughly cut in 3 tablespoons shortening. Next stir in ¾ cup of milk. This will be thinner than regular biscuit dough.
Say grace and dig in!
6 to 8 servings.

CHARLOTTE'S CUCUMBER SALAD

2 TO 4 CUCUMBERS
1 CUP BOILING WATER
¾ CUP SOUR CREAM
2 TABLESPOONS VINEGAR
1 TABLESPOON DILL SEED
1 TABLESPOON SUGAR
½ TEASPOON SALT
½ TEASPOON PEPPER

PEEL CUCUMBERS AND SLICE VERY THIN. Pour boiling water over them. Drain immediately and cover with ice water. Drain again and dry. Mix together sour cream, vinegar, dill, sugar, salt, and pepper. Toss with cucumbers. Chill 30 minutes and enjoy! *6 to 8 servings.*

CHARLOTTE'S CHOCOLATE CHIP COFFEE CAKE

¼ POUND SOFT BUTTER
3 EGGS
1 CUP SUGAR
1 TEASPOON SODA
1½ CUPS FLOUR
8 OUNCES SOUR CREAM
1 TEASPOON VANILLA
1 TEASPOON BAKING SODA
⅓ CUP BROWN SUGAR
¼ CUP WHITE SUGAR
1/2 CUP CHOPPED NUTS
1 PACKAGE (6 OUNCES) CHOCOLATE CHIPS
2 TEASPOONS CINNAMON

PREHEAT OVEN TO 350°. Grease and flour a 9 x 13 baking pan.

Cream together the butter, eggs, and sugar. Add soda, flour, and sour cream and blend well. Add vanilla and soda.

In a second small bowl combine the brown sugar, white sugar, nuts, chocolate chips, and cinnamon. Pour half of the batter in the baking pan and cover with half of the dry mixture. Gently smooth over with spoon and repeat with batter and dry mixture. Bake for 35 to 40 minutes. *10 to 12 servings.*

Driving into Carthage on the old alignment of Route 66, motorists can only imagine the nightly activity around the Riverside Inn that was built in the 1930s. It was off-limits to the younger generation because the nightclub sold alcohol. The building burned mysteriously one night in the late 1960s.

This low area next to the Spring River was subject to flooding and stranded countless impatient motorists through the years. The vintage Red Rock Motel still stands nearby.

Route 66 enters Carthage on Central, turns onto Main and leaves on Oak. Jack Sink ran a popular cafe at the bus stop for years and Ray Carter's C&W Cafe was a fixture on the square. Boot's Drive-In was a popular stop at the intersection of Highways 66 and 71.

Take time to admire the Jasper County Courthouse. The building, made from gray marble taken from local quarries, is a true work of art. The ancient clocktower still works and the elevator dates from 1917.

Belle Star, the notorious bandit queen, was born in Carthage where her father's hotel, on the north side of the court house square, was burned when the Civil War began. Years later, on that same square, a popular restaurant that was named for her also burned. The Shirley family moved to a farm near Allen, Texas, after Belle's brother was killed during the bloody war.

"Carthage Turnage Cafe 1/2 block south of Intersection
71 - Clean - Good Cooking - Reasonable."

(Highway Publicity Bureau's "Main Street of America" vintage map.)

Today, the Carthage Deli and Doughnut, on the northwest corner of the square, is a busy downtown lunch stop. The decor is right out of the 50s and includes a neon Route 66 sign, a vintage car booth, and old photographs and signs. The black and white checked floor and drugstore chairs add to the nostalgic atmosphere.

Carthage is an area art center, hosting several well-known resident artists in addition to Lowell Davis. Samuel J. Butcher first introduced Precious Moments porcelain figurines in 1978. Now his

Carthage chapel is open for daily tours and a well-stocked gift shop is located nearby. Tiffany's Restaurant forms an important part of the complex and offers good food in a relaxed atmosphere.

Historic 66 continues through Carterville and Webb City where the old Bradbury Bishop Drugstore is just off the old highway at Main and Daugherty Streets. At one time Webb City was also home to Babe's Drive-In.

Follow State Road 66 through Joplin toward the Kansas line. Law's Silver Castle was once located at 8th and Main. During the late 1940s the restaurant's varied menu included their famous "ring-cooked" steaks.

An earlier Joplin restaurant, Daniel's Grill, became one of the original "Chicken In The Rough" franchises in 1937. The combination of a half chicken, shoestring potatoes, hot rolls, and honey made an instant hit. Wilder's Cafe was also located on Main.

Joplin is the western gateway to the Ozarks. On the edge of an ore-producing region that extends through southwestern Missouri, Kansas, and into Oklahoma, the city sits atop countless abandoned mining tunnels. Cave-ins occasionally occur along Route 66 as limestone cavities give way. Drive quietly as you head into Kansas.

"Joplin, Missouri Bob Miller's Restaurant at 419 Main. AAA 3 blocks North of U.S. 66 Food you will remember. "Steaks, Fried Chicken Salads, and the Best Pastries."

(Advertisement for Travelmats, Inc.)

"Joplin Christman Cafeteria - One block East of 66 on 5th and Virginia. Instant service - Good food."

(Highway Publicity Bureau's "Main Street of America" vintage map.)

On 7th Street heading west out of Joplin, Dolly's Chili House, Bill's Hamburgers, the Top Hat Diner, Dixie Lee's Dine and Dance Bar and Dana's Bo Peep have all been a part of the old road at different times.

Today, Route 66 is a four-lane highway into Kansas lined with used car dealerships, automobile graveyards, relics of crumbling buildings, and mountains of weed-infested mine tailings. The human blight line hides the natural beauty of the nearby countryside.

At the "Old Route 66 Next Right" sign, turn onto a rare, surviving section of the original highway. A newer 66 alignment also heads toward Galena but this old, old road has somehow found protection and offers original pavement, complete with dangerous side lips. It also offers a few minutes for the imagination to take over, for this is land still haunted by the rough days of the mines, prohibition, and the Great Depression.

KANSAS

KANSAS. The oldest alignment of Route 66 enters Galena at the north end of town then makes a sharp left turn onto Main. While lead and zinc ruled Galena, the area's population soared to an estimated 15,000. Today, Main Street is lined with boarded-up brick buildings that recall the uproarious years when money bought short term pleasure and relief from prohibition, depression, work, and war.

Most of the saloons of Galena have faded into oblivion, but a ghosted sign on the Palace Drug is still visible and people still remember Link's Cafe. Dorotha Centers still greets people at the Golden Rule Dry Goods Store she inherited from her father. The store offers a nostalgic trip into the past.

Vi-D's Cafe is at 518 Main. The cafe is all that remains of the old Miner's State Bank, once located on the first floor of the three-story New Century Hotel. The hotel and bank were razed several years ago, leaving the annex where the cafe stands today. The huge walk-in vault was too large to move, so the original locking pins were removed and the vault became the safest pantry on Route 66! The vault opens into the front dining area and a peek inside reveals shelves ready for storing flour, lard tins, and seldom-used kitchen utensils.

Around the corner on Seventh Street, Howard Litch presides over the Galena Mining and Historical Museum, located in the old KATY Depot. His collection of one-of-a-kind tools and early-day memorabilia makes a fascinating visit into the time of the tri-state area glory days.

Next door is Katie's Hi-Winds Cafe and across the street is a pizza stop where, for twenty years, Brown's Cafe stayed open twenty-four hours a day. Brown's served both folks from the highway and teenagers who considered it their favorite late-night dining spot. Before Brown's, the cafe was Rosie's to travelers motoring east and west on Highway 66.

Hardworking Kansas citizens had concreted all thirteen and two-tenths miles of their length of Route 66 by 1929. The original saw-tooth strip still follows section lines, passes mountains of misplaced rock and near-forgotten cemeteries, and heads generally westward toward Oklahoma.

Between Galena and Riverton, a popular stop on the early highway was a motor court and gas station called Camp Joy. Even before I-44 came through in the 1960s, bypassing Kansas, the Camp Joy area had almost disappeared. Many local citizens referred to it as "Rest Awhile Hill" or "Rock-A-Bye Hill." Riverton, a tiny unincorporated community on the banks of the Spring River, makes one of the loveliest stops along historic Route 66.

A t the Spring River Inn, located on seven and a half acres next to the river, guests will find a delicious smorgasbord. The thirty-five-foot buffet table is loaded with home-cooked food. Cinnamon pull-apart bread and delicately browned squaw bread are among the house specialties. Mashed potatoes are real, noodles are made on site, and fresh fish is served nightly.

Spring River Inn has a colorful past. Land in this area was originally a buffer zone between Missouri and Indian territory, but by 1870 it became available for settlers. Mr. B.F. Steward began building the inn

as his private home in 1902. He sold it to the Joplin Country Club in 1905 for $1,500.

Mines flourished, a gigantic power plant was built nearby, and an electric railroad was added to connect the Country Club with Joplin ten miles to the east. The club became the social center of the area, boasting a "swimming tank," tennis courts, and boating facilities on the Spring River.

Hard times came with the depression and the club was sold to J.W. Grantham in 1932. It was used as a boating club for a while, then opened as a

restaurant in 1952. Judy Birk and her children have owned and operated Spring River Inn since 1970.

Open evenings each day except Monday, the Inn offers a spacious main dining room and three glass-enclosed porches with views of the river and grounds. A meal at Spring River Inn is truly a gourmet step into history. Chess pie at the inn makes a perfect ending for the evening's meal.

SPRING RIVER INN CHESS PIE

36 EGGS
4 TABLESPOONS VANILLA
¾ CUP CORN MEAL
¾ CUP LEMON JUICE
1 GALLON SUGAR
3¾ CUPS MILK
3 POUNDS BUTTER, MELTED

MIX THE ABOVE and pour into 11 unbaked 9-inch pie shells. Sprinkle pecans or coconut on top if desired. Bake 35 to 40 minutes in preheated 350° oven. *11 pies.*

ROUTE 66 CHESS PIE

2 CUPS SUGAR
1 TABLESPOON FLOUR
1 TABLESPOON YELLOW CORN MEAL
4 EGGS, UNBEATEN
½ TEASPOON VANILLA
¼ CUP BUTTER, MELTED
¼ CUP MILK
4 TABLESPOONS LEMON JUICE

COMBINE DRY INGREDIENTS and stir in eggs, vanilla, butter, milk and lemon juice. Pour into an unbaked 9-inch pie shell. Bake for 35 to 40 minutes in preheated 350° oven. *6 to 8 servings.*

ROUTE 66 COPPER PENNY SALAD

2 POUNDS FRESH CARROTS, SLICED
½ CUP DICED GREEN ONION
1 GREEN PEPPER, SLICED THINLY
1 CAN (10½ OUNCES) TOMATO SOUP
1 TEASPOON WORCESTERSHIRE SAUCE
½ CUP SUGAR
½ CUP OIL
1 TEASPOON PREPARED MUSTARD
½ CUP VINEGAR

COMBINE CARROTS, ONION AND GREEN PEPPER. Mix together the tomato soup, sugar, mustard, oil, vinegar, and Worcestershire sauce. Pour over carrot mixture. Toss lightly. Refrigerate overnight or longer. Drain before serving. *8 servings.*

Down the street is another one-of-a-kind landmark, Eisler Brothers' Old Riverton Store, built by Leo and Lora Williams in 1925. The Williams' location was originally a Standard Station. By 1932 they had added the Y Not Eat Barbecue. Isabell and Joe Eisler bought the location in 1973 and the market and deli are run today by Scott Nelson, their nephew. The old building is well maintained and still contains such authentic gems from the past as the original pressed tin ceiling. Nelson is president of the Kansas Route 66 Association and has an outstanding selection of highway memorabilia and souvenirs for sale.

A deli at the back of the market offers customers sandwich makings. The cool porch out front is furnished with white picnic tables and chairs, and icy-cold pop comes from a nearby antique cooler.

Stop in for a memorable visit.

Route 66 signs are in place all along the Kansas alignment of the historic road. Between Riverton and Baxter Springs, the old concrete truss "Rainbow Bridge" served travelers for years. A nearby cider stand did a thriving business since drivers had already slowed down to safely make the curves at either end of the bridge.

Baxter Springs, established in 1858, was an early-day cow town to drovers who made the long trip from Texas to Kansas City. When thousands of immigrant miners flooded into the area to work the turn-of-the-century lead and zinc mines, Cherokee County gained an even more rough-and-tumble reputation. Saloons and bawdy houses flourished, taking the workers' money on payday.

When the mines began to play out after World War I, strikes and poverty led to extensive bootlegging. Route 66 brought income, but it also provided a way to escape, so thousands went elsewhere in search of their American dream, finally leaving this tiny corner of Kansas to peaceful retirement.

Route 66 enters Baxter Springs in an area referred to as "Gasoline Alley," then curves left on 3rd Street and right on Military Avenue.

Dorothy Spencer Waddell grew up along Gasoline Alley, living in six different locations while her father, A.T. Spencer, ran gas stations and eating places on Route 66. Where the Frisco and Kansas City Southern Railroad crossed Route 66 as it curved onto 3rd Street, a hobo village grew up next to the highway in the 1930s. Mrs. Waddell says her mother couldn't hang clothes out on the line without losing some to passing vagrants. Her dad kept old clothes and suitcases in a back room to help the needy. He also fed folks when they were hungry and lent them money when they were broke. Several times he received letters from California repaying the loans he had made to folks moving west.

Pretty Boy Floyd gassed up regularly at Spencer's Shell station in the mid-1930s. Mrs. Waddell remembers him pacing in front of the window and talking to her while her dad serviced the car.

In 1944, the Spencers opened an authentic diner car cafe on a lot next to today's Auction Barn. Mr. Spencer found the old KATY passenger coach in Chetopa City, Kansas, and bought it in May of that year from William Lea for $250.

The heavy railroad car broke the axle on the mover's truck so it took a great deal of time and a lot of maneuvering to finally get it into place. The Spencers served hamburgers, hot dogs, and good chili from Spencer's Diner until they retired and locked the doors in 1962. The diner car was sold to a new owner who had it moved again, this time to its graveyard location on Highway 66, just inside the Oklahoma line.

Route 66 through downtown Baxter Springs is Military Avenue. At one time a streetcar ran through here, connecting the mining communities of Pitcher and Joplin. Bill Murphey's Restaurant is still on the corner of Military and 11th where the town's first bank used to stand.

Back in 1876, Jesse James and Cole Younger rode into town and robbed the bank of $2,900, then headed their horses south into Indian Territory. A hastily formed posse chased the thieves to a blacksmith shop about seven miles south of Baxter Springs where the outlaws quickly disarmed their pursuers. Shots were never fired and the money wasn't recovered. The posse returned to town safe but empty-handed.

Bill and Wanda Murphey moved to the historic corner location in December of 1941. The old bank had housed a sandwich shop during the 1930s. They opened Murphey's Restaurant and for thirty-five years served thousands of Route 66 regulars. Wanda sold out in 1976 and Alice Hampton owns Murphey's today.

Bill and Wanda satisfied their customers with good food and hard work. Wanda remembers that the interstate business fell off dramatically when Kansas was bypassed in the 1960s, but their regular highway customers still exited I-44 to eat at Murphey's just as they had during the glory days of the old road.

Wanda was noted for her superb pies. Some of her customers came in just to watch her put her special Slip Slide Custard Pie together. The crust and filling were baked separately and after the custard cooled, she would deftly slide each custard into a crisp shell.

MURPHEY'S SLIP SLIDE CUSTARD PIE

3 EGGS
½ CUP SUGAR
¼ TEASPOON SALT
2 CUPS MILK
1 TEASPOON VANILLA
SPRINKLE OF NUTMEG

BEAT EGGS SLIGHTLY. Add sugar, salt, milk and vanilla. Stir well to blend. Grease a 9-inch glass pie pan and set it in a pan of water. Pour custard mixture into pie pan and sprinkle with nutmeg.
Bake in a preheated 350° oven for 35-40 minutes or until the custard is firm to the touch. Cool thoroughly. Loosen custard around edges with a knife and slip into baked crust.

MURPHEY'S PIE CRUST

2 CUPS FLOUR
1 TEASPOON SALT
⅔ CUP SHORTENING
¼ CUP ICY COLD MILK

MIX FLOUR AND SALT. Add shortening and mix with 2 knives or a pastry blender until the mixture is the size of small peas. Add cold milk gradually until dough can be gathered into a ball. (All of milk may not be needed.) As soon as the dough holds together, stop handling.

Divide the dough into two balls and roll each one out from the center in each direction. For two single prebaked pie crusts, fit each circle of pastry loosely into a pie pan. Build a rim and pinch with thumb and forefinger. Prick well with fork and bake in preheated 450° oven for 10 to 12 minutes or until lightly browned. For a double crust pie, line a pie pan with one pastry circle, fill, and cover with the other circle of pastry. Pinch all around to close. *One double pie crust or two shells.*

Many other vintage Baxter Springs eating places are gone today, victims of the economy, declining population, and time. Travelers may remember the Merry Bales Hotel, Anna and Goldies, The Ranch House that was owned by the Murpheys, Gene Young's Luncheonette, Ma and Pa Lewis's cafe, and the Blue Castle.

Ralph and Frances Adams bought the Blue Castle Cafe soon after they married. They opened for business in January, 1947. The tiny eating place seated only thirty-two and the Adamses had an apartment in the back. Business was good so in 1956 they purchased the old Ritz Theater building, remodeled it and opened with seating for eighty-two.

Ralph, who loved to experiment, came up with a tremendously popular deep-fried boneless turkey. He knew he had a winner but didn't pursue marketing the idea. Years later, McDonald's brought out its similar Chicken McNuggets, an instant hit.

One of the most popular Sunday specials at the Blue Castle was Escalloped Turkey perfected by Gladys Jackson, Blue Castle cook for thirty-one years. Edna Abbott, another employee, made a celery seed dressing so popular that the Blue Castle bottled it for their customers.

The Adams' three children worked at the restaurant but didn't want to go into the business, so Ralph and Frances retired in 1980.

BLUE CASTLE CELERY SEED DRESSING

1 CUP SUGAR
1 TABLESPOON GRATED ONION
1 TABLESPOON SALT
¾ CUP VINEGAR
1 TABLESPOON DRY MUSTARD
1 TABLESPOON CELERY SEEDS
1 CUP OIL

COMBINE ALL INGREDIENTS but the oil in bowl of an electric mixer. Set mixer at low speed and combine. Then add oil very slowly and beat until all oil is combined. *2 cups.*

BLUE CASTLE
ESCALLOPED TURKEY

8 CUPS DICED, COOKED TURKEY
½ CUP MELTED BUTTER
2 CHICKEN BOUILLON CUBES
½ TEASPOON SALT
4 TABLESPOONS FLOUR
2 CUPS MILK
½ CUP BUTTERED BREAD CRUMBS

LIGHTLY COAT A 9- X 11-INCH CASSEROLE DISH with cooking spray. Fill dish with diced, cooked turkey. Make a white sauce by melting butter and adding bouillon cubes, salt, and flour. Stir in milk and cook until sauce is medium thick. Pour over turkey. Top with buttered bread crumbs. Bake for 30 minutes in preheated 350° oven. *8 to 10 servings.*

Margaret Mary Reddy, who passed away in 1992, remembered the excitement of the Route 66 Bunion Run that came through Baxter Springs in March of 1928.

The run was the biggest organized event ever to take place on Route 66. The transcontinental odyssey was begun on March 4 in Los Angeles by 275 men. Only one black runner remained by the time the group arrived in Miami, Oklahoma, an overnight stop for the group. Because black people weren't allowed to spend the night in Miami, the young runner was brought to Baxter Springs for supper and a bed. Mary Margaret said he eventually placed third in the race that netted Andy Payne, a Cherokee Indian from Foyil, Oklahoma, $25,000.

Before leaving Baxter Springs, stop at the excellent historical museum where much of the early area history has been captured in vignette form. Volunteers at the museum are capable and friendly.

Kansas holds a unique piece of Route 66 history. Take the old road and forget the interstate along here or you will miss an authentic part of mid-American culture.

OKLAHOMA

OKLAHOMA. Just inside the state line, standing between the old and new alignment of Route 66, the ghostly remains of Spencer's Diner sat abandoned for thirty years. The characteristic diner served hundreds of customers on Gasoline Alley in Baxter Springs.

But scrub oak and shoulder-high weeds claimed the shabby ruin. Even vandals, who broke the windows and left their graffiti behind, abandoned the old railway car. So in early 1993, an unknown owner bulldozed the rusty walls and carted off a memorable piece of Route 66 nostalgia.

Nearby, a rock fireplace and its crumbling chimney mark the location where Toots, a depression era roadhouse, once served celebrities like Mickey Mantle and Billy Martin.

Baxter Springs resident Margaret Mary Reddy remembered Toots well. "Toots was a one-of-a kind hostess," recalled Margaret Mary. "She entertained from her kitchen door just about any time of day. Folks served in the kitchen drank for free, but as soon as the roadhouse opened, they were quickly moved to the main bar and charged accordingly."

Toots was a buxom lady with an meticulous hairdo who often served guests in her chenille bathrobe. A big isinglass diamond was always pinned on her shoulder.

"Once when a friend heard Toots was to be raided that night, she offered her porch to store the liquor," Margaret Mary said. "Toots hastily moved the supply, but not before she had carefully marked the level in each bottle to make sure all the contents returned safely."

The bar itself was worth a trip to Toots'. It was inlaid with silver dollars and covered by glass. The old roadhouse was originally located in a small white building across the highway. When Toots moved to her new location, the bar went along.

Margaret Mary was at Toots' one night when the sheriff came in to make a raid. Margaret Mary walked right up to him, bent under his arm, headed for her car, and was never stopped or questioned. She said when the mines closed, people in the area turned to making whiskey for survival. Law officials knew people needed the money so bootleggers were often warned to "get the whiskey down the well, there's gonna' be a raid tonight."

Countless eating places have lived and died or disappeared along the eight-state path of old Route 66. This small area serves as a vivid reminder of the glory days as well as the desperation of the past. The cafe and roadhouse speak of the dreams of people we never knew and stand as a reminder of a past we will never experience but should not forget.

Quapaw, five miles into Oklahoma, is a lazy farming community that was once a vital part of the frenzied search for zinc and lead. Now, cattle graze on acreage in front of the elementary school and the tallest thing in town is the green and white water tower boasting the Quapaw Wildcats. At Dallas Dairyette, kids on bicycles stop by for "icees" on hot summer afternoons and local merchants share gossip over coffee.

Commerce, where the Turkey Fat Mine was centered, is on the outskirts of Miami and was home to the Black Cat Cafe for years. Today passing motorists stop at the Lil' Cafe for a bite to eat.

Downtown Miami is being revitalized around the Coleman Theater, a 1929 Spanish Mission structure complete with art deco designs and its own protective gargoyles.

The restaurant in the former Main Hotel and Coffee Shop is vacant now. The most recent tenants were Ernest and Tammi Soto who operated

St. James Fine Food. Ernest explained how hard it is for independent restaurant owners to stay in business today. "Fast food chains cater to casual dining, so fewer and fewer people dress up and come downtown," he said.

The old hotel was built in 1919 by the James family and has been host to several good restaurants during the years. In 1947, Bronson Edwards, a nationally known Ottawa Indian artist, painted murals around the dining room walls depicting his Indian heritage. The collection is part of the National Historic Registry.

ST. JAMES MARINATED CHICKEN

2 CUPS KRAFT CREAMY GOLDEN SALAD DRESSING
1 TABLESPOON VANILLA
DASH OF BASIL
DASH OF OREGANO
¼ CUP SOY SAUCE
4 TO 6 BONELESS CHICKEN BREASTS

COMBINE ALL INGREDIENTS. Marinate boneless breasts for 12 hours. Remove from marinade and grill chicken until done. To serve, sprinkle generously with Monterey Jack cheese and a slice of bacon that has been cooked to the rare stage. Slide chicken under broiler to melt cheese and crisp bacon. Serve on a bed of rice. *4 to 6 servings.*

Miami's Silver Grill served Route 66 travelers

FAMOUS FOR STEAKS AND CHICKEN DINNERS

BAKER'S CAFE

AIR CONDITIONED

BAKER'S CAFE

BAKER'S CAFE, Afton, Okla.

50 Miles West of Joplin and 80 Miles East of Tulsa on U. S. Hiways 66 and 69

region's finest. In March of 1929, the fourth annual U.S. Highway 66 convention was held at the hotel. The main focus of the meeting was to encourage paving of the 2,448 miles to "increase transient trade." When Route 66 was officially designated in 1926, only 800 miles of the new highway was paved.

Today, stop by the Pizza Hut at 101 A NW

from 1946 until it closed in 1964. The grill originally opened in 1941 as a part of the Silver Castle Lunch System.

Another favorite Miami eating place, also gone, was Ben Stanley's Cafe. Ben's advertisement read, "We Don't Fool You, We Feed You." Stanley, an early day U.S. Marshal, hired an English chef who served the finest food. The restaurant was very successful until the turnpike came through, rerouting Highway 66 traffic. After Ben closed the cafe and retired to his lakeside cabin, he became famous for the big feeds he prepared for his many guests.

Hotel Miami, built in 1918, was once one of the

in Miami where Renick and Jackie Kreeger have created at 1950s Route 66 mecca. The Kreegers are actively involved in the Oklahoma Route 66 organization and love to get acquainted with visitors.

Buffalo Ranch, on the outskirts of Afton, offers a petting zoo, totem pole, plenty of buffalo to photograph, and both a Western Wear Shop and Trading Post. When travelers are ready to eat, they can amble over to the Chuck Wagon Barbecue for some down home chili or buffalo burgers.

Afton was established in 1886. The old road through town is lined with empty shells that speak of a busier time. The two-storied Palmer House Hotel hosts a deteriorating sign and boarded windows that seal in a world of memories. At the Rocket Drive-In, hungry teens fill up on hamburgers at noon and return for snacks after school.

Afton was once home to Clint Baker's Cafe, reputed to have served some of the best food along Route 66. The cafe was recommended by Duncan Hines for at least nine years.

Clint's Cafe - On U.S. 66 Air conditioned - Steaks, Chicken and Seafood are our specialties - Also Fountain Service -Ample Parking - Breakfast, Lunch and Dinner - Clint Baker and Sons, Owners and Operators.

(Early Travelmat, Inc. advertisement)

Between Afton and Vinita is a section of the old road appropriately named Dead Man's Corner. A cafe served travelers near the corner in the early 1930s. Depression lingered and the location became the LJ Club before the little building was abandoned and disappeared.

On the outskirts of Vinita, the Little Cabin Creek Pecan Orchard Gift Shop makes a mouth-watering stop. Don and Michel Gray own forty acres of pecan trees that have supplied three generations of Highway 66 travelers. At the gift shop, guests can find a variety of pecan goodies and other Oklahoma products.

Don is a director in the Oklahoma Pecan Growers Association and loves to share his enthusiasm for pecans with hungry tourists. Michel has put together a couple of taste-tempting pecan cookbooks and shares these two favorite recipes, recommended by the Oklahoma Pecan Growers Association.

OKLAHOMA PECAN PIE

3 EGGS, LIGHTLY BEATEN
I CUP SUGAR
I CUP LIGHT CORN SYRUP
I TABLESPOON MELTED BUTTER
I TEASPOON VANILLA
I CUP PECAN HALVES OR PIECES
I UNBAKED 9-INCH PIE SHELL

BEAT EGGS, ADD SUGAR, CORN SYRUP, and butter and mix together until well blended. Stir in vanilla and pecans. Pour mixture into pie shell and bake in a preheated 350° oven for 45 to 55 minutes or until knife inserted halfway between center and edge comes out clean. Cool well on wire rack. Serve plain or with whipped cream. *6 to 8 slices*

OKLAHOMA MILLIONAIRES

1 CUP WHITE SUGAR
1 CUP BROWN SUGAR
1 CUP WHITE SYRUP
2 STICKS BUTTER OR MARGARINE
1 LARGE CAN EVAPORATED MILK
1 TEASPOON VANILLA
4 CUPS PECANS
1 PACKAGE (12 OUNCES) REGULAR CHOCOLATE CHIPS
1 PACKAGE (12 OUNCES) MILK CHOCOLATE CHIPS
3 OUNCES PARAFFIN

MIX SUGAR, SYRUP, BUTTER and 1 cup of the evaporated milk. Bring to a rolling boil and while keeping mixture boiling slowly, add remaining milk. Cook to 234° (soft ball stage). Add vanilla and pecans. Pour into a 9 x 9 inch or larger pan. Refrigerate for several hours. Cut into squares. Melt both packages of chips with the paraffin in a double boiler or the microwave oven. Dip squares in mixture and cool on waxed paper. *3½ pounds.*

Vinita, founded in 1871, is the oldest Oklahoma town on Route 66 and the self-proclaimed "Calf Fry Capitol of the World." The mid-September festival each year provides an authentic glimpse of Oklahoma's Western heritage. Regional teams vie for the title of Calf Fry Champions of the World and there is plenty of good food and entertainment for everyone willing to try new experiences.

This calf fry recipe comes from the Vinita Chamber of Commerce.

OKLAHOMA CALF FRIES

SLICE 2 POUNDS OF CALF FRIES ABOUT ¼ INCH THICK (they are easier to slice if slightly frozen.) Soak in an egg and milk mixture about 10 minutes. Roll each fry in a mixture of 1½ cups cornmeal, 3 cups flour, and 1 teaspoon salt. Fry in hot oil (350°) until golden brown. Enjoy!

For many years, the Grand Cafe at 117 East Illinois in Vinita was a Route 66 landmark. Mr. and Mrs. W.E. Updegraff first opened the cafe in 1914. W.E. died in 1922 and Mrs. Updegraff continued to operate the cafe while raising five children.

Mrs. Updegraff was featured in Robert Ripley's Believe It Or Not column in June of 1933. She won the honor for making sixty-six pies in forty-five minutes. The only mechanical help she had at the time was an electric mixer to whip the meringue. Mrs. Updegraff specialized in fourteen different kinds of pies and sold them whole for thirty-five cents or for ten cents a slice. She estimated that she had made in excess of 720,000 pies during her career. She ran the Grand Cafe until her retirement in 1947.

Archie and Lanoe Wilson bought the cafe in 1951 and ran the popular eating place for eighteen years. A number of passenger trains passed through Vinita each day and employees from the Grand Cafe met the trains with box lunches for sale.

Another vintage Vinita eating establishment, Clanton's, is still very much in business. Clanton's is one of the few eating places along Historic Route 66 that has been in business during the whole life of the old road. Tom and Linda Clanton run the cafe that was begun by Tom's grandfather, "Sweet 'Tater" Clanton, some 65 years ago.

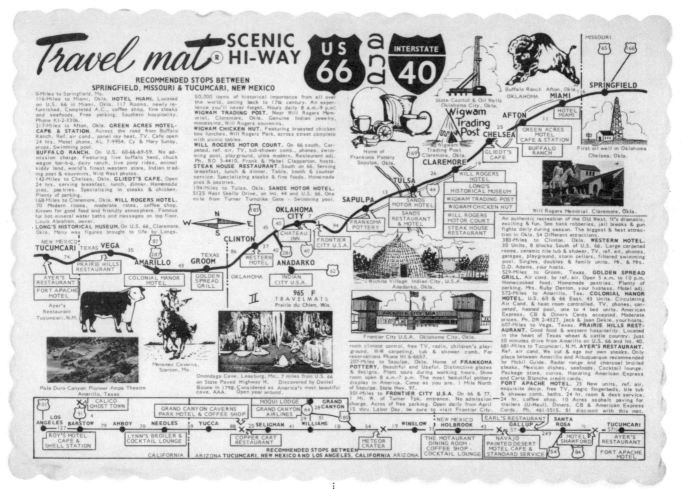

In addition to helping run the cafe that "Sweet Tater" started, his son Cleve helped build Route 66 through Vinita by driving a team of horses that leveled the roadbed. Tom followed his father in the cafe business when Cleve retired.

"We're a dying breed," Tom says. "There aren't many of us left who have spent all our lives in the restaurant business on this old road."

Clanton's has hosted governors and congressmen, local folks, and travelers. Its hometown atmosphere

is warm and comfortable. Tom says running a cafe means plenty of hard work. "A person has to love people to stay in the restaurant business," he said. Where else can you get such a good cup of coffee for thirty-eight cents, including tax!

Travelers who take I-44 out of Vinita will find the world's largest McDonald's spanning the four-lane interstate. The 29,135-square-foot structure was originally built as the Glass House, opening to the public in 1958. The building attracted worldwide

attention when the dedication was held there marking this section of I-44 as the "Will Rogers Turnpike."

Historic Route 66 signs can be found through the heart of Green Country. White Oak is only a shadow of a town today but Chelsea deserves a quick turn across the railroad. Sixth Street is lined with sturdy two-story buildings from the turn of the century. Two miles south of town the first oil well in Oklahoma was completed in 1889. It was only 36 feet deep. Today, Bonnie B's and Mel's Diner serve hungry folks on the highway.

At the first stop light in Claremore, Route 66 tourists can choose parallel routes through town. Swing north and curve onto J.M. Davis Boulevard to travel old, old Route 66. Lynn Riggs Boulevard is the newer road. Riggs was a Claremore native and author of "Green Grow the

Lilacs," the story on which Pulitzer Prize winning *Oklahoma!* is based. Claremore deserves several stops. The J.M. Davis Gun Museum houses a unique collection of firearms and fills a block between the two main thoroughfares.

Barely a block from the museum, The Pits Barbecue stands on the corner in an unpretentious cinder-block building. Barbecue is serious business in Oklahoma and The Pits is one of the best. The sign out front says, "Barbecue That Is." There's good food inside.

Jim May, the owner, says his barbecue is prepared Texas style--with no seasoning other than hickory smoke. The meat may take as long as thirty hours to reach perfection. Jim uses family recipes and says he cooks by the "pinch and taste" method.

Claremore folks who remember the "good ole days" always mention the Linger Longer, as the granddad of good barbecue in Eastern Oklahoma. The Pits is housed in the same building as the old Linger Longer. After this old classic went out of business, several others tried the location. May has found the right combination to compete and survive.

Will Rogers was born between Claremore and Oologah. Turn north on Will Rogers Boulevard to visit his memorial and museum, located on a twenty-acre plot he once owned.

The Hotel Will Rogers, designed in the Spanish motif, was completed in 1929, just in time for the depression. Despite hard times, it provided fifty-eight years of continuous service to thousands of railroad and highway tourists who often came to take the radium water baths. Like so many other old hotels, it stands behind boarded windows, hiding secrets from a long-gone era.

On the south edge of town, just across the railroad track from Route 66, is Cotton Eyed Joe's, another serious barbecue stop. Todd Dost owns the restaurant that was started by his father-in-law, Joe Henderson. The restaurant used to be Henderson's home but was remodeled in barbecue revival style when he began the business. Since that time, an extra room has been added and Dost and his wife have furnished it with Western art, vintage signs, cooking utensils, and tools.

Barbecued ribs are a specialty, slow smoked in the old-fashioned manor by manager Russ Riffle, who also runs the barbecue pit out back. Russ also prepares the secret barbecue sauce that makes the ribs so succulent. The recipe is a family secret but guests can buy jars of the sauce and special meat rub to take home.

COTTON EYED JOE'S BAKED BEANS

2 CANS (16 OUNCES EACH) PORK AND BEANS
⅛ TEASPOON SALT
3 ½ TABLESPOONS BROWN SUGAR
2 TABLESPOONS WORCESTERSHIRE
¼ CUP BARBECUE SAUCE*
1 TEASPOON POWDERED MUSTARD
3 DROPS LIQUID SMOKE
1 TEASPOON POWDERED ONION

COMBINE ALL INGREDIENTS IN A LARGE CONTAINER and bake at 300° for one hour.
*Cotton Eyed Joe's private brand is suggested.
10 servings.

Verdigris is a sleepy community named for the nearby river. At one time five cafes, three filling stations, and two wrecker services lined Route 66 along here.

Catoosa, a rare inland "Port City," is home to the turn basin for the Kerr-McClellan Arkansas River

Will Rogers, State Memorial, Claremore, Oklahoma

Drive In Entrance To Meramec Caverns, America's First Proposed Atomic Shelter, Deep in the Ozarks-Stanton, Mo.

Jesse James' Hideout

H & M REST. — CONSUMERS CAFE — 46 — 26 — BOYER HOTEL COURT & REST. — ROYCE CAFE — 12 — 108 — 27 — OKLAHOMA CLAREMORE — CLINT'S CAFE — 51 — 41 — BOB MILLER'S RESTAURANT — 73 — COLONIAL HOTEL — 155 — SNELL'S CAFE

WEATHERFORD OKLA. — EL RENO OKLA. — OKLA. CITY. — EDMOND OKLA. — TULSA OKLA. — AFTON OKLA. — JOPLIN MO. — SPRINGFIELD MO. — SULLIVAN MO.

Navigation System. The basin forms the farthest inland port in the nation. Route 66 crosses the navigation system bridge immediately east of the twin "erector set" spans over the Verdigris River.

At the west edge of the twin bridges is Molly's Landing, an upscale restaurant with an unexpected twist. A retired Mississippi River push boat, the Molly Smith, is moored on the river. Restaurant patrons can have drinks in the nearby "tastefully cluttered," barn-sized log cabin or find a delicious meal on the boat by following a winding path through oak and redbud to the water's edge.

Linda Powell and her sons have created this unexpected get-away where quality steak and seafood is served nightly except Sundays.

The 119-foot Molly Smith was built in 1949 and for thirty years pushed large oil barges up and down the Mississippi. Powell's brother found the boat for sale in Houston. "After Hurricane Alicia left the boat out of water in 1984, the owners were more than willing to quote a sale price," said Powell. "The Molly Smith made the two-week trip up the river as part of a barge tow."

The location is perfect for Route 66 history buffs. The river near here has a solid rock bottom and was once an old Indian crossing. Later, a way house was built for travelers who needed to ford the Verdigris by wagon. The turn-in to Molly's Landing is part of the original Route 66 and some of the old paving is still visible as the road wraps around the hill behind the restaurant. An original Route 66 bridge was just a few hundred yards north of the spot where the Molly Smith is moored, but no sign of it remains.

Stop at Molly's Landing for a one-of-a-kind Route 66 experience.

MOLLY'S LANDING MARINATED MUSHROOMS

1 ½ CUPS VEGETABLE OIL
½ TEASPOON DRY MUSTARD
1 ½ CUPS VINEGAR
1 ½ TABLESPOONS FRESH GARLIC, MINCED
2 MEDIUM ONIONS, MINCED
3 TABLESPOONS SUGAR
2 TEASPOONS WORCESTERSHIRE
1 TABLESPOON SALT
1 POUND FRESH MUSHROOMS, CLEANED

COMBINE ALL INGREDIENTS EXCEPT MUSHROOMS. Pour mixture over mushrooms and marinate for 24 hours in the refrigerator. *5 to 6 servings.*

Nearer Catoosa, an abandoned water park sits in a lonely glade lined with persimmon thickets. A big blue whale and decrepit Noah's Ark remind folks of better days. Across the highway, in the location that originally housed Wolf-Robe's Indian Trading Post, new owners, Doug and Pam Jennings, have opened the Arrowood Trading Post. The Jennings specialize in Indian art and silver and occasionally serve squaw bread and other Indian dishes when they have special showings. Stop by — these are enthusiastic Route 66 supporters!

Turning west at the only stop light in Catoosa, Route 66 motorists will find Lil' Abner's Sweet

Shoppe. The tiny building, surrounded by a caliche parking lot, has been home to a variety of eating places since its birth back in the 1950s as the Town and Country Cafe.

Clara Rider began cooking there soon after the cafe opened. When she took over management, she added her name and called it Clara's Town and Country.

Clara is from the old school. She had a computer memory and never wrote down an order. "I remember cooking twenty five breakfasts at a time," she recalls, "and I never sent out an incorrect order."

Interstate truckers used to line their rigs along the narrow highway by day and young couples courted in the booths at night. Dwight Sappington met his future bride at the cafe back in the early 1970s and even held a mock wedding there before the real ceremony.

Through the years, the cafe has had customers from around the world and local folks have learned to call it home. "I had a wonderful time while I worked there," Clara recalled. "There were lots of special people I grew to love."

CLARA RYDER'S "VEAL" BIRDS

PUT ROUND STEAK THROUGH A TENDERIZER TWICE. Cut it into four 6-inch squares. Dredge with flour then salt and pepper to taste. Sear on grill then lightly fill each with cornbread dressing. Roll and piece each with toothpicks. Place birds in

baking dish and cover with 2 to 3 cups of beef gravy. Bake in preheated 325 ° oven for 45 minutes. Serve on a bed of rice. *4 servings.*

Tulsa was the home of Cy Avery, an early entrepreneur and highway supporter who is often referred to as "The Father of the Mother Road." It is largely through Avery's efforts that Route 66 became a federal interstate highway in 1926.

The 1926 alignment through Tulsa was on Admiral, a mile to the north of 11th Street. At the corner of Admiral and Mingo, Avery owned a service station, tourist court, and the Old English Inn. Ruth Sigler Avery, his daughter-in-law, says, "It was a lovely place, just far enough east of town to make a nice trip. People would drive out on Sunday after church, have a leisurely dinner, and enjoy the countryside on their way home."

ELECTRIC TOURIST PARK ALL MODERN CONVENIENCES—GAS.

A HIGH GRADE OF GAS AND OILS.

OLD ENGLISH INN, LUNCHES AND DINNERS.

AVERY SERVICE STATION, 6 MI EAST OF TULSA ON HIGHWAYS Nos 7—11—12.

Mrs. Avery remembers the efficient lady who operated the restaurant. "She always had crisp, white linens at every table," she said. "And there were always small vases of fresh flowers in season."

The Old English Inn opened in 1920 and was razed to make way for a traffic circle in 1943.

OLD ENGLISH INN "ROUTE 66" ROLLS

from Mrs. J. Leighton (Ruth Sigler) Avery

½ CUP SHORTENING
½ CUP SUGAR
2 CUPS HOMOGENIZED MILK
½ CUP MASHED POTATOES
1 CAKE YEAST
2 TABLESPOONS WARM WATER
2 EGGS, BEATEN
4 CUPS SIFTED FLOUR
2 TABLESPOONS BAKING POWDER
1 TABLESPOON SODA
2 TABLESPOONS SALT
2 CUPS SIFTED FLOUR

WARM SHORTENING, SUGAR AND MILK in saucepan until shortening is melted. Add mashed potatoes and cool. Dissolve yeast in 2 tablespoons warm water and add to beaten eggs. Add this to first mixture.

Sift 4 cups flour with baking powder, soda, and salt. Stir liquid mixture into these dry ingredients. Put into a large bowl and let rise in warm surroundings to twice bulk. This is a sponge. Cover overnight with light cloth.

The next morning add remaining 2 cups of sifted flour to the sponge and knead until satiny. Put the dough in a greased bowl and let rise in warm surroundings. Knead on lightly floured board. Form into rolls. Place these rolls on a greased pan and let stand 5 minutes in warm surroundings until double in size. Bake 15 minutes at 425°. *Rolls for 10 people.*

Eleventh Street replaced Admiral as a Tulsa thoroughfare and Admiral shows its age today. Many business tenants have forgotten the history made along the asphalt out front. Abandoned motor courts and unloved buildings are scattered among comeback hopefuls on the city route. However, local Route 66 Association members have banded together in a strong group to plant trees in the median and clean up seedy areas. At the busy corner of 11th and Memorial, the Route 66 Cafe and Drive-In survived until 1955. A big sign out front advertised an "Air-conditioned Dining Room." McCollom's Restaurant in the 5700 block of East 11th is also closed. A few struggling elms survive on the vacant lot next door where the Will Rogers Motor Court served travelers for more than thirty years.

The Route 66 corner that most folks remember for good food in Tulsa is 11th Street and Yale Avenue where the Golden Drumstick served chicken dinners from the late 1940s through the 1960s. The cafe met immediate success, due in part to Bob Latting, the "first Tulsa television personality" who was one of the restaurant owners. Lee and Lois Apple and their son, Ed, purchased the Golden Drumstick in 1958. Much of the early Route 66 traffic had moved to the city's bypass by that time, but the Apples had outstanding food and developed a large patronage.

The Golden Drumstick was a favorite stop for hometown regulars after church on Sunday. Ed "Strangler" Lewis always ate with the Apples when he was in town. Lewis, a giant of a wrestler, was one of the world's highest paid athletes at one time. And rodeo great Jim Shoulders stopped by when he performed at the nearby fairground rodeos. Shoulders made a habit of counting his winnings at the dining table. University of Tulsa athletic teams also made the restaurant a regular meeting place. The Golden Drumstick's success was due in part to "the best fried chicken in the world" along with great onion rings and hot apple pie. Its salad dressing was considered the finest in town.

GOLDEN DRUMSTICK BLUE CHEESE DRESSING

¼ POUND BLUE CHEESE, MELTED
I CUP SALAD DRESSING
½ CUP OIL
I SCANT TABLESPOON LEMON JUICE
I CUP SOUR CREAM
GARLIC POWDER TO TASTE

MELT THE BLUE CHEESE ON SIMMER or use the microwave on low power. Add remaining ingredients and stir vigorously to blend. Store in covered container in refrigerator until needed. *2 ¾ cups dressing.*

After Lee Apple's death, the Golden Drumstick was closed. In the mid-70s it reopened as the Middle Path Cafe, offering vegetarian and health food. The Middle Path became a victim of the oil recession but its food is

well remembered The recipe that follows makes a thick soup. Thin it with broth if you like. Vegetable stock may be substituted for the water and bouillon.

MIDDLE PATH GUMBO

⅓ CUP RAW BROWN RICE
7 CUPS WATER
I ½ TEASPOONS VEGETABLE BOUILLON
½ CUP DICED GREEN PEPPER
½ CUP CELERY
½ CUP DICED ONION
I ½ TABLESPOONS MARGARINE
I ½ CUPS DICED FRESH TOMATOES
½ CUP CHOPPED GREEN CHILIES
2 CUPS TOMATO SAUCE
I TEASPOON SALT
I TEASPOON PEPPER
½ CUP FROZEN CORN
2 CUPS SLICED OKRA, FRESH OR FROZEN

IN A SKILLET, STIR-FRY RICE WITHOUT OIL UNTIL GOLDEN. In a large pot, combine water and bouillon and bring to boil. Add rice and simmer. In skillet, saute green pepper, celery, and onion in margarine until tender-crisp. Add tomatoes and chilies and bring to boil. Add to rice in soup pot. Add salt, pepper and tomato sauce; simmer until vegetables are tender. Add corn and okra and simmer until done. Garnish servings with parsley if desired. *3 quarts or 10 to 12 servings.*

MIDDLE PATH
HOT TODDY BREAD

3 CUPS WARM WATER
2 PACKAGES DRY YEAST
1 TEASPOON GROUND GINGER
½ CUP HONEY
¼ CUP MOLASSES
3 CUPS WHOLE WHEAT FLOUR
½ CUP MASHED POTATOES, WITH SKINS
2 CUPS ANY COMBINATION OF WALNUTS, CASHEWS,
SUNFLOWER SEEDS
2 TO 4 CUPS UNBLEACHED WHITE FLOUR

IN A LARGE MIXING BOWL, combine water, yeast, ginger, honey, and molasses. Set aside and allow to soften until bubbly.
When ready, add whole wheat flour, potatoes and ground mixture. Add enough unbleached flour to make a stiff dough. Sprinkle 1 cup of the unbleached flour on a bread board or pastry cloth and turn dough onto it. Knead until dough is smooth and elastic. Place in greased bowl, turning to coat the top. Cover the bowl with towel and let rise in a warm place (85°) until double in bulk (about 1 hour). Punch dough down to original size. Divide into half and shape into 2 loaves. Place in 9 x 5 x 3 greased loaf pans. Let rise again until double (about 1 hour). Bake in a preheated 375° oven for 45 minutes. If desired, dough may be divided into thirds and baked in three 8½- x 4½ pans. *2 large loaves.*

Set in the morning shadow of the University of Tulsa's Skelly Stadium, the Metro Diner serves good food in a glitzy, neon roadhouse atmosphere. This classic diner is cast in the "trolley car" mode with comfortable booths and plenty of 1950 memorabilia on the walls.

The exterior of the Metro Diner is shiny aluminum siding, accented with glass brick and plenty of neon lights. The diner was built on the site of a gas station that served Route 66 customers for many years and the owners incorporated some of the building materials from the old station. The diner is a favorite with Tulsa University students and neighborhood residents.

Sandwiches, chicken fried steak, and chicken fingers are regulars on the menu, with a Blue Plate Special always posted near the door. Chicken salad sells out every day. Homemade cobblers and rich cream pies are dessert favorites. Don't even think about counting calories!

METRO DINER
CHICKEN SALAD

2 ½ POUND CHICKEN
1 CUP FINELY DICED ONION
1 CUP GRATED CHEESE
½ CUP CHOPPED PECANS
1 CUP FINELY DICED CELERY
½ TEASPOON SALT
½ TEASPOON GARLIC POWDER
¾ TEASPOON ONION POWDER
¾ TEASPOON PEPPER
1½ CUPS SALAD DRESSING

BOIL THE CHICKEN, COOL, BONE AND CHOP into ¼ inch pieces. Add onion, cheese, pecans and celery. Blend well. Add remaining seasonings and mix. Stir in salad dressing and blend thoroughly. *10 servings.*

Bama Pie, Inc., with main ofices at 2727 East 11th, is another Route 66 success story. Paul and Lilah Marshall moved to Tulsa in 1937 and established a tradition of excellence for their pastries and sweets. Today, trailer loads of their fine products are delivered across the continental United States each day. In addition to their famous pecan pies, Bama makes cookies, turnovers, biscuits, and ready-to-use pie and tart shells.

Just west of the Bama complex is a tiny jewel resurrected from the past. The 1935 vintage building was a Silver Castle outlet for years and is now home to the Route 66 Diner. Debbie Higgs bought the old structure in 1988. The popular eating place is filled to capacity each day. Debbie's mother, Dorothy Crane, bakes all the bread for the diner and Debbie's newer Downtown Route 66 Diner. A host of regulars and Route 66 tourists keep the four tables and eleven counter stools occupied and when customers leave, they're sent on their way with a friendly, "Bye y'all, come back soon."

One of the specials at the Route 66 Diner is Philly Chicken. Since Debbie usually cooks without a recipe, she wrote it out for the first time for Suzanne Holloway, Food Editor for the *Tulsa World*, when Suzanne featured the cafe in a column.

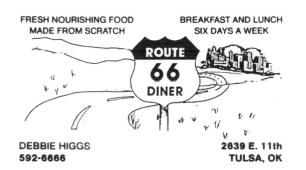

ROUTE 66 DINER PHILLY CHICKEN

½ CUP CELERY, CHOPPED
½ CUP ONION, CHOPPED
¼ OF A MEDIUM GREEN PEPPER, CHOPPED
3 TABLESPOONS VEGETABLE OIL
½ TEASPOON TARRAGON
¼ TEASPOON LEMON PEPPER
2 CLOVES GARLIC, MINCED
1 PINT HEAVY CREAM
1 PACKAGE (8 OUNCES) CREAM CHEESE, SOFTENED
¾ CUP MILK
1 CHICKEN, COOKED, SKINNED AND DEBONED (APPROXIMATELY 3 CUPS DICED)
¼ CUP PARMESAN CHEESE
WILD RICE OR PASTA

IN A LARGE SAUCEPAN, saute the celery, onion and pepper in vegetable oil. Add the tarragon, lemon pepper and garlic. Cook until vegetables are tender. Add cream, cream cheese, milk and chicken and heat to simmer but do not boil. Sprinkle with Parmesan cheese and serve over wild rice or pasta. *6 to 8 servings.*

Many Route 66 merchants in this area are slowly creating a needed facelift along the historic street. One of the best, The Browsery, is located in a unique old building constructed in the late 1920s.

Near the center of town, 11th Street makes a slight jog where a dazzling art deco building stands boarded and unloved. The tower, with red and blue polychrome terra cotta ornamentation, is yearning for renovation.

The old structure epitomizes the dilemma of preservation. When it opened in 1929 as a farmers market, its owners supplied groceries for much of Tulsa. Depression closed the market's doors but the building got a new, but short life as Club Lido, a fancy ballroom. Since then, it has a variety of tenants. Local architects call the building vulnerable and irreplaceable. It is a part of Route 66 history that should not be lost.

Visitors to Tulsa should exit Route 66 along here to take advantage of two world-class opportunities, the Thomas Gilcrease Museum and Philbrook Museum of Art. Both offer collections that shouldn't be missed. Excellent light luncheon facilities are available.

On the old, old Admiral route, Hatfield's Hamburgers, home of "The Real McCoy," serves their juicy version in a former Dairy Queen location. Other vintage Route 66 eating places on Admiral include Hank's Hamburgers (since 1949), Ike's Chili House, Wings Hamburgers, and the Eastside Cafe.

From Admiral, the 1926 route through downtown Tulsa turned onto 2nd Street, zig-zagged to Detroit, 7th Street, Cheyenne, and back to 11th Street before crossing the Arkansas River.

With the old configuration in mind, Debbie Higgs opened her Downtown Route 66 Diner at 2nd and Elgin to complement the Route 66 Diner on 11th Street. The old building is on a sunny corner with plenty of windows. Decor is black and white and there is a wide variety of memorabilia for sale. Downtown office workers have found her location and the *Tulsa Tribune* ranked the food as excellent. Homemade bread, beans, and meat loaf are always on the menu. Mashed potatoes are for real and desserts include a great apple pie and pineapple cobbler.

Debbie is an entrepreneur of the first order. The Route 66 name has garnered well-deserved publicity and her menu capitalizes on 66 with twenty-six items that have prices ending with sixty-six-cents. Beans are on the menu every day. After all, Route 66 was the depression road and beans carried Okies through the lean years. Debbie doesn't presoak the beans for her Downtown Route 66 Diner Brown Beans, but allows them to become tender as they simmer.

DOWNTOWN ROUTE 66 DINER BROWN BEANS

1 POUND BROWN BEANS
4 QUARTS WATER
1 LARGE HAM BONE
1½ ONIONS, CHOPPED
2 TEASPOONS MINCED GARLIC
1 TABLESPOON SALT
¼ TEASPOON PEPPER

WASH AND PICK OVER BEANS. In a large pot, cover beans with water. Add other ingredients and simmer over low heat for 6 hours, adding water as needed. Do not stir.

Across the street from the diner is an abandoned blue dome gas station. Built in 1925, it was Tulsa's first filling station to feature compressed air pumps and restrooms with hot and cold running water. Today, the building is less valuable than the land it stands on.

In downtown Tulsa, The Minck's Cafe - "Eat the Blue Willow Way" - $.50 to $.75 - soup to dessert complete - 109-111 East 3rd or 15 East 4th Street.

(Vintage Route 66 road map)

When Johnny Harden moved to Tulsa in 1939, he took a job at the Pig-in-the-Pen Cafe, a truck stop and diner on Route 66 in west Tulsa. By 1941 he had opened his first hamburger stand, Johnny's Gyp Joint. It wasn't long before his logo, a big happy face world, appeared above Harden's Hamburgers at 4004 East 11th Street. This Route 66 location was second home to several generations of Will Rogers High School students.

In 1955, Harden added chicken to the menu and became the first Kentucky Fried Chicken franchise west of the Mississippi. Harden had thirteen outlets when he gave up the franchise to serve chicken under his own name. Today, Harden's daughter, Pat Clark, owns Harden's Fried Chicken on old Route 66 in west Tulsa, only a mile from where Johnny Harden got his start over fifty years ago.

Billy Ray's Barbecue is a family-owned business entrenched on Highway 66 in West Tulsa for a decade. Billy Ray's is noted for top quality meat, authentic hickory smoking, and a great sauce from Grandma's secret recipe. At Billy Ray's, the potato salad, barbecued beans, and coleslaw are almost as popular as the meat, and every meal is served with pickles and crisp sweet onions.

BILLY RAY'S BARBECUE COLESLAW DRESSING

1 CUP SUGAR
¼ CUP CIDER VINEGAR
6 TABLESPOONS SALAD OIL
1½ TEASPOONS SALT
2 CUPS MAYONNAISE
½ POUND SHREDDED CABBAGE

COMBINE SUGAR WITH VINEGAR, OIL, AND SALT until sugar is dissolved. Add mayonnaise and mix well. Pour over cabbage and stir to combine. *8 to 10 servings.*

Where refineries and a power plant curl around the west bank of the Arkansas River, a long-time neighborhood park has been renamed to honor Route 66 and Cy Avery. Nearby, in the heart of Red Fork, Ollie's Restaurant has become a friendly neighborhood retreat with a mom-and-pop atmosphere. Ollie's is about 300 yards south of the first oil well in Tulsa County. This 1901 discovery well, the Sue A Bland #1, triggered the search that led to an eventual oil bonanza.

Ollie's is built from native stone in the true old roadhouse tradition. Decor can be summed up in one word: trains. A couple of miniature Garden scale models run on clear plexiglass above the booths. Suspension and supports are designed so everyone gets a good view as John Gray, the restaurant owner and train enthusiast, mans the controls. Warm cinnamon rolls at Ollie's come big and gooey with light layers that pull apart. Linda Gray, who works alongside her husband, says this recipe makes enough for half a day at Ollie's. Leftovers become bread pudding, an Ollie's favorite tradition.

OLLIE'S RESTAURANT CINNAMON ROLLS

3 QUARTS MILK, SCALDED AND COOLED
1½ CUPS YEAST
4 CUPS SUGAR
3 EGGS
35 CUPS FLOUR

ADD YEAST TO THE MILK AND LET STAND TO PROOF. Combine sugar, eggs, and flour. Add milk and yeast mixture and knead to combine. Let dough rise in warm place until doubled in bulk. Roll out to ¼ inch thickness. Cover with melted butter and a mixture of cinnamon and sugar. Roll dough and cut into ¾ inch slices. Place on greased baking sheets and let rise again for 30 to 40 minutes. Bake for 8 to 10 minutes in a preheated 375° oven. Serve warm.

ROUTE 66 CINNAMON ROLLS

5 CUPS FLOUR
1 PACKAGE DRY YEAST
1 CUP MILK
⅓ CUP MARGARINE
⅓ CUP SUGAR
½ TEASPOON SALT
3 EGGS
¾ CUP BROWN SUGAR
1 TABLESPOON CINNAMON
4 TABLESPOONS FLOUR
⅓ CUP MARGARINE
½ CUP RAISINS
½ CUP CHOPPED PECANS
1 TABLESPOON MILK OR LIGHT CREAM

IN LARGE MIXING BOWL combine half the flour and the yeast. In a saucepan heat the milk with margarine, sugar, and salt until margarine has melted. Add to flour mixture. Add eggs and beat with electric mixer for about 4 minutes. Stir in remaining flour.

Turn dough out on floured surface and knead until smooth and elastic, 3 to 5 minutes. Shape into ball, place in greased bowl and let rise in warm place until double, about 1 hour.

Combine brown sugar, cinnamon and flour. Cut in margarine until crumbly. Set aside.

Punch dough down, turn out on lightly floured surface and roll into a 12-inch square. Sprinkle filling over dough; top with raisins and pecans and roll up, pinching edges to seal. Slice into eight 1 1/2 inch rolls. Arrange, cut side up, in a greased 13 x 9 x 2 baking pan.

Cover and let rise again until nearly double. Brush dough lightly with milk and bake in a preheated 375° oven for 25 minutes or until lightly browned. Brush again with milk or cream and remove from pan to cool on wire rack. Drizzle powdered sugar glaze on top if desired. Serve warm. *8 large rolls.*

The 33rd West Avenue Exit from Interstate 44 is where summer travelers can head for Discoveryland, a unique outdoor amphitheater where the Rogers and Hammerstein musical *Oklahoma!* is performed each summer evening except Sunday. The play is preceded by a typical Western barbecue and offers one of the best evenings of outdoor entertainment along Route 66.

Drivers heading west toward Sapulpa will find Route 66 is the "free road" into town. Well-placed Historic Route 66 markers make excellent guides. A working oil well is on the north right-of-way and a barn painted with "Meramec Caverns, Stanton, Missouri" is to the south of the highway. This segment of Route 66 between Tulsa and Oklahoma City is one of the most scenic along the whole length of Route 66.

Entering Sapulpa, drivers will find a true Route 66 jewel, Norma's Diamond Cafe, located across the street from the cemetery. Norma and her husband Bob opened the cafe in 1950 and until the turnpike went through, they stayed open twenty-four hours a day. Drivers can't miss their cinder-block building with the bright orange front and a sign in the window, "99 Cent Breakfast!" Norma says the special breakfast is her trademark. It's so popular, she can't afford a change.

Opal Glenn has been Norma's cook for twenty-six years. Bob now spends most of his time at his sporting goods and U-Haul business next door. At one time, Bob ran an adjoining filling station. Big trucks parked up and down the highway to eat Norma's good food while Bob serviced the rigs. Bob usually took the truckers' pictures and had copies ready for them the next trip through.

At Norma's Diamond Cafe, beans are always simmering on the back of the stove and Norma has "Red Top" ready to serve. This specialty is a combination bowl of half stew and half chili, always served with piping hot cornbread. Another unique feature at Norma's are the dishes. Every order is served on distinctive Frankhoma Pottery, made within a mile of her Route 66 location.

NORMA'S OKLAHOMA CHICKEN

8 CHICKEN BREASTS, SKINNED
1 CAN CREAM OF CHICKEN SOUP
1 CUP WHITE COOKING WINE
1 TABLESPOON BASIL
SALT AND PEPPER TO TASTE
1 JAR (3½ OUNCES) CHOPPED PIMENTO, DRAINED
1 CUP SOUR CREAM
WILD RICE

PLACE CHICKEN BREASTS IN A LARGE PAN so that meat is in a single layer. Combine soup, wine, basil, salt, and pepper. Pour mixture over chicken and cover container with foil. Bake for 1 hour at 300°. Remove from oven and spread with pimento and sour cream. Return to oven to keep warm. Serve chicken on a bed of wild rice. *8 servings.*

OPAL'S SWISS STEAK

2 POUNDS ROUND STEAK
SHORTENING FOR BROWNING
1 CUP CHOPPED GREEN PEPPER
½ CUP CHOPPED ONION
SALT AND PEPPER TO TASTE
2 CUPS TOMATO SAUCE

BROWN STEAK IN A LARGE SKILLET using a small amount of shortening. Add green pepper and onion and season with salt and pepper. Pour enough sauce over steak to cover it. Reduce heat to simmer, cover container, and cook slowly for 1 hour. *8 servings.*

Sapulpa was once home to the Dixieland Amusement Park. Built in the 1920s, the park featured a huge swimming pool — some say the largest in the state — fed by natural springs. The flow of water diminished when the interstate went through nearby, forcing the park to close in 1951. In 1965, the Dixieland opened as a steak house but was closed forever in 1978. Many stories surround the old Dixieland, including the one that says John Dillinger and his gang sometimes stopped there to eat. Today, the pool is filled with old cars and ghosts whisper through the encroaching weeds.

Route 66 passes through Kellyville, across Polecat Creek, and into Bristow where many of the settlers have Lebanese and Syrian ancestry. Their good food reflects a heritage of dishes like tabouli, stuffed cabbage, and honey cakes.

Opal Lyon's father was a Lebanese grocer in Bristow for many years. Opal's husband worked for him after they married but the young couple soon had an opportunity to buy Congers Confectionery on Route 66. There was a fountain on one side and Opal sold gifts and stationery supplies on the other. A friend who owned the White Way Cafe encouraged them to add chili and sandwiches to the menu and Opal began to bake pies. "I practiced on my young customers who sometimes had to use knives to cut the tough crusts," she said.

Opal says their rent was paid with "marble boards" and slot machines called "one-armed johnnies." By 1932, they had saved enough to buy the Lyons Cafe. As business increased, they stayed open longer and remodeled to accommodate more customers. For years, Opal went to work at four a.m. to make pies and cinnamon rolls. "I remember serving 'poor boy' milkshakes for a nickel, popcorn to nearby movie patrons, and providing curb service for folks who didn't want to come inside," she said. "And on Christmas eve, we always served free eggnog to everyone who stopped by." The Lyons retired in the mid-70s and Opal still works at the Bristow Senior Citizens center. Her pie-making skill is well known throughout the area. Opal uses Wyman's Maine blueberries for this pie.

Just down the street, Jack Abraham and his wife ran Bristow's J&J Cafe for years and the Hamburger King was located down the block from the J&J Cafe. Opal remembers, "My father ground the meat for the Hamburger King at his grocery back in the 1930s and charged ten cents a pound."

On the west edge of town, the Anchor Drive In has served hungry customers for over forty-one years. George and Margaret Shamas started the tiny hamburger haven and their children, George, Linda, and Sharon, run it today. An early 1980s edition of the *Tulsa World* ran a contest searching for the best hamburgers in the state and named the tiny Anchor "Number One in Oklahoma."

OPAL'S
BANANA BLUEBERRY PIE

¾ CUP SUGAR
3 HEAPING TABLESPOONS FLOUR
⅛ TEASPOON SALT
1 CAN (15½ OUNCES) BLUEBERRIES
2 TEASPOONS LEMON JUICE
4 TO 6 BANANAS
2 BAKED 8-INCH PIE SHELLS
1 PINT CREAM, WHIPPED
5 TABLESPOONS SUGAR

COMBINE THE SUGAR, FLOUR, AND SALT. Add the blueberries, including the juice, and cook slowly until the mixture thickens. Remove from heat and add the lemon juice. When mixture cools, slice the bananas into the baked pie shells and pour half the berry mixture over each pie. Beat the sugar into the whipped cream and top the pies. *2 pies*

In the roadside restaurant tradition, the Anchor Drive In doesn't look like much from the outside — it's a plain white stucco box with a tiny sign. Inside, there are four booths with a few stools at the counter, but folks concentrate on good food. Barbecue at the Anchor is as popular as the hamburgers and George's original recipe is still dished out to second generation customers. Stop by and sit a spell at the picnic table out front.

From Depew to Stroud, road enthusiasts will find some old, old Route 66 paving segments that parallel the highway. The road is choked with weeds and cut into short strips. In Stroud, the Rock Cafe has been a part of Route 66 history since it opened on July 4, 1939. The Rock was built in giraffe stone modern by Roy Rives and is owned today by Ed and Aleta Smalley. Ed's relationship with The Rock started years ago when he washed dishes there, working the night shift from six p.m. to six a.m. for a dollar a shift. Ed met his wife, Aleta, at The Rock on April 4, 1946, the day he returned from service after WW II.

Mamie Mayfield remembers leasing the Rock Cafe in 1959. Coffee was a nickel and rent remained at $80.00 a month until she retired July 14, 1983. Mamie says cross-country truck drivers from both coasts knew about the Rock and would stop in for a hot meal and good coffee. After the Turner Turnpike came through, she served fewer and fewer folks, but she will always remember the days when trucks lined the street and the old cafe was humming.

New managers have opened The Rock again. Stop by, find a table behind the lace-curtained windows, and reflect on earlier days.

ROCK CAFE OLD FASHIONED GREASY HAMBURGER

¼ POUND COARSELY GROUND BEEF
½ TEASPOON SALT, OR TO TASTE
¼ TEASPOON PEPPER
1 TEASPOON FINELY CHOPPED ONION

MIX ALL INGREDIENTS, lightly pat into a burger about ½ inch thick. If you want a juicy burger, don't pack the meat. If the meat is too lean, mix a little ground suet with the patty. Fry patty on grill or in iron skillet for a few minutes, turn and cook a few minutes longer. Overcooking dries out the meat.

Lightly butter the top and bottom of a bun, place on grill until golden brown. Spread mustard on bottom half, pile with chopped onions, pickles, and meat patty. Spread mayonnaise or mustard on top half of bun. Pat the top of the bun with a spatula loaded with hamburger grease. Provide lettuce, tomato, and catsup to be used as desired.

Another memorable Stroud cafe, the White Way, operated for forty years. The original owner, Carl Thomas, named the cafe for the fancy new lights when they were installed on Main Street. The cafe burned in 1936 and was moved to the Burford building where a faded sign still remains above a restored Coca-Cola advertisement.

For years, the Coney Island Cafe on East Main was known as the best place in Stroud for squaw bread. Guy Whistler searched for a specialty when he opened the Coney Island. One day he sampled Flossie Lawson's grandmother's squaw bread and knew he had a winner. Guy took the recipe with him when he moved his business to the Black Hawk Cafe.

GRANDMA WYCKOFF'S SQUAW BREAD

2 CUPS FLOUR
1 TABLESPOON BAKING POWDER
1 CUP SOUR MILK
3 TABLESPOONS LARD
FAT FOR FRYING

COMBINE FLOUR, BAKING POWDER, MILK AND LARD. Knead on bread board until soft. Use more flour to hold together if needed. Cover and let stand 10-15 minutes. Pinch off dough and roll into thin strips 6-8 inches long and 3-4 inches wide.
Heat fat to about 400° and fry strips to a pretty dark brown color. *10 pieces*

Dan's Barbecue Pit is serious business in Davenport. Dr. Rich Davis, author of *The Great American Barbecue Book,* listed Dan's as one of the ten best barbecue outposts in the country in 1988. John and Alice Vandever bought the unpretentious stop in 1981 when John decided he had all the truck driving he wanted. The Vandevers had eaten regularly at Dan's for twenty years before they decided to invest in the building, the former owner's secret recipes, and a pile of hickory stacked out back. The gamble paid off. Folks drive from all over the country to eat at Dan's. A few even stop by in helicopters. The crusty ribs, savory brisket, hot links, and shredded pork are dished out in hearty portions. John and his son Mike prepare the meat with their secret blend of spices and depend on hickory smoke for flavor, adding sauce at serving time. Beans, salad, cinnamon rolls, and great desserts accompany the barbecue. You won't go hungry here!

DAN'S PEANUT BUTTER DESSERT

1 CUP CHUNKY PEANUT BUTTER
8 OUNCES CREAM CHEESE
½ CUP POWDERED SUGAR
1 LARGE CONTAINER OF COOL WHIP
GRAHAM CRACKER CRUST

CREAM PEANUT BUTTER WITH CREAM CHEESE AND SUGAR. Fold in Cool Whip and pour into a 13 x 9 inch baking dish lined with graham cracker crust. Sprinkle top with graham cracker crumbs. Refrigerate until served. *10 to 12 servings.*

Chandler was once home to the popular Tiny Ritz Cafe near the Route 66 curve in the southwest part of town. Elsie Ward, who worked there as a teenager, remembers the constant crowd since there were only three booths and a counter. The short order menu included hamburgers and T-bone steaks with all the trimmings. On a hanging sign, easily seen from the highway, "Old King Beer," was advertised. Local residents say it was made in Oklahoma City and tasted pretty awful.

Elsie remembers working fifteen-hour shifts in the grim years before electric fans. Whatever the weather, The Ritz was open and busy twenty-four hours a day. Elsie shares this salad recipe from Route 66 days. Poke grows wild in Oklahoma and is found in abundance every spring.

If you are gathering your own poke greens, harvest them only when they are very young and pick only the tops. Immerse the fresh greens in boiling water for one minute, then drain and continue with the instructions as given for canned poke greens.

Canned poke may be difficult to find, but the greens are still canned in season by Griffin's in Muskogee, Oklahoma.

TINY RITZ POKE SALAD

USE A 16-OUNCE CAN OF POKE GREENS. Rinse in cold water, drain, and put in a skillet with a small amount of bacon grease. Cook down for approximately 10 minutes; add salt to flavor and vinegar to taste.

The Lincoln County Historical Society has an outstanding museum on Route 66 in Chandler. The building was constructed of large sandstone blocks in 1897 and is on the National Register of Historic Places. It has been home to the James Restaurant, Murphy's Grocery, a bakery, and a variety of other businesses. Behind the museum is the only brick outhouse in Oklahoma, thought to be built between 1903 and 1912, still containing the original French fixture.

At one time, a number of other cafes and hotels were scattered along Route 66 in Chandler. Travelers may remember the Childress Cafe, J&E Cafe, Betty's Grill, Red Wing Cafe, and the Lewis Cafe where "the coldest beer in town" was served. Chandler's St. Cloud Hotel was one of the earliest hotels in the state.

The Court House Cafe, an especially popular stop, was torn down in 1969. The three story structure was built in 1904 as an opera house that attracted first class productions. It became the Egbert Hotel, then the Mack Hotel, and finally the Court House Cafe. The building had a banquet room that seated a hundred.

On the last deadly curve leaving Chandler, PJ's Bar-B-Cue can be found in an old Route 66 filling station. While at PJ's, take a look at a Route 66 landmark — the plastered over crack in the wall where a daredevil driver crashed into the station years ago.

P.J. BoBo opened the popular barbecue spot in 1986. She's a true Chandler native — her family staked their claim south of town during the land run of 1889. P.J. left town for a while to do some modeling in California before returning home to go into business. Food service appealed to her and hard work has made PJ's a success.

Her son, Mike Grayson, oversees the barbecue pit and turns out exceptional ribs and beef brisket, slow cooked over hickory smoke just as his grandfather taught him. P.J. makes their special barbecue sauce from a secret recipe she learned from her father, Winfield Riley. P.J.'s husband, Lonnie, and her brother, Steve Riley, are also involved in the business. Steve is the artist who did the Route 66 mural out front.

There's nothing fancy about the location or decor. The old filling station still has the original pressed tin ceiling with a cornice banding and plastered walls. Old Coca-Cola advertisements provide color, and customers can eat at oilcloth covered tables or sit out front where the pumps used to be. A collection of antique pop bottles line a shelf above the kitchen window. P.J. says her customers find them all over the country and bring them in to add to her collection.

If PJ's Barbecue Sauce isn't available for Sweet and Sassy Chicken, another good barbecue sauce may be used.

P.J.'s Barbecue Sweet and Sassy Chicken

1 FRYER, CUT IN PIECES AND SKINNED
1½ TEASPOONS GINGER
1 CUP BROWN SUGAR
¼ CUP SOY SAUCE
½ TEASPOON GARLIC POWDER
½ CUP PJ's BARBECUE SAUCE
2 CUPS WATER
DASH OF SALT
½ TEASPOON BLACK PEPPER

PREPARE CHICKEN AND PLACE IN SHALLOW PAN. Combine remaining ingredients and pour over chicken. Cover container and place in refrigerator. Allow to marinate for at least 3 hours or preferably overnight. Turn chicken several times. When ready to cook, remove chicken from marinade and place in an uncovered baking pan in preheated 350° oven for one hour. If preferred, cook on outdoor grill away from the flame
4 to 5 servings.

Warwick, Wellston, and Luther survive as sleepy farming communities. One steps back in time along here. There are small country cemeteries, pecan groves, the inevitable abandoned buildings, and dogs asleep in the street. A lonely Amtrack car sits in a field where motorists turn onto Luther's main street.

The famous round barn stands next to the road in Arcadia but travelers may have their minds on food if the wind is just right and good food

is cooking at Larry's Barbeque. The old location once housed the office for an abandoned moter court. The decor at Larry's is plain vanilla. Orders are taken at an unadorned counter and there are only a handful of tables, but business is brisk since former tenants, Bob and Ursula Taylor, put the location on the map for monumental barbecue.

Bob has moved Bob's Barbecue further west on Route 66 to 2nd Street in Edmond where he continues to smoke unbelievably tender whole beef loins, as much as 300 pounds at a time. Bob cuts most of the wood, green hickory, from his own property. He takes as long as thirty to forty hours to smoke the huge loins over massive beds of coals.

Pork ribs, Polish sausage, turkey, and chicken take less time but all receive his masterful attention. Ribs come out crusty and brown outside with the interior pink and juicy. Bob smokes barbecue without adding sauce, allowing customers to apply their own to taste. And what a sauce! It could be the standard by which others are measured — it's made by the Selmon family, as famous in Oklahoma for football as for their barbecue expertise.

Bob buys only select cuts of meat, from a packing house that can fulfill his exacting standards. Ursula is just as particular about the quality of the potato salad they sell. Potato salad at Bob's is made in quantity. Try it when a crowd is coming!

BOB'S BARBECUE POTATO SALAD

ENOUGH POTATOES TO FILL A 5 GALLON CONTAINER
16 HARD-COOKED EGGS, SLICED
2 CUPS ONION, FINELY CHOPPED
1 QUART SWEET RELISH, WITH JUICE
2 QUARTS SALAD DRESSING
1 CUP MUSTARD
SALT AND PEPPER TO TASTE

BOIL POTATOES UNTIL TENDER, then peel and slice while hot. Add eggs, onion, relish, salad dressing and mustard. Salt and pepper to taste. Allow salad to season in the refrigerator. If the salad is too stiff, boil 2 cups of water and immediately pour over the mixture, stirring in quickly.

ROUTE 66 POTATO SALAD

2 POUNDS POTATOES
3 HARD-COOKED EGGS, SLICED
¼ CUP FINELY CHOPPED ONION
½ CUP RELISH, WITH JUICE
½ CUP SALAD DRESSING
¼ CUP MUSTARD
SALT AND PEPPER TO TASTE

FOLLOW DIRECTIONS FOR BOB'S BARBECUE POTATO SALAD. *6 to 8 servings.*

Old Route 66 came into Edmond on 2nd Street then turned abruptly south. Most of the vintage cafes along the highway have fallen to urban renewal, but old timers still remember the 66 Highway Cafe that was built in 1927 on the corner of 2nd and Broadway and The Lone Elm, down the street.

The Wide-A-Wake Cafe is also gone, but Cleo Noe Lamson, who owned the Wide-A-Wake from 1931 until 1972, has vivid memories of the years she spent serving hungry truckers on Route 66. "I sure did a lot of hard work in there," she recalls. "We kept the cafe open twenty-four hours a day, seven days a week and even did all our own laundry. My husband and I worked the daytime shift while his brother and wife operated the cafe at night."

Cleo's mother-in-law built the little cafe called the Night and Day in 1927. She encouraged the Noes to move home from Hobbs, New Mexico, to help manage it when her first tenant's lease ran out. Wide-A-Wake was selected as the new name and an owl was added to the sign out front. Their slogan became "Stay Awake and Eat at the Wide-A-Wake."

Truckers often parked outside the restaurant to sleep and one of the Noes would always wake them up, serve their breakfast, and send them on their way.

Cleo says they started the cafe without any money. "We went to Watkin's Grocery where we got credit for the first week. When we paid the bill, we could buy again," she said. Business grew and they soon hired a cook who stayed with them for twenty years. At one time the Wide-A-Wake offered curb service and provided tables outside. The cafe seated only thirty-one, so extra space was appreciated.

Inside the cafe, the walls were lined with pictures

On Highways 66 and 77
Edmond, Oklahoma

of the truckers who ate with them. Many times the drivers returned to show the pictures to their families or look for old friends. Cleo had never worked in a cafe and had eaten in very few when she went to work at the Wide-A-Wake. At first, her husband did most of the cooking while she waited on tables. But Cleo learned quickly. For years, her box of handwritten recipes stayed in the cafe kitchen for reference. No plate lunch ever went out without meat, mashed potatoes with gravy, and two vegetables. Cleo has cooked thousands of chicken-fried steaks, but her personal favorite continues to be salmon croquettes. Here are two of her specialties.

WIDE-A-WAKE COLE SLAW DRESSING

1 CUP MAYONNAISE
1 TABLESPOON VINEGAR
½ TEASPOON GARLIC POWDER
½ TEASPOON CELERY SEED
½ TEASPOON SUGAR
⅓ CUP BUTTERMILK

COMBINE MAYONNAISE WITH VINEGAR, garlic powder, celery seed, and sugar. Stir in buttermilk, adding more or less to make pouring consistency. *2 cups*

WIDE-A-WAKE BARBECUE SAUCE

3 TABLESPOONS ONION, FINELY CHOPPED
½ TEASPOON SALT
4 TABLESPOONS CELERY, FINELY CHOPPED
½ TABLESPOON CAIN'S BARBECUE SPICE
¼ GREEN PEPPER, FINELY CHOPPED
2 CUPS CATSUP
¼ CUP VINEGAR
1 TEASPOON MEAT SMOKE
1 TEASPOON FLOUR
¼ CUP WATER

COMBINE ALL INGREDIENTS and cook slowly for 40 minutes.

Store covered in refrigerator until needed.
2½ cups.

Crawford Noe, owner of the Wide-A-Wake, and Royce Adamson, owner of Royce Cafe, were best of friends and often hunted and fished together. Noe's enthusiasm for the restaurant business influenced Adamson to build the Royce Cafe in 1934, just as business from the oil industry began to flourish in the area.

Royce put his family to work, hired good-looking college students to wait tables, and stayed open 24 hours a day. He and his wife, Neva, soon enlarged the original cafe, adding meeting rooms on each side. A local artist painted Western scenes along the walls. Bus tours, ball teams, touring musical groups, and Route 66 customers found their way to the Royce along with one notorious gangster. The evening John Dillinger stopped in for coffee, Adamson was warned not to call the authorities at

risk of his life. Seeing two guns pointed his way from the windows of a long, black car with curtains, he was more than willing to comply.

Royce's son-in-law, Jimmy Tindall, was manager and an excellent cook. He supervised the kitchen and the quality food caught the eye of Duncan Hines, who included the Royce in his book of recommendations. Tindall made fiery chili and served it with ice cold beer. His blue cheese salad dressing was another favorite and he sold it by the jar to customers who could not coax the recipe from him. His wife, Eileen Royce, is sharing it now along with a favorite of Duncan Hines, the Royce Chocolate Angel Pie.

ON U. S. HIGHWAY 66 AND 77 . . . EDMOND, OKLAHOM

ROYCE CAFE BLUE CHEESE DRESSING

4 OUNCES BLUE CHEESE, CRUMBLED
1 QUART MIRACLE WHIP DRESSING
2¼ TEASPOONS ONION POWDER
1 TABLESPOON GARLIC POWDER
1 TEASPOON PAPRIKA
1 TEASPOON SAVORY SALT

BLEND TOGETHER AND REFRIGERATE before serving over salad. *5 cups.*

ROYCE CAFE CHOCOLATE ANGEL PIE

½ CUP SUGAR
⅛ TEASPOON CREAM OF TARTAR
2 EGG WHITES
½ CUP NUTS, CHOPPED
¾ CUP SEMI-SWEET CHOCOLATE BITS
3 TABLESPOONS HOT WATER
1 TEASPOON VANILLA
1 CUP HEAVY CREAM, WHIPPED

SIFT TOGETHER THE SUGAR AND CREAM OF TARTAR. Beat egg whites until stiff but not dry. Add sugar while beating and continue to beat until smooth and glossy. Line a greased 9-inch pie pan with meringue. Sprinkle with chopped nuts. Bake in 275° oven for 1 hour or until delicately brown. Cool thoroughly.

Melt chocolate in microwave or double boiler. Stir in water and vanilla and mix thoroughly. Fold chocolate into whipped cream. Fill shell and chill in refrigerator 3 to 4 hours. *1 nine-inch pie.*

Dinner Country Style

ALL-YOU-CAN-EAT!
12.95 per person, children under twelve 5.50
Here's how it works—You get a big platter of meat (beef ribs, brisket, and sausage), and generous bowls of potato salad, cole slaw, and beans. NOTE: When ordering Country Style, it's all for one and one for all. No individual beef rib, brisket or sausage platters may be ordered at the same table.

Sorry, no doggy bags on Country Style seconds.

Barbeque

Served with our homemade potato salad, cole slaw and beans.

BEEF RIB PLATTER 10.95
Three large beef ribs.
BABY BACK RIB PLATTER 12.95
A full rack of lean, tender Baby Back pork ribs.
BEEF BRISKET PLATTER 10.95
A generous portion of extra lean sliced beef brisket.
SAUSAGE PLATTER 7.95
Our own special recipe thick-cut link sausage.
MIXED PLATTER 10.95
One large beef rib, sliced beef brisket, and sausage.
CHILD'S PLATE 4.25
For children 12 and under.
CHICKEN PLATTER 8.95
Half a smoked chicken. NOTE: The pinkish color of the meat is a result of our slow smoking process.

Blue Plate Specials

Served with a large baked potato (with your choice of butter, sour cream, chives, or cheese), cole slaw, and beans.

SMOKED PRIME RIB
16-ounce 15.95
8-ounce 11.95
Smoked to perfection and served with au jus and creamy horseradish sauce.

SMOKED PORK TENDERLOIN
Half a pound 11.95
Quarter pound 9.95
Delicately smoked tenderloin served with au jus and our special barbeque sauce.

A la Carte

Homemade Bread
White or Whole Wheat!
loaf 3.50
half loaf 1.95

Jumbo Baked Potato
with your choice of butter,
sour cream, chives,
or cheese
2.50

Mushrooms
Cooked in butter
and red wine
3.95

All our food items require special preparation, and to insure freshness we cook a limited quantity each day. Should the demand for certain items be especially high, on occasion we may sell out.

From Edmond, Route 66 drops into Oklahoma City on Kelly and Lincoln Boulevard, takes 23rd Street to May in the Crown Heights neighborhood, then shoots north to 39th and out through Bethany. The path of Route 66 through the capital has suffered through urban renewal and new expressways.

The County Line, just off Kelly at 1226 NE 63rd makes a fascinating stop and the food is good.

The restaurant features prime rib, barbecue, great homemade bread, and massive glasses of iced tea.

The County Line is a restaurant with a past. Built before the depression by local residents, it was known as the Kentucky Club for many years. The restaurant has changed hands several times, partially burned and been rebuilt, had a questionable reputation, and in its old age has finally become a respected presence in the city.

The building is long and narrow with private dining alcoves along each wall. There is a window in each. Longtime patrons tell of prohibition days when Texas bootleggers knocked discreetly on the windows to supply customer needs.

At one time, trap doors were installed underneath some of the tables in case law officials decided to drop by. The central portion of the restaurant was originally a dance floor where patrons could meet attractive employees who made rooms available downstairs.

Business boomed during prohibition, but time and owners changed. Now the popular restaurant is often host to fans from nearby Remington Park Race Track. The private booths, once named for horses, echo with new stories of daring and skill.

Another nearby attraction is the Oklahoma Cowboy Hall of Fame. The museum makes a good stop any time of year, but the third Saturday of July, the Hall of Fame is host to the Oklahoma State Championship Chili Cookoff. Each year the competition grows larger. Currently, over 100 cooks vie for the state title and a trip to the International Chili Championship in Terlingua, Texas, in November. All activities are held on the grounds of the museum and the public can sample the entries for a small fee that is donated to charity. Here is the 1988 and 1989 Oklahoma State Championship Chili Recipe as prepared by Deborah St. John, a member of the Heart of Oklahoma Chili Heads Club.

Add more cayenne pepper if you want hotter chili.

OKLAHOMA CHILI

3 POUNDS LEAN BEEF (¼ INCH CUBES OR CHILI GROUND)
1 TEASPOON WORCESTERSHIRE SAUCE
1 CAN (4 OUNCES) DICED GREEN CHILIES
1 CAN (8 OUNCES) TOMATO SAUCE
1 CAN (10½ OUNCES) BEEF BROTH
1 TABLESPOON ONION POWDER
2 TABLESPOONS PAPRIKA
1 TEASPOON CAYENNE PEPPER
2 TEASPOONS BEEF BOUILLON CRYSTALS
1 TEASPOON CHICKEN BOUILLON CRYSTALS
2-3 ADDITIONAL CANS BEEF BROTH

ADDITIONAL SEASONINGS

6 TABLESPOONS CHILI POWDER
1 TEASPOON MSG
4 TEASPOONS GROUND CUMIN
1 TEASPOON SALT
1 TEASPOON GARLIC POWDER
1 TEASPOON WHITE PEPPER OR TO TASTE
1 CAN PINTO BEANS (OPTIONAL)

SPRAY LARGE SKILLET OR ROASTING PAN WITH NONSTICK SPRAY. Brown meat using medium heat and drain grease. Add Worcestershire sauce, green chilies, and tomato sauce with 1 can of beef broth and bring to boil. Add dry ingredients and return to slow boil. Cover and cook for 1½ hours. Add additional beef broth during this time if needed and stir occasionally to prevent scorching. After 1½ hours cooking time add additional seasonings.

Cook all above ingredients for approximately 30 minutes, adding beef broth as needed for desired consistency. Reduce heat to obtain a slow boil.
Approximately 6 cups chili.

Beverly's Pancake Corner, at 2115 NW Expressway, is the final resting place for a Route 66 classic that celebrated a 70th birthday in Oklahoma City in 1991. Beverly's is home base for "Chicken In The Rough," the first franchised food chain in the United States. The story that began in 1921 tossed a bombshell into American food habits.

Beverly and Rubye Osborne opened their first cafe at 209 W. Grand. Osborne is said to have borrowed $15.00 from the milkman, pawned Rubye's engagement ring, and sold the car to make a down-payment on the six-stool shop. They offered 19-cent meals and the tiny cafe was soon filled to capacity. It was here, in 1921, that the Osbornes developed their pancake specialty.

With the profits, they bought a second cafe on Route 66. It became the famous original drive-in home of "Chicken In The Rough." The cafe at 2429

North Lincoln began with four booths and nine stools. The Osbornes built it into a giant that seated 1100 people and regularly hosted state executives, film stars, and the traveling public. The building was razed in 1961 to make way for construction of the state capitol complex.

The name and fame of "Chicken In The Rough" was adopted by accident. While driving toward California in 1936, Beverly hit a bump and Rubye spilled the box of chicken they had packed for lunch. When Rubye retrieved the battered pieces, she is said to have remarked, "This is really chicken in the rough." The comment sparked an idea that revolutionized American eating habits.

During the 20s and early 30s, Emily Post dictated that chicken should be eaten with silverware. The Osbornes dared to disagree. They returned home from their trip and began serving half a fried chicken on a platter with shoestring potatoes, rolls and honey — all finger food with a bonus of no silver to wash. At fifty cents a serving, "Chicken In The Rough" became an instant hit.

Beverly Osborne patented his grill and trademark and began to add new locations. By 1937, Osborne had chicken franchises on Route 66 in Arizona, Illinois, Missouri, and Oklahoma. The chain grew to over 156 franchises and included Hawaii and South Africa. There were seven locations in Oklahoma City.

The classic cigar-smoking golf-club wielding ruffled rooster appeared at every restaurant selling the famous chicken. Osborne paid a commercial artist $7.50 to design the original sign.

In 1974, Osborne sold his franchise rights to Randy Shaw, who had become a partner in 1947. Shaw bought out Osborne's remaining restaurants and today he oversees Beverly's Pancake Corner

BEVERLY OSBORNE

MRS. OSBORNE

where the original Chicken In The Rough recipe is as popular as cvcr. Many third generation customers stop at the Pancake Corner for good breakfasts and the ever-popular chicken.

Rubye loved to write poetry. For many years there was a small card with one of her inspirational poems and a blessing for the meal at each table. She also designed their own Christmas cards. Several times the card included this recipe for her divinity candy.

Rubye suggested that you make this candy on a day low in humidity.

RUBYE OSBORNE'S CHRISTMAS DIVINITY

3½ CUPS SUGAR
1 CUP WHITE CORN SYRUP
½ CUP WATER
½ TEASPOON SALT
3 EGG WHITES
1 TEASPOON VANILLA
WALNUTS OR PECANS TO TASTE

COMBINE SUGAR, CORN SYRUP, WATER, AND SALT. Place over medium heat, allow to come to boiling point. Continue cooking, stirring occasionally until a few drops will form a brittle ball when dropped in cold water (265°).

Meanwhile, beat egg whites until stiff. Pour syrup into whites in fine stream while beating until candy loses its gloss. Stir in nut meats and vanilla and drop quickly on waxed paper or pour into a buttered pan and cut into squares. *About 40 pieces.*

A newcomer on Oklahoma City's west side is Meiki's Route 66 Restaurante, offering Italian food made to order by Kam Meiki. When Meiki decided to move his Italian restaurant to the 39th Street location several years ago, he began searching for the perfect name.

A chance meeting with Bob Waldmire, traveling Route 66 artist extraordinaire, provided the inspiration for the Route 66 name. Waldmire was in Oklahoma City doing sketches along the historic route and Meiki took him home for dinner. Waldmire's enthusiasm spawned the new restaurant's identity.

Meike decorated his restaurant with Route 66 memorabilia and his wife designed their award winning menu. They even inscribed the Route 66 logo in the floor.

Meiki doesn't cut corners in preparing his favorite Italian specialties. Each order of fettucini is made in a separate skillet to ensure perfect sauce. Garlic is peeled and freshly grated. Meiki uses a secret recipe for individually prepared manicotti, and all dinners are served with hand-basted baguette toast. Stop by for a taste of ethnic 66 at its best!

MEIKI'S ROUTE 66 FETTUCINI ALFREDO

5 OUNCES FETTUCINI PASTA, PRE-COOKED
1½ TEASPOONS UNSALTED AA BUTTER
⅓ TEASPOON FRESHLY GROUND GARLIC
4 OUNCES HEAVY WHIPPING CREAM
DASH OF SALT
DASH OF WHITE PEPPER
1 TABLESPOON SOUR CREAM
1 TEASPOON GROUND PARMESAN CHEESE
1 TEASPOON GROUND ROMANO CHEESE

BRIEFLY HEAT MEDIUM SKILLET; ADD BUTTER. Over low flame, coat bottom of skillet with butter and add garlic. Stir until sautéed, then add cream. Increase flame slightly and heat, stirring constantly. Add salt, pepper, and sour cream and bring to heat while stirring. When sour cream is completely blended, combine and stir in cheeses. Stir pasta into sauce over low flame. Serve immediately. *1 serving.*

Many Route 66 eating places have come and gone along Route 66 in Oklahoma City due to urban renewal and freeway construction. O'Mealey's Cafeteria opened in the early 1940s at 2400 Classen Boulevard where it crossed Highway 66. The popular cafeteria later became The Classen Cafeteria, featuring chicken pie and pastries. The cafeteria closed for good in 1967.

Jean's, on Highways 66 and 77, was an unusual early-day eating place. Jean's postcards advertised, "When in Oklahoma City, dine at Jean's, where you will see a collection from the Southwest too wonderful for words to describe; meet Jean in person." The restaurant decor included hunting trophies and firearms that hung from the ceiling. Jean Van Almen served quality food. Guests didn't forget the place!

"Tis the Taste that Tells the Tale" was the motto at Garland's Drive-In Restaurant at 22nd and Broadway. The drive-in was operated from 1939 until 1950 by Garland Arrington. The art deco structure featured a tower and popular corner entrance. Patrons could eat inside amidst floral wallpaper and wrought-iron furniture or take advantage of curb service. When tipping became a part of the meal service, no matter what the bill, ten cents was considered the "right amount." Early-day car hops at Garland's dressed in patriotic sailor outfits with short skirts and white boots.

From 1930 until it closed in 1974, Dolores, The Unusual Sandwich Mill, served folks near the state capitol at 33 NE 23rd Street. The restaurant featured corn-fed Kansas City steaks in addition to a wide sandwich menu. There was a popular drive-in at the back.

DOLORES RESTAURANT BRANDY SAUCE

1 CUP SUGAR
1 TABLESPOON CORNSTARCH
¼ TEASPOON SALT
1 TABLESPOON BUTTER
1 CUP BOILING WATER
¼ CUP BRANDY

MIX SUGAR, CORNSTARCH AND SALT. Add butter and boiling water. Mix well and cook together 6 minutes or until clear.

Add brandy after you remove saucepan from heat. Serve warm over cake or pudding. *8 to 10 servings.*

Brown and white Historic Route 66 signs guide travelers on NW 37th Street into Bethany, a community founded in 1906 by members of the Nazarene Church. Crossing the North Canadian River and Lake Overholser, drivers continue into Yukon, the Czech Capital of Oklahoma. Route 66 passes between towering elevators. On the north is the Mid-Continent Farmers Co-op and to the south, a huge neon sign proclaims, "Yukon's Best Flour, No Finer or More Modern Mills in America." At night, the mill's neon lights can be seen for miles.

The first Saturday in October, Yukon residents celebrate their heritage with a Czech Festival. The celebration features street dances, handmade crafts, and plenty of Czech food. Beginning two months before the festival, volunteers work in shifts to make thousands of kolaches, the traditional Czech pastry. Here is a typical recipe shared by Mrs. Louis Krivanek whose father-in law made the Oklahoma run of 1889 and settled in Yukon.

YUKON KOLACHES

2 PACKAGES DRY YEAST
¼ CUP WARM WATER (110-115°)
2 CUPS MILK
½ CUP BUTTER OR MARGARINE
½ CUP SUGAR
⅓ CUP SHORTENING
1 TEASPOON SALT
1 EGG, BEATEN
2 EGG YOLKS, BEATEN
7 CUPS FLOUR
1 TABLESPOON MELTED BUTTER
1¼ CUPS PASTRY FILLING
(POPPY SEEDS, PRUNES, APRICOTS, OR FRUIT PRESERVES)

DISSOLVE YEAST IN WATER; SET ASIDE. In a medium saucepan heat the milk, butter or margarine, sugar, shortening, and salt until warm (120-130°), stirring constantly. Transfer to a very large mixing bowl. Stir in the dissolved yeast, egg, and egg yolks. Gradually stir in 5 cups flour to make a soft sponge. Cover and let rise in a warm place until the dough just starts to rise (20-30 minutes). Stir in remaining 2 cups flour to make a soft dough. Cover and let rise in a warm place until double (about 45 minutes). Stir dough down. Cover and let rest 10 minutes.

Turn out onto a floured surface and roll to ¾ inch thickness. Cut with a 3-inch round cutter. Place 3 inches apart on greased baking sheets. Brush with melted butter or margarine. Cover and let rise until nearly double (about 30 minutes). Using a floured finger or the back of a spoon, make a depression in the center of each and fill with about 2 teaspoons of the pastry filling. Bake in 375° oven 12-15 minutes or until golden brown. Remove from baking sheets and cool on wire rack. *About 28 kolaches.*

On Main Street in Yukon, J.E. Bennett has dished out hamburgers and coneys at Johnnie's Grill for over twenty years. The tiny storefront location provides a few tables next door, all served through a window just large enough to pass the orders through. Bennett began his food service career in 1949 at the Yukon Cafe across the street from the grill. A world of Route 66 traffic has passed before his doors!

El Reno is a city that remembers Route 66 and its history. Don't miss the Canadian County Museum and Heritage Park where an 1890s town has been resurrected. And don't miss the El Reno Hotel, built in 1892. El Reno claims the title, "Onion Fried Burger Capital of the World." Onion fried burgers were first cooked in 1926 at the Hamburger Inn; the idea caught on quickly. Now folks around the world come back to the city the first Saturday in May for Onion Burger Day.

After World War II, when Route 66 was humming with cars, at least a dozen onion burger grills satisfied hungry travelers in El Reno. Today three remain. Johnnie's Grill is perhaps the best known. Johnnie Siler opened his grill in 1948. When he retired in 1967, Otis Bruce took over the reins at the popular stop. Regulars at

Johnnie's don't even bother to order, the employees know what they want and serve it up hot and fast. Substantial orders of french fries accompany the burgers, all served up on old-fashioned burger-yellow paper in plastic baskets.

For coney lovers, the El Reno version includes cabbage slaw and chili, developed as a depression era mainstay around town.

If you miss Johnnie's Grill, keep an eye peeled for Robert's Grill or Sid's Diner. Both serve versions of the famous burger. The method of preparation varies a little, but experience seems to be the key to excellence. The meat is freshly ground, tossed on a grill at exactly the right temperature, and partially flattened. A handful of thinly sliced or chopped onions go on top, followed by more serious flattening. The burgers are served up hot with all the trimmings.

OFFICIAL EL RENO BIG BURGER

150 POUNDS FRESH GROUND BEEF
SALT AND PEPPER TO TASTE
150 POUNDS OF ONIONS, SLICED
PLENTY OF PICKLES AND MUSTARD
ONE 110-POUND BURGER BUN
LOTS OF WORK

COOK BEEF ON A 9-FOOT GRILL. Situate the bun and serve 300 hungry folks.

Hensley's Restaurant is another transplanted Route 66 original that stands behind a big oil derrick on I-40 at El Reno's Country Club Exit. H.M. Hensley began his restaurant career at the Consumer's Cafe, an addition to his service station on Route 66 at Elm and Hoff in El Reno. The restaurant has been moved, enlarged several times, and undergone a name change to follow the traffic and accommodate a growing clientele.

The first Consumer Cafe had ten stools at the counter where hamburgers and big slices of pie sold for ten cents each. Back then, Mrs. Hensley made the pies at home. Today, Hensley's Restaurant serves 750 to 1000 customers a day and is open round the clock.

Linda Kelly, Hensley's daughter, attributes its success to lots of hard work and good home cooked meals. The pie chef at Hensley's has been a valued employee since 1947 and Kelly says sixty per cent of her staff have been with her over five years.

At Hensley's, pie crusts are made from scratch and chicken and noodles are hand rolled in the old-fashioned way. Bread, rolls, and mouth-watering cinnamon buns are made on site. Linda prepares her own blue cheese dressing and one of the house specialties is a scrumptious peanut butter pie. If this doesn't sound good enough to make you hungry, try these two favorites, scaled to family-size portions.

HENSLEY'S APPLE MUFFINS

1½ CUPS FLOUR
½ CUP SUGAR
1 TEASPOON CINNAMON
¼ TEASPOON NUTMEG
½ TEASPOON SALT
1 TEASPOON BAKING POWDER
½ CUP NUTS, CHOPPED
½ CUP ORANGE JUICE
⅓ CUP COOKING OIL
2 EGGS, BEATEN
½ TEASPOON VANILLA
1½ CUPS GRATED RAW APPLE

Preheat oven to 375°. Coat twelve 2½ inch muffin tins with nonstick spray. In mixing bowl, combine dry ingredients and stir in nuts. Blend thoroughly. In a separate bowl combine remaining ingredients. Make well in dry ingredients and stir in apple mixture just until moistened. Do not overmix. Spoon batter into tins, filling three-fourths full. Bake for 20 minutes. *12 large muffins.*

HENSLEY'S CHICKEN ENCHILADA CASSEROLE

8 OUNCES TORTILLA CHIPS, LIGHTLY CRUSHED
I LARGE ONION, DICED
⅓ STICK MARGARINE
3 CUPS DICED COOKED CHICKEN
½ CUP CHICKEN BROTH
I CAN (10½ OUNCES) MUSHROOM SOUP
I CAN (10½ OUNCES) CHICKEN SOUP
I CAN (10 OUNCES) DICED TOMATOES AND GREEN CHILIES
I½ CUPS CHEESE, GRATED

PLACE HALF THE CRUSHED CHIPS in bottom of a greased 9 x 12 baking dish. Sauté onion in margarine. Combine all remaining ingredients and stir to combine. Pour mixture over crushed chips. Sprinkle remaining chips on top. Bake uncovered for 30 minutes in a preheated 350° oven. *8 to 10 servings.*

"The Oxford Cafe - One-half block North of 66 on Brickford Street Service 6 am to 8 pm - Good Clean Cooking"

(Old highway map advertisement)

At Hinton junction, Leon and Ann Little ran a popular cafe, sold gas, and had a few motel rooms from 1934 until 1962. Clarence Pleake drove a Greyhound bus back then between St. Louis and Amarillo. Clarence says he stopped regularly at Leon's place to let his bus cool off after making the Canadian River grade. He knew pie at Leon's was top-notch and always suggested his passengers have a piece while they waited.

In Hydro, the Johnson Peanut Company has been buying area growers' crops since the 1940s. Earl Johnson moved his storage facilities to the Route 66 location in 1963 and his children run the plant today, buying 7,000 tons of raw peanuts each year. Judy Pitt, one of the owners, distributes a good recipe booklet put out by the Oklahoma Peanut Commission.

ROUTE 66 NEVER FAIL PEANUT BRITTLE

3 CUPS WHITE SUGAR
I CUP WHITE CORN SYRUP
½ CUP WATER
3 CUPS RAW PEANUTS
I TABLESPOON BUTTER
I TEASPOON SALT
2 TEASPOONS SODA

BOIL SUGAR, CORN SYRUP, AND WATER UNTIL THREAD SPINS (234° F.). Add peanuts, stir continuously after peanuts are added. Cook until mixture turns a brownish gold. Take from heat, add butter, salt, and soda. Pour onto buttered board. Cool and break into pieces. *2 ½ pounds*

Just down the road, stop to visit with Lucille Hamons, who began selling gas to Route 66 travelers in 1941, fourteen years after the old station was built.

Lucille's is one of the oldest establishments still

operated by an original owner along Route 66. Lucille has a lot of Route 66 memories to share. She'll fix you a sandwich, pull out a cold drink and sit awhile at one of the oilcloth covered tables to reminisce. Lucille has a great collection of Route 66 memorabilia and a story with every piece.

LUCILLE HAMONS' PICKLED OKRA

1 CLOVE GARLIC PER PINT
1 HOT PEPPER POD PER PINT
1 TEASPOON DILL SEED PER PINT
⅔ CUP VINEGAR PER PINT
⅓ CUP WATER PER PINT
1 TEASPOON SALT PER PINT
SMALL WHOLE OKRA PODS

PLACE GARLIC AND HOT PEPPER in bottom of sterilized jars. Wash okra; remove most of stems but leave tops on each pod.

Pack okra tightly in jars and add dill seed. Bring vinegar, water, and salt to boiling point. Simmer for 5 minutes. Pour boiling brine to within ½ inch of top. Put on caps, screw bands firmly tight. Process in boiling water bath 5 minutes.

While in Weatherford, stop by the Out to Lunch Grill. Just the name captures the imagination. It's a good place for a friendly meal or a cup of coffee. Decor is simple but includes some interesting old license plates dating back to 1925 and a great collection of antique toy tractors. A big sign on the back wall proclaims "Nothing Runs Like a Deere."

The Mark, built in 1959, is thought to be the oldest restaurant in Weatherford still in business along the highway. The motel next door helps to provide a continuous stream of customers.

Although it has been torn down in the name of progress, old road enthusiasts will remember Weatherford's Porter House Restaurant, opened by Mr. and Mrs. Laverne Snow in 1949. The Snows named it for Mrs. Snow's father who was also in the restaurant business. The Porter House began with two booths and seven stools and eventually grew to a seating capacity of 144. "We worked there ten years, seven days a week without taking a vacation," Juanita remembers.

Juanita Snow says The Porter House was the first restaurant in the area to include a salad bar and buffet, and the first to serve Broasted Chicken. She bought the broaster after sampling the new cooking technique in Colorado and says the key to quality broasted chicken was following directions carefully. Her broasted chicken was marinated for twenty-four hours, dredged in a special flour mixture then quick-cooked in fresh shortening.

"I'll always remember the day Route 66 closed." Snow said. "It was at 11 o'clock on December 23, 1966. I cried and cried and thought we were ruined. Some guy from down the road came in and said he would give us six months to close. He made me so mad, I determined right then to stay."

Juanita says they had better business after I-40 opened than they ever expected. The economy was good, locals ate out more, and people still got off the interstate. She and Laverne retired in 1973. Their restaurant and motel have been replaced with a mini-market.

Another unique Weatherford diner owned by the Snows was the Cliff House that once stood at 305 W. Main. It was a Valentine System Diner, about 10 x 25 in size and prefabricated in Wichita, Kansas. The Snows hauled the portable diner to Weatherford from its original location in El Reno in 1961 and called it the Little Porter House. The interior was stainless and the tiny diner sported an early drive-through window.

When the Snows sold it to Clifford Harris, he changed the name to the Cliff House. This type of tiny diner was an immediate success along the highway because Americans on the go didn't want a leisurely meal. The diner operated until 1984.

PORTER HOUSE HOT CAKES

2 CUPS FLOUR
2 TABLESPOONS SUGAR
4 TEASPOONS BAKING POWDER
½ TEASPOON SALT
2 EGGS, BEATEN
2 CUPS MILK
2 TABLESPOONS MELTED BUTTER
½ TEASPOON VANILLA
DROP OF YELLOW FOOD COLORING

SIFT FLOUR, SUGAR, BAKING POWDER and salt together in a mixing bowl. Combine eggs, milk, melted butter, vanilla, and food coloring and whisk until smooth. Make a well in dry ingredients and add the liquid, beating rapidly until well moistened. Coat griddle with vegetable spray and heat to medium high. Bake on hot griddle until bubbles appear, then flip. Cook other side until golden brown. *18 three-inch hot cakes.*

Clinton is home to Pop Hicks Restaurant, a Route 66 institution since 1936. The cafe serves good home-cooked meals in a down-home friendly atmosphere. It's the kind of place where folks who polished off a massive breakfast at seven return by mid-morning for another cup of steaming brew accompanied by a cinnamon roll and the latest local news.

Pop Hicks was an early owner of the restaurant who gave it his name when he married the widow of the previous owner. The name became so firmly associated with good food that later owners kept it.

Howard and Mary Nichols operate the restaurant with their son, Ernie, and grandson, Rocky. Mary, who taught them both to cook, says Rocky has become the best cook in the family. A good burger plate is on the menu for $3.50. Mary also serves many favorites from her English home, including Yorkshire Pudding and Shepherd's Pie.

POP HICKS RESTAURANT — Hiway 66 — Clinton, Okla.

MARY NICHOLS' SHEPHERD'S PIE

1½ POUNDS GROUND MEAT
2 SMALL ONIONS, CHOPPED
¼ CUP BOUILLON
1 CAN (16½ OUNCES) ENGLISH PEAS
4 TO 5 CARROTS, THINLY SLICED
2 CUPS GRAVY
8 POTATOES (2½ POUNDS) MASHED AND SEASONED
SALT, PEPPER AND BUTTER TO TASTE

COOK MEAT AND ONIONS IN ¼ CUP BOUILLON until well done. Drain and season. Place mixture in an 8 x 11 baking pan, cover with layer of carrots and peas. Prepare two cups medium thick gravy using bouillon to flavor. Pour hot gravy over meat and vegetables. Mash potatoes, seasoning with a little milk, salt and pepper. Spread potatoes over meat mixture and dot top with butter. Bake 1 hour in a preheated 300° oven. *8 servings.*

Clinton is home to an excellent Western Trails Museum. A large area of the building is devoted to Route 66. Gladys Cutberth, a Clinton resident and widow of former U.S. 66 Association president Jack Cutberth, donated her husband's extensive collection to the museum.

Just west of Clinton at the Parkersberg Road exit from I-40 is Jiggs Smokehouse. Old 66 is the south access road along here, so let your nose lead you across the highway to this mouth-watering stop. George and Virginia Klaassen make an exceptional barbecue sauce to go with their specialty. George uses mesquite coals to smoke brisket and hickory to prepare jerky and hams.

A whole array of famous folks have stopped by their log cabin location. Autographed pictures cover the walls. The food is down-home good and the tantalizing aroma of barbecue can't get any better than this. If you can't find Jiggs, substitute another good quality barbecue sauce.

JIGGS SMOKE HOUSE BARBECUE BEANS

1 GALLON PORK AND BEANS
1½ CUPS JIGGS BARBECUE SAUCE
2 TABLESPOONS SORGHUM
2 TABLESPOONS BROWN SUGAR

COMBINE PORK AND BEANS IN A LARGE CROCK POT and heat slowly until ready to serve. *20 servings.*

The Country Dove Gift Shop and Tearoom on 3rd Street in Elk City offers unexpected delights. Located in an early 1920s prairie home, Glenna Hollis and Kay Farmer have assembled a whimsical collection of gifts and collectibles that appeal to the most discriminating buyer.

The two-story home, built by Anna L. and W.C. Jones, Sr., is typical of construction during the roaring twenties. It features clapboard construction, a large front porch, high ceilings, a low-pitched hip roof with unusual dormers, and double-hung sash windows. The Country Dove is a place to feed the soul as well as the body. After a leisurely tour through the upstairs galleries, stop for a light lunch in the tea room where the menu is designed to pamper and delight. This French Silk Pie is worth the trip by itself.

COUNTRY DOVE FRENCH SILK PIE

NUT CRUST

1 STICK BUTTER, MELTED
1 CUP FLOUR
⅔ CUP FINELY CHOPPED NUTS

FILLING

¾ CUP BUTTER
1⅓ CUPS SUGAR
2 TEASPOONS VANILLA
2 SQUARES UNSWEETENED CHOCOLATE, MELTED
AND COOLED
3 LARGE EGGS

WHIPPED CREAM

½ PINT WHIPPING CREAM
¼ CUP SUGAR
1 TEASPOON VANILLA
CHOCOLATE SHAVINGS

COMBINE CRUST INGREDIENTS AND BLEND WELL. Pat thin layer of mixture into bottom and sides of a 10-inch pie pan. Bake in preheated 350° oven for 20 minutes. Allow to cool.

CREAM BUTTER AND SUGAR THOROUGHLY. Blend in vanilla and chocolate and mix well. Add eggs one at a time, beating with mixer on high speed for at least 5 minutes after each addition. Pour mixture into a pie shell and chill in refrigerator for several hours or overnight. The crust and filling freeze well at this STAGE IF MAKING the pie ahead of time.

WHIP CREAM TO SOFT PEAK STAGE. Add sugar and vanilla and continue to whip until cream stands in firm peaks. Spread over pie and grate sweetened chocolate on top. *8 servings.*

Elk City's Old Town Museum and the Anadarko Basin Museum of Natural History provide a graphic account of the area's farm and ranch economy and a fleeting experience with the wealth of gas.

On the far western edge of Elk City, Queenan's Indian Trading Post stands empty and abandoned. The Route 66 landmark was built by Reese and Wanda Queenan in 1948. For years the Queenan's offered tourists a wide selection of Indian goods.

They also sold apple and cherry cider. Many cider booths sprang up all along the old road, but this was one of the best. Wanda Queenan still has her home behind the deserted trading post and spends much of her time at the Old Town Museum.

Gene Hill, who died in 1992, remembered those early Route 66 days, too. Gene retired in 1990 after spending thirty-nine years in the cafe business around Sayre.

Hill bought the Rainbow Cafe in 1951. Later, he and his wife, Hazel, also operated Gene's Cafe, the Silver Grill, and a cafeteria. The Family House Restaurant now operates in one of his old locations.

"The first Christmas we were in business, we served holiday traffic for twenty-four hours without taking a break," Gene said. "We never really caught up and were almost too tired for a late celebration ourselves."

Another time, a blizzard in the Texas Panhandle stranded motorists throughout Western Oklahoma for several days. There weren't enough motel rooms available so many folks just stayed at his cafe. Gene recalled one fellow didn't believe his warnings and headed West early one morning, only to return that night, a real believer in what he had been told about blizzards on the Great Plains.

Before leaving Sayre, stop by the Owl Rexall Drug to have something cold at the soda fountain. The original oak shelves and marble-topped back fountain are still in place. A picture of the old building, taken about 1906, stands at the pharmacy counter.

Erick is home to the Beckham County Honey Festival, featuring tours of a working honey farm, a parade, cookery contests, and live entertainment. A honey farm has been located near Erick for over thirty years. Ben and Margie North operate the farm today and sell their pure clover and alfalfa honey, and delicious honey treats all year long. For those missing the festival, highway signs clearly direct travelers to the honey farm. The Beckham County Extension Clubs sponsor a cooking contest at the festival. Here is a first prize recipe courtesy of the Erick Chamber of Commerce.

BECKHAM COUNTY HONEY ROSE CHEESE CAKE

½ CUP SHORTENING
1¼ CUPS SUGAR
¼ CUP HONEY
2 EGGS
1 TEASPOON LEMON EXTRACT
1 TEASPOON ORANGE EXTRACT
2 CUPS FLOUR
1 TEASPOON CINNAMON
⅓ TEASPOON SALT
1 CUP BUTTERMILK
1 TEASPOON VINEGAR
1 TEASPOON BAKING SODA
1 TEASPOON RED FOOD COLORING

CREAM CHEESE FROSTING

1 PACKAGE (3 OUNCES) CREAM CHEESE
1½ CUPS POWDERED SUGAR
1 TEASPOON WARM WATER
1 TEASPOON VANILLA

CREAM TOGETHER THE FIRST SIX INGREDIENTS. Sift flour, cinnamon and salt together. Add alternately with part of the buttermilk to creamed mixture. Add vinegar and soda to the last part of buttermilk and mix well. Add red food coloring to complete mixture and pour into 7½ x 11 greased pan. Bake in preheated 350° oven for about 30 minutes, or until toothpick inserted comes out clean. Soften cheese. Add sugar, water, and vanilla. Beat until creamy and spread over cake.

Cal's Country Cooking has been an Erick landmark since 1946. For thirty-three years, Cal served his memorable food on old Route 66, but when the interstate bypassed Erick, he knew he had to follow the crowd. So Cal designed a sprawling log cabin restaurant, spent two and a half years helping to build it, and opened at Exit 7 on I-40 in October of 1979. Cal is an entrepreneur who gets to work by five each morning and personally supervises preparation of his famous ham and beans, chicken-fried steak, breads, and homemade desserts.

One wall at Cal's is a who's who of famous guests: Dale Robertson, Richard Thomas, Jessica Lang, Randy Travis, Hoyt Axton, Dennis Weaver, and home town boy, Roger Miller. Next to their pictures, Cal has framed articles from the *Interstate Gourmet, The Daily Oklahoman,* and *Oklahoma Today,* where he has won awards.

Cinnamon rolls served at Cal's are designed for hefty appetites and dozens of mouth-watering loaves of homemade bread go home each day with contented customers. Some folks come back regularly just for Cal's cornbread, always served with ham and beans. Folks would have to hunt a long time to find better down-home country fare.

CAL'S MOCK LOBSTER SALAD

½ POUND CRACKERS, CRUMBLED
1½ STALKS CELERY, CHOPPED
1 SMALL ONION, CHOPPED
3 HARD-COOKED EGGS, CHOPPED
1 CUP MAYONNAISE
½ TEASPOON CELERY SEED
¾ CUP TOMATO JUICE
1 CUP CANNED TOMATOES
SALT AND PEPPER TO TASTE

COMBINE CRACKERS WITH CELERY, ONIONS, AND EGGS. Blend mayonnaise with celery seed, tomato juice, and canned tomatoes. Stir into first mixture and season to taste. *8 servings.*

At the state line, take a detour through the dying town of Texola. Vernon Baily once ran Texola's Longhorn Trading Post. Bill's Cafe also took a turn serving road traffic. For awhile, the Hitching Post Bar was considered a last chance saloon since travelers heading west couldn't buy another beer before reaching Amarillo. On the Highway 66 curve leaving town, the Last Stop Bar has a fresh sign painted on the front wall.

There's no other place
Like this place
Anywhere near this place
So this must be the place.

Driving west on old 66, you'll be in Texas in less than five minutes.

TEXAS

TEXAS. Here, cowboys are for real and "Y'all come" is sincerely meant. Barbecue and black-eyed peas have replaced the chuckwagon image of beans and burnt cow. The Panhandle is one of the nation's leading beef production areas and steaks are good and plentiful.

Route 66 originally crossed the Texas Panhandle in 178 miles. About ninety percent of the old road can be traveled today. Highway 66 is the south service road as it enters Texas and is in good condition past the tiny community of Alanreed.

The first Route 66 community in Texas is Shamrock, where the U Drop Inn opened for business on April 1, 1936. Standing at the intersection of two cross-country highways, the building is one of the most unusual examples of art-deco architecture in the nation. Two polished green tile domes beckon customers to stop and stay awhile. Only the red neon lights that once outlined the domes are missing.

John and Bebe Nunn, the original owners, were in business before Highway 66 was paved in front of their cafe. "In 1938 we had a big celebration when paving was completed through here. There was a parade, a banquet, and an all-night dance in the streets," Bebe said.

For many years, the U Drop Inn was the classiest place to eat between Oklahoma City and Amarillo. During the busiest Route 66 years, the Nunns employed twenty cooks.

John Nunn never forgot a face and never met a stranger. He and Bebe served good home-style food. They were especially famous for freshly cut steaks and clean service. All their waitresses wore starched uniforms and aprons, had hair nets under their caps, and wore hose with their practical shoes.

Bebe Nunn remembered the heavy holiday traffic during those early days. "On Labor Day weekends,

Penny postcards marked the way: Devil's Elbow region in Missouri and Santa Monica beach and pier.

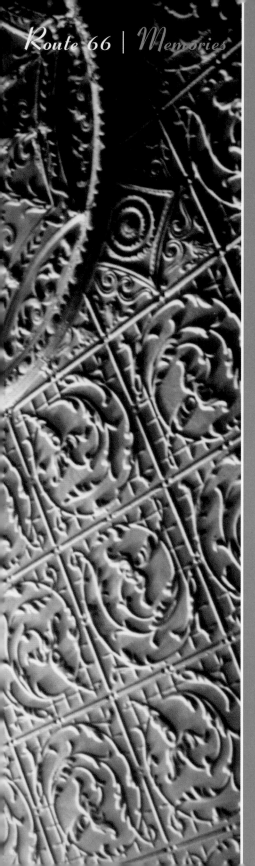

Many of the old cafés and filling stations along the way had patterned tin ceilings. John's Modern Cabins, Clementine, MO; G.I. Joes billboard, Lexington, IL.

For years, fantastic neon guided the way by night.

Comfort food along the Mother Road. (clockwise from top left) Rock Café, Stroud, OK; Steak n' Shake, Springfield, MO; Caveman Bar-B-Q and Steak House, near Lebanon, MO; Red Cedar Inn, Pacific, MO; U Drop Inn, Shamrock, TX.

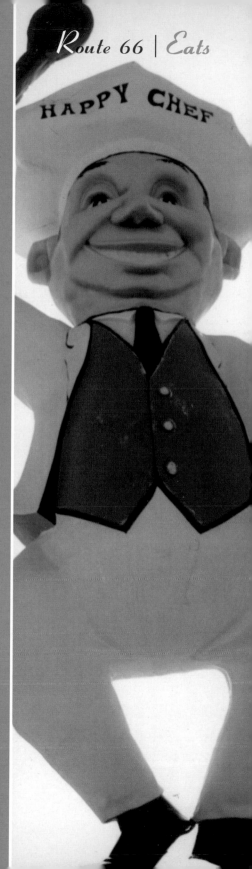

(clockwise from top left) Cozy Dog Drive In and Supply Company, a classic in Springfield, IL; Lincoln Dining Room, Springfield; the happy fat man advertisements for the Club Café made Santa Rosa, NM famous. The café is gone today.

(side) Granny's Country Kitchen, Chandler, OK; (top left) Coca-Cola sign inside P.J.'s Bar-B-Q in Chandler, OK; (bottom) Travis Dillon and Ted Drewes at Ted Drewes Frozen Custard, St. Louis, MO.

(top) Icicle-clad Ted Drewes Frozen Custard, a top flavor of the road; (bottom) Joe and Aggie's Mexican Food in Holbrook, AZ; (side) 66 Diner in Albuquerque, NM.

Pitstops of the past. (top right) Old Soulsby's Service Station, Mount Olive, IL; (middle) gas station near Odell, IL; (bottom) gas station, Mclean, TX—at the heart of Old Route 66.

(top) Coral Court Motel, St. Louis, MO; (bottom) Boots Motel, Carthage, MO.

(top) Wagon Wheel Motel, Cuba, MO; (bottom) Blue Swallow Motel, Tucumcari, NM: both still in operation today.

(top) Route 66 Motor Tour in Illinois; (bottom) near Devil's Elbow, MO.

(top) Oatman Road, AZ; (bottom) Chain of Rocks Bridge, linking Illinois and Missouri. Open to non-vehicular traffic as of April 2000, this is now the longest pedestrian bridge in the world.

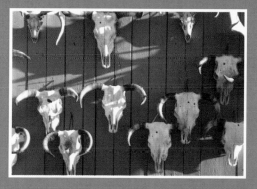

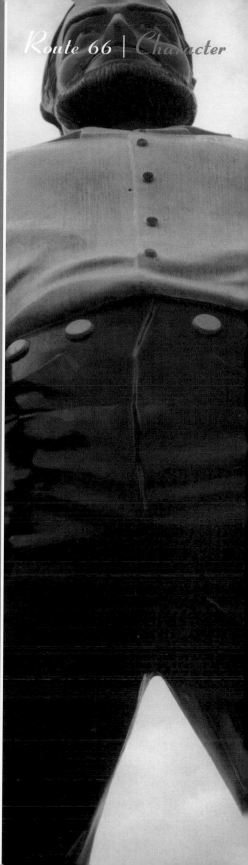

(top) The Wigwam Motel, Holbrook, AZ, still open today and a popular stop, just down the street from Joe and Aggie's Café. (bottom right) Santa Fe, NM; (bottom left) Launching Pad Drive-In, Wilmington, IL; (side) Paul Bunyon, Flagstaff, AZ.

(side) Ed Galloway's Totem Pole, Foyil, OK; (clockwise from top) Blue Whale, Catoosa, OK; Big Boy can still be found in several locations in Illinois and Missouri; Betty Boop, Polk-a-Dot Drive-In, Braidwood, IL.

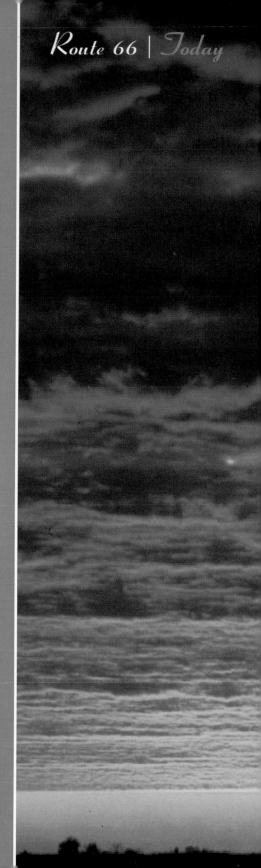

(top left) A restored Coca-Cola sign on the Buford Building, once home to the White Way Café in Stroud, OK; (bottom) El Rancho Hotel, Gallup, NM.

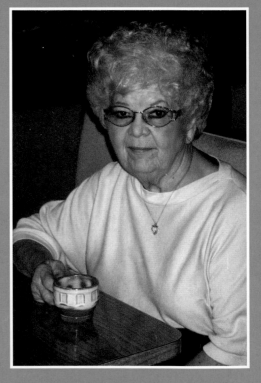

(top, and bottom left) Juan Delgadillo's Snow Cap in Seligman, AZ; (bottom right) Norma Hall, Norma's Diamond Café, Sapulpa, OK.

local service club members gathered on the vacant lot just east of the U Drop Inn to serve free slices of watermelon to passing motorists," she said. "It was a welcome rest for travelers and our way to advertise the quality melons that grow so well around here. Travelers remembered and came back to see us year after year." Mrs. Nunn, a Texas Route 66 Hall of Fame member, passed away in 1992.

The old restaurant has changed names and had several new owners in over half a century of service. James and Ann Lunsford took the reins in 1991. James now presides over the kitchen, where he has built a reputation for masterful baking. Ann says she is content with working out front since she is in charge of the kitchen and the kids at home.

Today's U Drop Inn offers the friendly,

courteous service the Nunns established. The atmosphere is relaxed and home-town comfortable. Stop by for a giant dose of Route 66 nostalgia.

Really **FRESH** *Coffee!*

Bottled Drinks
Ice Cold

U Drop Inn Banana Cake

½ CUP BUTTER
1½ CUPS SUGAR
3 LARGE EGGS
2 CUPS FLOUR
2 TEASPOONS BAKING POWDER
¾ TEASPOON SODA
½ TEASPOON SALT
¼ CUP BUTTERMILK
1 TEASPOON VANILLA
1 CUP MASHED BANANA

Caramel Icing

¼ CUP BUTTER
½ CUP BROWN SUGAR
. ⅛ CUP MILK
½ TEASPOON VANILLA
1 CUP POWDERED SUGAR
PINCH OF SALT

CREAM TOGETHER THE BUTTER AND SUGAR until light and fluffy. Beat eggs lightly and add to creamed mixture, blending well.

Sift together dry ingredients and add alternately with buttermilk and vanilla, beginning and ending with flour. Fold in bananas and stir to blend. Pour batter into two greased 8-inch cake pans or one 9 x 13 baking pan. Bake for 35 to 40 minutes in a preheated 350° oven. Frost with Caramel Icing.

For the icing, melt butter in saucepan and add brown sugar. Cook over low heat, stirring constantly, for 2 minutes. Add milk and allow to come to a boil. Immediately remove from heat and allow to cool before adding vanilla, sugar, and salt. Beat well and frost cake.

U Drop Inn Pineapple Cake

2 CUPS FLOUR
2 CUPS SUGAR
2 TEASPOONS BAKING SODA
PINCH OF SALT
2 EGGS
1 CAN (20 OUNCES) CRUSHED PINEAPPLE, UNDRAINED
1 TEASPOON VANILLA

FLOUR AND GREASE A 9 x 13 BAKING PAN. Combine flour, sugar, soda, salt, eggs, pineapple, and vanilla. Pour into pan and bake in preheated 350° oven for 40 minutes. Top with your favorite cream cheese or coconut frosting.

BEBE NUNN'S CHICKEN AND RICE CASSEROLE

1 FRYER, CUT IN PIECES AND SKINNED
1 CUP UNCOOKED RICE
1 CAN (10½ OUNCES) MUSHROOM SOUP
1 CAN WATER
1 TABLESPOON DRY ONION SOUP MIX
SALT AND PEPPER TO TASTE

SPRAY AN 8 X 11 BAKING DISH WITH NONSTICK SPRAY. Add uncooked rice and place chicken pieces over rice. Salt and pepper to taste. Combine soup, water and onion soup mix and pour over chicken and rice. Bake uncovered in preheated 350° oven until done, about 1 hour. Casserole should be nicely browned on top.

After the Nunns retired, the U Drop Inn became the Tower Cafe. Grace Bruner made the Tower a Greyhound bus stop in 1960. Some of her most memorable guests were Indian children from New Mexico and Arizona who were bused to reservation schools in Oklahoma each fall.

TOWER CAFE HEAVENLY HASH

2 CUPS WHIPPING CREAM
½ CUP SUGAR
I TEASPOON VANILLA
I CAN (20 OUNCES) CRUSHED PINEAPPLE
I PACKAGE (6¼ OUNCES) MINIATURE MARSHMALLOWS
½ CUP CHOPPED PECANS

Whip the cream until it stands in soft peaks. Add sugar and vanilla and continue whipping to blend. Fold in drained pineapple and marshmallows. Sprinkle pecans on top or add to mixture. *12 servings.*

Marie Taylor is another longtime Shamrock resident who has managed a Shamrock eating place almost continuously since she and her husband opened their first cafe on Highway 87 in 1935. They later bought the Casey Steak House on Highway 66 and when it burned, she took over management at the Western Restaurant across the street from the U Drop Inn.

Although several years past the age when most people retire, Marie loves her job and says she has outlasted her daughter in Amarillo who retired last year.

Marie remembers she and her husband installed the first dishwasher in Shamrock, and they had the first air-conditioned cafe. "That air conditioner was a real drawing card for folks who wanted to cool off awhile. It was worth every penny," she said. "Our winters can be as extreme as the summers," Marie said. "One time the train was stalled here because of a terrible blizzard. We couldn't get our car out and an old man with a team of mules and a wagon helped my husband get through from the cafe to feed the hungry passengers."

Marie says that Route 66 days brought busloads of tourists through Shamrock at mealtime. Drivers would stop near the intersection of 66 and 87 and passengers would flock in all directions to eat. "We usually knew they were coming and would be prepared with lots of sandwiches and cold drinks," she said.

WESTERN RESTAURANT BROWNIES

I STICK MARGARINE, MELTED
I CUP SUGAR
4 EGGS, BEATEN
I CAN (5 OUNCES) HERSHEY SYRUP
I CUP FLOUR
¾ TEASPOON BAKING POWDER
I CUP PECANS, CHOPPED
6 TABLESPOONS MARGARINE
6 TABLESPOONS MILK
I½ CUPS SUGAR
½ CUP MILK CHOCOLATE CHIPS

PREHEAT OVEN TO 350°. Grease and flour a jelly roll pan. Combine margarine, sugar, eggs, and syrup, beating thoroughly. Combine flour and baking powder. Add to syrup mixture and stir in chopped pecans. Pour into pan and bake for 25 minutes. Cool.

In a small saucepan, combine margarine, milk and sugar and bring to rolling boil. Let boil for barely 1½ minutes, then stir in chocolate chips. If cooked too long, the sugar will crystalize. Frost brownies. *30 to 36 brownies.*

During the boom years of the 1940s, Shamrock had over 20 eating places. The Porterhouse Drive-In and the Dixie Cafe were popular stops. The Dixie was a block west of the U Drop Inn and advertised "Fried Chicken and Hot Biscuits our Specialty - Rotary and Lions Service Clubs. We Welcome Chartered Buses and Serve Children's Portions."

Today, Mitchell's Family Restaurant and the North 40 Steak House catch much of the traffic on I-40. Both are good spots to eat but lack the nostalgia found a few blocks south on the old roads.

Before leaving Shamrock, take time to drive south on Highway 83 through the old downtown section and look up at the tallest water tower in Texas, 181 feet. Able to hold 50,000 gallons, it is a realistic reminder of the dust bowl days.

In McLean, there are two museums, both well worth the traveler's time. On the east side of town, in an old brick building the size of a city block, is the Devil's Rope and Texas Old Route 66 Museum. The museum includes the Texas Route 66 Hall of Fame. A restored 1930-vintage cafe makes an unusual addition. Visitors can wander in, have their pictures made at the counter and relive the days of linoleum floors, ice boxes, and coffee cream served in reusable glass containers. In the same building, the American Barb Wire Collectors Society has assembled a massive display of old tools and old ways, sure to fascinate.

On Main Street, the McLean-Alanreed Historical Museum offers viewers another realistic glimpse of the pioneer past in the Texas Panhandle.

McLean was home to the first Phillips 66 station in Texas, built in 1926 and operated into the 1970s.

Local residents have restored the tiny station to its early 1930 appearance. It is on the south side of the street as travelers leave town. Because McLean is near the halfway point on a trip along Route 66, the town slogan has appropriately become, "McLean, Texas — at the Heart of Old Route 66."

At one time Sophie Hutchinson ran Cafe 66 on Main Street, Bob Massy owned the McLean Cafe and Grace Bruner presided over the Greyhound Drug.

Grace, who died of a heart attack in 1992, was a member of the Texas Route 66 Hall of Fame. She recalled building a lunchroom in the basement of the drugstore so McLean teenagers would have a special place to eat. She called it the Tiger's Den and supplied comic books, posters, and music for entertainment. Grace also remembered catching one teenager with five funny books under his coat as he left the Den. She confiscated them and sent him on his way. Years later, he became a Highway Patrolman and regular customer at her Tower Cafe in Shamrock. When he married Grace's best waitress, she loved to remind him about taking things away from her.

Grace said the most popular item on her menu during the 1950s was the "Tower Special" that included a 3½ ounce steak she dipped in milk and flour before frying. She served the steak over toast and added a green salad and French fries. Homemade golden fried onion rings were piled on top. Salad dressing and catsup went along with each dinner and she sold the meal for $1.95.

Today, early risers in McLean find that first cup of coffee at the Cowboy Cafe. By sunrise, the parking lot out front is full of pickups and the tantalizing aroma of frying bacon draws an assortment of hungry dogs to lounge around the back entrance.

Alanreed was once the home of the Reptile

Ranch, a tourist stop where a huge carved snake stretched into the air in front of the "museum" and trading post. Untold carloads of children urged their dads to stop for pictures with the snake. Business was profitable until I-40 came along. The new alignment meant Dad had already missed the turnoff before the kids spotted the snake. The old building is empty today, and the snake stands entombed at the McLean Route 66 Museum.

The landscape is determinedly flat by the time travelers reach Groom. Only occasional houses and surrounding elm trees blemish the horizon. In the summer, distant mirages form giant mirrors to reflect the incredibly blue sky, and in winter there is no protection from icy "northers" that send bone-chilling winds whipping across the highway. Tumbleweeds roll across the road to entangle themselves in the barbed-wire fences and unwary motorists are often hit by a barrage of the prickly balls. At the leaning Britton Water Tower, travelers find a startling reminder of man's ability to create marketing gimmicks. The tower stands at a precarious angle just north of the I-40 Groom exit where the foundation is all that remains of a once prosperous fast food joint and service station.

Ruby Denton owns the Golden Spread Grill in Groom where she began serving Highway 66 customers in 1951. She bought the attractive, uncluttered cafe in 1957. Ruby works from 6 a.m. until 10 p.m., seven days a week, taking off for only a few minutes each afternoon to rest. "It's a good life," she says, "my customers come back because they like my home cooking and I'd rather live here in Groom than any place else in the world."

When I-40 bypassed Groom, business all but disappeared. Ruby said she was too set in her ways to move and couldn't afford an interstate location anyway. Her business today is primarily local folks who come in to catch up on area news while they eat.

Ruby also has a regular group of I-40 customers who stop each fall on their way to Arizona for the winter. In the spring they return going northeast. When someone asks Ruby what her specialty is, she has a standard reply, "Anything you order."

"I can't change the menu," she says. "Folks around here have it memorized. They expect Mexican food on Mondays, chicken and dumplings on Fridays, and chicken and dressing every other Sunday." Fresh black-eyed peas are standard summer fare. During the heyday of Route 66, traffic through Groom supported several cafes, including the Ranchhouse, the Sportsman, Wards, the Longhorn, and Homer's. There was even a 66 Hotel. By the time I-40 came through in June of 1980, there were still three cafes and a drive-in. Ruby is the survivor.

GOLDEN SPREAD PECAN PIE

3 EGGS
½ CUP WHITE SUGAR
1½ CUPS DARK KARO SYRUP
PINCH OF SALT
½ CUP OR MORE PECANS
1 UNBAKED 9-INCH PIE SHELL

PREHEAT OVEN TO 350°. In a medium mixing bowl, beat eggs until creamy. Add sugar, syrup and salt. Blend well to dissolve sugar. Pour mixture into unbaked pie shell and top with pecans. Bake 45 minutes to 1 hour or until set. *8 servings.*

As the name of Ruby's restaurant indicates, this area of the Texas Panhandle is called the Golden Spread. At harvest time in June and July, a blanket of ripe wheat covers the incredibly flat tableland as far as the eye can see.

The 1926 alignment of Route 66 passed through Amarillo on 3rd Street but was moved to Amarillo Boulevard (N.E. 8th Street), turned south on Fillmore to 6th Street and headed west toward the state line. Later, Route 66 stayed on Amarillo Boulevard all the way through town. Ruth's Steaks was located at 5106 Amarillo Boulevard for thirty years. Ruth made history on Route 66 by serving nothing but good steak. Just across the street was the Aviatrix, an Amarillo landmark with a story of its own.

In the late 1930s, Earl Hooper and his brothers built a small drive-in on pasture land across from English Airfield on Amarillo Boulevard. Earl named the cafe the Aviatrix and designed a long cement ramp out front. His waitresses skated up and down the ramp, serving "Chicken on the Wing" to patrons in their cars. The oblong plates were heavy pewter and spoons extending on each side made the dishes actually look like an airplane. There was room for sixty to seventy customers inside for those who preferred tables.

In 1940 Carlton Scales and his mother, Iweta, bought the cafe and turned the Aviatrix into a Texas panhandle showplace. Enlarged to seat six hundred, it became the most elaborate ballroom and supper club in the Panhandle. The Aviatrix served banquets, wedding parties, convention goers, and visiting dignitaries until it closed for good on August 5, 1989.

Scales organized a five-piece orchestra soon after the showplace opened and he continued to delight dancers through the mid-60s. Big band celebrities were regulars at the Aviatrix. Louis Armstrong, Duke Ellington, Harry James, the Dorsey brothers, and Spike Jones all took their turn at the microphone.

"It was a family dance hall," Scales said. "We had couples from the air base as well as whole families who would come out to celebrate Grandma and Grandpa's anniversary."

The Aviatrix was a family affair for the Scales, too.

"My aunt, my mother's sister, was the oldest hat-check girl in the country. She was still checking hats and coats every Saturday night at the age of ninety-eight. She would dance anytime she was asked, but usually dozed off after ten p.m. and had to be waked up so customers could retrieve their hats and coats," Scales said.

In 1952, the Aviatrix burned to the ground but was completely rebuilt. In the 1970s Scales switched to country-western music to keep up with popular trends.

Through the years, thousands of Amarillo Air Base personnel and Panhandle residents made this Route 66 classic a Texas favorite.

Amarillo has always been a center for interstate traffic. At the intersection of Fillmore and Amarillo Boulevard, U.S. 60, 66, 87, and 287 met in a constant traffic snarl for years. Back in 1967, gasoline on the corner sold for 29.9 cents and cafes around the area stayed open twenty-four hours a day.

Bob Dowell's Cafe was located on that busy corner, "Where Tourists and Texans Dine." Dowell masterminded a highway survey one year that indicated east or westbound travelers were primarily going to visit relatives or seek new jobs. They had less money to spend than north- or southbound motorists, who were usually going to spend the winter in a warmer location and were more willing to leave their travel dollars in Amarillo. Dowell found more cars traveled east and west so local businessmen benefitted equally.

Dowell opened his first restaurant in Amarillo in 1948 and had three locations on Highway 66 at one time. His last restaurant was on the interstate west of Amarillo.

"When I opened my first place, there weren't any chains," Dowell said. "My place was just plain vanilla, but we served good food. We got the traffic because we didn't have to compete with those big boys running the chains." To attract businessmen, Dowell provided plug-in telephones in booths so that calls and appointments could be taken care of while dining.

For four decades in Amarillo, Dowell was one of the city's biggest boosters. He never met a stranger and was an enthusiastic member of the Texas Route 66 Hall of Fame. "I always loved to travel 66," he said "I have lots of good friends up and down the route, and lots of memories. I used to stop at the cockfights at Old Endee and eat great Mexican food in Santa Rosa."

Bob Dowell's restaurants were known for good steaks and some of the best homemade pastries in Amarillo. His famous salad dressing remains a secret, but he shared this Mexican food recipe just a few months before he passed away in March of 1992.

BOB DOWELL'S TACO MEAT

1¼ POUNDS LEAN GROUND BEEF
1 TABLESPOON GARLIC POWDER
½ CUP CHOPPED ONIONS
1 TEASPOON SALT
1 TEASPOON BLACK PEPPER

THOROUGHLY MIX ALL INGREDIENTS. Cook well, either on top of stove or in a slow oven. Drain any excess grease.

Break meat into small pieces with fork or spoon. Serve on buffet with crisp fresh taco shells, grated cheese, chopped tomatoes and lettuce, more onion if desired, and a big bowl of taco sauce. *8 Texas size tacos.*

Amarillo Boulevard became home to Beans and Things in 1979 when Wiley Alexander decided to go into the barbecue business. Alexander had recently resigned from the police force and he and a friend were looking for a new challenge. Since Alexander already owned land on Amarillo Boulevard, old Highway 66 became the logical location for their new "pure Texas" venture.

"I had never even made a sandwich when we started," Alexander says. "That first day, the meat was done and on the chopping board, but I hadn't cut it up when about thirty customers lined up out front. I had to learn fast."

Alexander not only learned fast, he learned well. Several years ago Jane and Michael Stern came through Amarillo and stopped at his take-out counter to pick up some barbecue. They drove away but soon returned for more. The Sterns wrote up Beans and Things as one of the best barbecue spots they had ever found. "I wasn't even there," Alexander says, "Or if I was, they never introduced themselves. But I'm sure glad they liked my food."

Alexander has recently retired, but the girls who have leased his business are carrying on with his good barbecue and chili recipes. At 1700 Amarillo Boulevard East, Beans and Things can't be missed. A fat cow stands atop the building.

BEANS AND THINGS BARBECUE SAUCE

2¼ CUPS CATSUP
2¼ CUPS WATER
2 TEASPOONS BEEF BROTH
3 TABLESPOONS BROWN SUGAR
½ TEASPOON WORCESTERSHIRE
2 SHAKES TABASCO
1 TABLESPOON LEMON JUICE
½ TEASPOON LIQUID SMOKE
1¼ TEASPOONS DRY MUSTARD
1 TEASPOON CHILI POWDER
½ TEASPOON GARLIC POWDER
1 TEASPOON BLACK PEPPER
¼ TEASPOON CAYENNE

COMBINE ALL INGREDIENTS IN LARGE SAUCEPAN and bring to boil then simmer for 15 minutes. Cool and store in refrigerator until needed. *1 quart.*

BEANS AND THINGS CHILI

4 POUNDS COARSE GROUND BEEF
1 TABLESPOON CHOPPED GARLIC
1 ONION, CHOPPED
1 TABLESPOON CHILI POWDER
1 TEASPOONS RED PEPPER
1 TEASPOON BLACK PEPPER

1 TEASPOON CRUSHED RED CHILI PEPPER
1 CAN (10 OUNCES) ROTEL TOMATOES
1 TEASPOON OREGANO
1 TEASPOON GROUND CUMIN
1 TEASPOON SALT
1 TABLESPOON PAPRIKA

BRAISE MEAT UNTIL BROWNED. Add garlic and onions and continue cooking until onions are clear. Add remaining ingredients and cover with about 2 inches of water. Cook until meat feels heavy on the bottom, about 2 hours. *12 to 16 servings.*

Longchamps Dining Salon opened on Amarillo Boulevard in 1945 as an elegant seafood restaurant recommended by AAA and Duncan Hines. The Homer Rices bought the restaurant in 1947 and changed the name to Rice's Dining Salon in 1953. Wes Izzard, former editor of the Amarillo Daily News, described the 5000 bulb billboard atop Rice's as "the largest restaurant sign between New York and Los Angeles." It remained a landmark and beacon for hungry people until the Rices retired in 1978.

Mrs. Rice continues to be proud of the varied menu, often saying their guests could eat 78 different times in the restaurant without ordering the same thing. "We always used linen table cloths and napkins," Mrs. Rice says, "And we used Rogers silverplate at the tables."

Homemade chicken noodle soup was a house specialty and cobblers were the most popular dessert. Mrs. Rice taught the cook to make her mother's turkey dressing and says she had more compliments on the dressing than almost anything else they served.

Homer Rice remembers the week the Detroit Lions were in Amarillo for an exhibition game. "I said I would feed them all they could eat and that was a big mistake," he recalls, "After they had eaten all our steaks, they wanted to know what was next. That's when I got out the chicken."

RICE'S DINING SALON TURKEY DRESSING

4 CUPS CRUMBLED CORNBREAD
4 CUPS LIGHTLY TOASTED BREAD, CUBED
1 LARGE ONION, CHOPPED
1 CUP CELERY, CHOPPED
1 LARGE DILL PICKLE, DICED
2 CUPS TURKEY BROTH
2 EGGS, WELL BEATEN
2 TEASPOONS SAGE
SALT AND PEPPER TO TASTE
ADDITIONAL BROTH AS NEEDED

COMBINE CORNBREAD AND BREAD IN LARGE MIXING BOWL. In medium saucepan, add onion, celery, and dill pickle to turkey broth. Bring to boil, cooking until barely tender. Cool slightly and pour over bread mixture.

Add beaten eggs, sage, salt and pepper, and enough additional broth to make a slightly moist mixture. Pour dressing in a greased 9 x 11 baking dish. Bake in preheated 350° oven for 30 minutes. *8 to 10 servings.*

The Madsen Dining Room opened on Amarillo Boulevard in 1936. "Mother" Madsen specialized in chicken dinners accompanied by honey butter, hot biscuits, and elegant pastries. Amarillo also had a Fred Harvey Coffee Shop, Mexican Inn, Ding How and Hong Kong Restaurants, Mason's Cafe, the Dream Diner, Myers Fried Chicken, and Underwood's Barbecue. The Hackney Club served dinner guests who loved to gamble and was occasionally raided.

The Rainbow Cafe has a special story, reflecting Wilbur Wood's lifetime love for food and the people he served. Wood moved to Amarillo as a young boy from Mounds in Indian Territory. When World War I broke out, he was underage but enlisted anyway. When Wood's feet began to give him problems, his captain suggested he apply to be a cook. He immediately found his place and wrote home to his mother to send recipes. Before long the men were eating better than the officers and Wood was transferred to the officers' mess. After the war he tried several other civilian jobs, but finally borrowed enough money to build the Rainbow Cafe at 315 N. Fillmore. He opened July 13, 1935. Wood said thirteen was his lucky number so he installed thirteen stools at the counter. His specialties were fried chicken, chili, and the pies he learned to make from his mother and perfected while in the service.

During World War II, Wood raised chickens behind the cafe to ensure a regular source of meat and eggs. He bought beef halves and cut the steaks

himself. Many of his customers ate at the Rainbow every day, bringing their families on weekends. When they cashed their paychecks with Wood, he deducted the weekly bill and returned the balance. The Rainbow was open twenty-four hours a day, seven days a week, closing only at Christmas.

RAINBOW CAFE OSGOOD PIE

1 CUP RAISINS
⅓ CUP SUGAR
1 TABLESPOON FLOUR
½ TEASPOON NUTMEG
1 TEASPOON CINNAMON
¼ TEASPOON SALT
1⅓ CUPS SOUR CREAM
½ CUP CHOPPED PECANS
3 EGG YOLKS, BEATEN
1 TABLESPOON MELTED MARGARINE
1 TEASPOON VANILLA
1 9-INCH PIE SHELL, BAKED
3 EGG WHITES
⅓ CUP SUGAR

POUR BOILING WATER OVER RAISINS; let stand 10 minutes and drain. Combine raisins, sugar, flour, cinnamon, nutmeg and salt in saucepan until thoroughly mixed. Add sour cream, pecans, egg yolks and margarine.

Cook over medium heat until thick, stirring frequently. Remove from heat and allow to cool slightly. Add vanilla. Pour mixture into baked pie shell. Make meringue by beating egg whites to soft peak stage. Add sugar and continue beating until stiff peaks form. Spread on top of pie and brown in preheated 350° oven for 10 to 12 minutes. *6 to 8 servings.*

Two exceptional entrepreneurs established another Amarillo first on Route 66. In 1930, O.R. Tingley and John Dinsmore capitalized on the sandwich craze that had begun to sweep the country. They developed and marketed pig hip sandwiches made with "tender blue ribbon pig hips." They opened two locations in Amarillo, one at 5th and Pierce and another in the heart of San Jacinto.

Using the slogan, "They made their way by the way they're made," the men "borrowed" a recipe developed by Dinsmore's brother in Pittsfield, Illinois. Ernie Edwards, of Broadwell, Illinois, who takes credit for originating the pig hip sandwich, calls these Amarillo entrepreneurs "about three branches off the family tree."

The secret sauce took two people to prepare. One cook beat the egg mixture while the other slowly added oil. If not done correctly, the whole mixture would curdle. It was unthinkable in post-depression days that a whole recipe of the precious sauce might be wasted.

The pig hip sandwich consisted of thin, succulent slices of pork on a toasted bun and was topped with the secret sauce, lettuce, and tomato slices.

Ansley's Musical Pig Shop, the last of the original pig hip shops, was one of the most popular drive-ins in Amarillo. At Ansley's, carhops yelled orders to the cook in their own "lingo," never wrote down an order, and always provided fast, accurate service. Local teenagers made it a favorite stop.

Several Amarillo cafes have adapted their own versions of the popular pig hip sandwich. The Blue Front Cafe offers what is considered the best by many long-time enthusiasts. Their gastronomic resurrection is the Porker Delight, complete with a

secret sauce. The sandwich is accompanied by crisp, Curly Q Tators, another nice piggy touch. It still takes two people to prepare the sauce — one to stir and one to pour oil.

A great breakfast selection draws local businessmen, who regularly return for coffee breaks by mid-morning at the Blue Front. A Route 66 eating place for forty years, the cafe was originally across the street from its present 801 West 6th Street address. The bright blue door and window facings remain and Curt Johnston, the current owner, sees no reason to change his two best hallmarks. The legendary Porker Delight, complete with the slogan, "The Secret's in the Sauce," will be around and doing well for a long time to come.

BLUE FRONT CAFE CHEESE AND BACON SOUP

1 PACKAGE (24 OUNCES) CREAM SOUP BASE*
1 GALLON WATER
1½ POUNDS GRATED CHEDDAR CHEESE
3 CUPS COOKED DICED POTATOES
1½ POUNDS BACON, FRIED AND CRUMBLED
⅓ CUP BACON DRIPPINGS
1 TEASPOON SALT
1 TEASPOON WHITE PEPPER
2 TEASPOONS MINCED ONION
MILK TO DESIRED CONSISTENCY

FOLLOW PACKAGE DIRECTIONS TO PREPARE SOUP BASE. It should be thick. Add grated cheese and stir over low heat until cheese is melted and smooth. Stir in bacon drippings and blend well. Add remaining ingredients, stirring with wire whisk. Thin to desired consistency with milk. Remove from heat and serve.

*Cream soup base is available at selected groceries. Several brands are available including Tone's and Today's. This recipe can be cut in size easily and freezes well. *1½gallons.*

Sixth Street in Amarillo is a microcosm of the history of Route 66. Many of the buildings are shells of businesses which once supported the traveling community. A Main Street revitalization program and enthusiastic merchants have revived this west Amarillo business strip. It is now a valued center for antiques, collectibles, and distinctive eating places. Merchants are capitalizing on the colorful history of the area. They enjoy telling stories like the one from the 1930s about Cecil Bradford who sometimes stood on the roof of his grocery store and threw live chickens into the crowd while announcing his store specials.

The Nat, a San Jacinto cornerstone at 6th and Georgia, was another Panhandle phenomenon. Built in the 1920s, the front resembled a Moorish-Camelot castle and the sides and rear imitated a steamship with porthole windows. The Nat was first a natatoriam offering indoor swimming, but when that didn't pay, the pool was covered and it became a ballroom. Top bands from the 30s and 40s performed at the Nat. Benny Goodman, Harry James, Louis Armstrong, Count Basie, and Paul Whiteman all took their turns. A supper club on the second floor served adults on weekends and local teenagers who danced there during the week.

Age and disrepair have claimed the singular structure. It has been condemned as dangerous and faces a questionable future today.

Next door, the Alamo Bar has survived since the 1930s. It is the oldest surviving bar in Amarillo and

is undoubtedly housed in one of the most unusually designed buildings.

In the heart of the revitalized section of 6th Street, the Golden Light Cafe is an old-fashioned "greasy spoon" believed to be the oldest restaurant in Amarillo continuously operating in the same location. The modest, unadorned cafe was established in 1946 by Chester "Pop" Ray and his wife, Louise. Actually, Pop was sick when the big day finally came, so his son, Charles, opened the doors for the first time. With some hamburger meat and buns, Charles grossed $10.48 that first day. The cafe has had several owners since Pop retired in 1957 but Marc Reed, who owns the cafe today, continues to serve the great hamburgers that Pop was famous for. The chili recipe has changed with the owners but continues to be the best kept secret around the place.

Marc says hungry tourists won't go wrong on any of his specials: Flagstaff Pie, Chicago Beans, Route 66 Chili, and Half Way to Albuquerque Burritos. Better take a nap before you head out!

The decor at the Golden Light is plain, the cooking good and there is an eclectic crowd: businessmen in suits and ties, joggers cooling off with big glasses of tea, and cowboys in well worn boots and jeans. All come back; homely places sometimes offer the best kept secrets.

GOLDEN LIGHT SIXTH STREET SPECIAL

1 QUARTER-POUND HAMBURGER PATTY
1 LARGE SLICE SWISS CHEESE
½ CHOPPED TOMATO
¼ CUP SOUR CREAM
DASH HOT SAUCE
1 LARGE FLOUR TORTILLA

COOK AND SEASON A LONG, NARROW HAMBURGER PATTY on grill. Top meat with cheese during last minute of cooking. Place meat, cheese, chopped tomato, sour cream and hot sauce on large flour tortilla that has been heated. Wrap and serve while hot.

Down the street is the Neon Grill and Fountain. Eating at the Neon is almost as good as a View Master trip back in time. All the fixtures are authentic. The soda fountain came from an early drugstore, complete with a marble top counter. Original Hamilton Beach malt mixers are used. Cokes are mixed with syrup before the carbonation is added. Dishes and glassware are copies of originals that stand behind the bar. A Wurlitzer Jukebox plays tunes from the 1940s.

Chocolate malts at the Neon are better than memory, and Cokes are the real thing. The wall decor features antique soft drink advertisements and the tables and chairs are ice cream parlor design. Jim Elder, the owner, patterned his eatery after a 1940s picture of the old Neon Cafe, once located on the same site. It's a place to stop and stay awhile.

Although gone today, the Mason Cafe once stood across the street from the Neon. The Mason hosted one of the National Route 66 Association meetings and many old road enthusiasts remember

that some of the best chicken-fried steak ever served on Highway 66 was dished up there.

If you're looking for proof that the real west is still alive, stop at the Big Texan Restaurant on I-40. The Big Texan offers the ultimate Texas challenge — consume a 72-ounce steak dinner in accordance with the house rules, and the meal is free! Motivation to succeed is the $43.25 price tag for failure. Since owner Bob Lee initiated the offer, over 5,000 have accomplished the feat. In addition to the steak, a shrimp cocktail, baked potato, salad, and roll must be consumed in one hour. Cincinnati Red pitcher, Frank Pastore, did it in 11 minutes. In 1983, a 110-pound woman writer from the Wall Street Journal did the job and later wrote a story about her experience. The youngest to succeed so far is an eleven-year old, 135-pound boy. The oldest is a sixty-three-year-old grandmother. About one customer a year chooses to eat the 4½-pound steak raw.

For real cowpokes and those who yearn for the old days, the Big Texan hosts a Cowboy Poet's Breakfast every Saturday morning. A Texas size buffet is spread for the crowd and everyone, from the well-known to the unknown, is welcome to perform.

The main dining room at the Big Texan is decorated in early miscellaneous memorabilia. Take a tour after you have eaten. Everything from the elaborate collection of mounted heads to beautifully framed turn-of-the-century ladies' wear is authentic. A really big Texan occasionally ambles through the dining rooms on his stilts and strolling Western musicians offer Texas harmony. For those lucky enough to be there on the right night, a melodrama takes place in the big back dining room in conjunction with Amarillo Little Theater, complete with plenty of popcorn to throw at the bad guys.

Bob Lee, the Big Texan's founder, was an entrepreneur in the true Texas spirit. He moved to Amarillo in 1959 and opened his first Big Texan Steak House on the Amarillo Boulevard section of Route 66 because he recognized that travelers from other parts of the world expect to find big cowboys and big steaks in Texas.

When I-40 construction began, Lee knew he would have to follow the traffic. So he borrowed money, bought several old buildings at Pantex Village where government employees had lived during World War II, and with a handful of carpenters, his eight children and his wife, built the new Big Texan. The restaurant opened in March of 1971 to instant success.

A disastrous fire resulted in the Big Texan complex being rebuilt bigger and better than ever. Today, Lee's wife and children operate the amazing business and have Texas-sized plans for the future. The Big Texan is an experience that shouldn't be missed.

Before every meal, guests chow down on big plates of "Texas Caviar" complete with jalapeño peppers and Texas flags. Here's how it's made. To prepare your own caviar, try the scaled down recipe for a smaller crowd:

72OZSTEAK1HR.
The Big Texan

THE BIG TEXAN "TEXAS CAVIAR"

1 GALLON BLACK-EYED PEAS, DRAINED
5 MEDIUM JALAPEÑOS, MINCED
1 SMALL WHITE ONION, CHOPPED
2 CUPS ITALIAN DRESSING
2 GREEN BELL PEPPERS, CHOPPED
¼ CUP SEASONED SALT
½ CUP CHILI POWDER
½ CUP GROUND CUMIN
1 TEASPOON GROUND RED PEPPER

ROUTE 66 BIG TEXAN "TEXAS CAVIAR"

2 CANS (16 OUNCES EACH) BLACK-EYED PEAS, DRAINED
1 MEDIUM JALAPEÑO, MINCED
¼ SMALL WHITE ONION, CHOPPED
⅓ CUP ITALIAN DRESSING
½ GREEN BELL PEPPER, CHOPPED
1 TABLESPOON SEASONED SALT
2 TABLESPOONS CHILI POWDER
2 TABLESPOONS GROUND CUMIN
¼ TEASPOON GROUND RED PEPPER

COMBINE BLACK-EYED PEAS WITH REMAINING INGREDIENTS. Serve chilled with corn chips. *Texas-sized recipe makes 5 quarts. Smaller recipe makes 5 cups.*

Less than half an hour south of Amarillo is another unique Texas experience. Palo Duro Canyon offers a huge dose of history, spectacular scenery and an outdoor production of Paul Green's musical drama, *Texas*. The extravaganza begins with a horseman racing along the edge of the 600-foot canyon wall behind the outdoor stage. Throughout the evening, dramatic lighting and sound blend with nature's elements. A Texas-style barbecue dinner is served before the show. To get to Palo Duro, turn south off I-40 to I-27, then take SR 217 into the park.

Route 66 west of Amarillo is the north access road of I-40, except for a short distance where it disappears near the famous Cadillac Ranch.

Near the Cadillac Ranch, where an RV Park is located today, the Tip Top Cafe served knowledgeable roadies for 28 years. Mae and Lance Pollard built the little cafe at the end of World War II and the Tip Top soon became known as one of the best pie stops along Route 66.

Truckers came in from across the country to eat Mae's coconut cream and chocolate pies. Delbert Trew, Texas Route 66 Association President from McLean, remembers stopping at the Tip Top with his dad to buy whole pies. "We would split it and eat the whole thing while driving old 66," he said.

The Pollards are retired now and live nearby. "I can't make pies like those anymore," Mae said. "My success was due to fresh whole milk and eggs. We had two Jersey cows and our own chickens out back. I used to put five egg whites into the topping for each one of those pies and I made all my crusts from lard."

The Pollards say another secret of their success was a limited menu. Lance built a barbecue pit out back and bought only the best quality meat from Pinkney Packing Company for his T-bone steak plate. Sunday was turkey and dressing day and there was always a hot chicken sandwich plate.

When I-40 came through, the highway department bought their cafe and moved it away to make room for progress. The Pollards retired to Colorado but soon returned to their Texas home near Route 66.

Jesse's Cafe has been another good place to eat in the Western Panhandle since Jesse Fincher and his partner opened their first cafe in Adrian soon after Jesse was discharged from service in World War II. Jesse's years as an army cook paid off. He quickly became known for his pies, succulent plate lunches, and perfect hot rolls. Banquets and service club meetings became a specialty. Jesse added a second cafe in Wildorado in the late 1960s. Jim Helmes owns the popular stop today. It's a favorite with truckers as well as area farmers and ranchers. Stella Horton cooked for Jesse in Adrian and shares his recipe for beet pickles.

JESSE'S CAFE BEET PICKLES

I GALLON CANNED BEETS, UNDRAINED
I CUP VINEGAR
¼ CUP PICKLING SPICES TIED IN CHEESECLOTH
I CUP SUGAR

COMBINE ALL INGREDIENTS AND BRING TO SLOW BOIL. Simmer 10 minutes, then let cool with the pickling spice remaining in the liquid. When cool, remove spices and store beets in refrigerator until ready to serve.

When Lena Gray worked for Jesse, apple pie à la mode was one of the best sellers. Her apple pies began with canned apples. Lena always added a cup of sugar, a teaspoon of cinnamon and about three pats of margarine. A little cornstarch dissolved in apple juice thickened the liquid.

Lena made pie crusts at Jesse's, 30 to 40 at a time. She always began with six pounds of margarine and worked in enough flour to make a pebbly consistency. A touch of salt, a little sugar, and barely enough water to dampen the ingredients completed the process. Lena says almost any pie is good if the crust is made right.

A big sign out front at both Jesse's Cafe locations always said, "Ho' Made Pie." The same sign is still out front in Wildorado today.

For over a third of a century, Route 66 travelers stopped at Krahn's Cafe and Truck Stop in Vega.

Built in the 1930s, the location was originally Jerry's Cafe. When Don and Ann Krahn bought the cafe in 1950, Route 66 business was booming so they added the truck stop and stayed open 24 hours a day, seven days a week. The comfortable cafe was the place area ranchers completed cattle deals and local high school students met friends. The Krahns were second parents to many of the students.

"We had all kinds of highway customers, too," Don remembers. "When they would come in and forget their kids, we'd get in the car and run them down. We sent one lady off to have a baby once and had to keep her boy for a while. We took him home and Ann washed his clothes and fed him good before his dad finally came back to pick him up."

Ann says she had customers who drove all the way from Albuquerque to eat her pies. She also remembers the days she got up at 3 a.m. to start cooking. She served a specialty each day and says her Thursday enchilada dinners were about the most popular.

KRAHN'S CAFE ENCHILADA CASSEROLE

1½ POUNDS LEAN GROUND BEEF
SALT AND PEPPER TO TASTE
1 MEDIUM ONION, CHOPPED
3 CUPS GRATED CHEESE
2 CANS (10 OUNCES) ENCHILADA SAUCE
1 CAN (2¼ OUNCES) CHOPPED GREEN CHILIES
12 CORN TORTILLAS

BROWN GROUND BEEF IN SMALL AMOUNT OF SHORTENING. Drain fat and season meat with salt and pepper to taste. Meanwhile chop onion and grate cheese. Heat enchilada sauce; stir chilies into ground beef. Heat small amount of oil in skillet. Using kitchen tongs, dip each tortilla in hot oil until softened, about 15 seconds. Drain on paper towel. (Tortillas can also be heated in microwave for 4 minutes on medium). Using tongs, dip tortillas into warm enchilada sauce, place in greased 8½ x 13 casserole and spoon about ¼ cup of meat and ¼ cup cheese onto each tortilla. Roll tortillas around mixture; continue until all tortillas are filled. Sprinkle onion over enchiladas; cover with any remaining cheese and enchilada sauce. Bake for 15 to 20 minutes in preheated 350° oven. Serve hot with beans or rice and a green salad.
6 to 8 servings.

Paving of Highway 66 began in the western part of the Texas Panhandle in 1936. The next year the Cozy Cafe opened in Adrian, but the cafe met its end in ashes several years later. When the owners rebuilt, they named their new eatery the Old Route 66 Cafe. But most folks called the new cafe the Bent Door, and the name stuck.

The name *The Bent Door* was perfect. When Amarillo Air Force Base was dismantled, one of the buildings to be carted away was the airfield control tower. The inexpensive shell came to rest where the old Cozy Cafe had stood. Windows sloped inward toward the bottom in the control tower, so the door had to match. The unusual configuration made the handle a little awkward, but folks didn't seem to mind. "The Bent Door stayed open twenty-four hours a day then," says Stella Horton, who worked at Jesse's and the Bent Door for years. "There wasn't even a key to the cafe. When we closed in respect for local funerals, we just stuck a kitchen knife in the door beside a note that said we'd be back

Stella remembers a load of high school seniors from the east coast who stopped at the cafe one day. A local cowboy was sitting at the counter in his regular outfit including chaps, boots, and hat. The group got very excited that they had finally found a real Texas cowboy and they all had their pictures made with him. She thinks he even took them out to his ranch to ride horses for a while.

The Bent Door served good food to weary travelers and local farmers until the interstate bypassed Adrian. The local domino crowd, who kept a table busy in the back room, could no longer support the business. Even the pool room in the basement where Percy Gruhlkey sometimes played fiddle, couldn't attract enough folks to keep the little cafe open.

Today, what's left of the Bent Door stands hidden behind shoulder high weeds and assorted junk, a sad tribute to glory days on the old highway.

Stella Horton has retired but will always remember the hundreds of Lemon Meringue Pies she made at Jesse's and the Bent Door.

BENT DOOR LEMON MERINGUE PIE

1½ CUPS SUGAR
6 TABLESPOONS CORNSTARCH
1½ CUPS BOILING WATER
3 EGG YOLKS
3 TABLESPOONS BUTTER OR OLEO
4 TABLESPOONS LEMON JUICE
1½ TEASPOONS GRATED LEMON PEEL
1 NINE-INCH BAKED PIE SHELL

MERINGUE
3 EGG WHITES
¼ TEASPOON CREAM OF TARTAR
6 TABLESPOONS SUGAR

MIX SUGAR AND CORNSTARCH. Stir in boiling water and cook over direct heat, stirring constantly, until mixture thickens and boils. Set over boiling water for 10 minutes longer. Beat egg yolks until frothy and slowly stir in a little of the hot mixture. Blend the eggs with the sugar and cornstarch mixture and continue cooking over boiling water for another 5 minutes. Stir in butter or oleo, lemon juice and grated peel. Pour into baked pie shell and cover with meringue. Bake in preheated 425° oven for 5 minutes or until delicately browned.

Beat egg whites until frothy. Add cream of tartar and continue beating until mixture is stiff. Add sugar one tablespoon at a time until meringue holds a peak. *6 to 8 servings.*

Much of the western half of the Texas Panhandle was once part of the XIT Ranch that comprised three million acres and extended 200 miles north and south along the Texas, New Mexico border. In some places along here, barbed wire stretched 150 miles without a break. The XIT came into existence as payment for granite to build the Texas State Capitol Building.

This is Llano Estacado country, the land of the staked plains — land as flat as it comes. It is also land of the tumbleweed, cocklebur, and devil's claw. The sky here offers an ever-changing panorama of beauty. Area residents declare the sunrises and sunsets are the most spectacular in the world.

Just past Adrian, the tableland gives way to a

dramatic drop over the caprock and a breathtaking panorama of space. Astride the Texas and New Mexico border and barely a part of Deaf Smith County, Texas, is Glenrio, "so far in the northwest part of Deaf Smith County that most people don't even know it's there," said Homer Ehresman, a longtime Glenrio resident.

Today, the Ehresman family lives in a comfortable farm home amidst the memories of the three eating places, motel, and bar that provided their Route 66 income for over forty years.

Route 66 was still a dirt road all the way to Amarillo when the Ehresman's opened their first cafe on the New Mexico side of the line in 1934. When the highway was paved in 1937, they fed the road crew three meals a day, all they could eat, for a dollar a day.

The Ehresman's sold their New Mexico business and moved away when they heard the first threats of an interstate, but when nothing happened for a few years, they built the Texas Longhorn Cafe and a

motel on the Texas side of the line. By the time I-40 left Glenrio to weeds in 1973, the Ehresman's son Allen and his wife had built another motel and cafe at New Endee, a few miles west. That, too, stands empty today.

As travelers cross over the Texas border, an old 66 signpost of plain white wood marks the division between Deaf Smith County, Texas, and Quay County, New Mexico. Across the street are the shells of a bank, train depot, hotel, filling stations, cafes, and a gift shop that flourished and died. The tall sign that used to boast of the Last Motel in Texas and First Motel in Texas is falling apart.

NEW MEXICO

NEW MEXICO. The mystique of New Mexico begins at the state line. This is a land where nature's artistry comes in giant doses. It's the state of the Camino Real, the Santa Fe and Ozark Trails, and Historic Route 66. In New Mexico, the chili pepper and the pinto bean reign supreme.

Begin the trek into New Mexico on an authentic strip of original Route 66 by taking the once-paved road from Glenrio through Old Endee to San Jon.

San Jon's mayor, Fern White, remembers the time when her tiny community had two hotels and several cafes. At the two story Ozark Hotel, family-style meals were served in the dining room, complete with starched white tablecloths and napkins.

The White Cafe, run by the mayor's mother-in-law, opened in San Jon in the early 1920s. The Mint and California Cafes were in operation while Route 66 was being paved in the 1930s. Later, the Circle M opened for a short time and the Silver Grill did a thriving business on the highway.

Fern worked as a waitress for her aunt at the California Cafe in the mid-1930s. She remembers her aunt baking lemon, chocolate, and coconut pies that all looked alike after they were crowned with thick meringue topping. To identify the contents, she sprinkled coconut on one, swirled high peaks on the chocolate pie, and marked slices through the lemon meringue.

Today, local farmers and ranchers sip coffee and exchange news at the Rustler.

WHITE CAFE LEMON MERINGUE PIE

1½ CUPS SUGAR
5½ TABLESPOONS CORNSTARCH
1½ CUPS HOT WATER
3 EGG YOLKS, SLIGHTLY BEATEN
3 TABLESPOONS BUTTER
4 TABLESPOONS LEMON JUICE
1 BAKED 9-INCH SHALLOW PIE SHELL

MERINGUE

3 EGG WHITES
¼ TEASPOON CREAM OF TARTER
6 TABLESPOONS POWDERED SUGAR

MIX SUGAR WITH CORNSTARCH IN SAUCEPAN. Gradually stir in hot water, making sure mixture is smooth. Cook over moderate heat stirring constantly until mixture thickens and boils. Boil for 1 minute. Remove from heat and beat ½ cup hot mixture into bowl of slightly beaten egg yolks. Then add slowly to remaining hot mixture in saucepan, beating constantly. Cook 1 minute while continuing to stir. Blend in butter and lemon juice and pour into pie shell.

To make meringue, beat egg whites until frothy. Add cream of tarter, then gradually add sugar. Continue beating until mixture is stiff and glossy. Bake 5-8 minutes at 475°.

SILVER GRILL BARBECUE SAUCE

¼ POUND BUTTER OR OLEO
3 TABLESPOONS VINEGAR OR LEMON JUICE
1 TABLESPOON WORCESTERSHIRE SAUCE
½ CUP CATSUP
½ CUP WATER

MELT BUTTER OR OLEO and mix with other ingredients. Use on chopped roast for sandwiches or for barbecuing chicken or other meats. *1½ cups.*

Ten miles south of San Jon, the Caprock Amphitheater is open summer weekends to tell the story of Billie the Kid. A catered barbecue is served before each starlight production.

Tucumcari is twenty-five miles to the west. Signs along the interstate still proclaim, "Tucumcari Tonight, 2000 Rooms!" More than fifty motels once lined the Tucumcari city route. Today, Tucumcari boasts twenty-six motels and seventeen restaurants.

At the Blue Swallow Motel, Lillian Redman presides over the front desk as she has since 1958 when her husband bought the time-honored motor court as a wedding present. She remembers the days when Route 66 traffic traveled bumper to bumper along Tucumcari Boulevard in front of her motel.

"Route 66 is a long ribbon of friends for me," she recalls. "This old highway still ties the country together." Lillian also remembers her eight years as a Fred Harvey waitress on Route 66. "I applied to become a Harvey Girl right here at the Harvey House in Tucumcari," she said. "They sent me to Kansas City for three months of training before I could go to work."

Her generation of applicants had to meet rigid standards to be accepted for training. Girls had to be single, meet strict height and weight requirements, be willing to travel and move frequently, and at first, they could be no more than thirty years old. The classes Lillian took lasted eight hours a day for three months and she had to pass an examination to graduate. Emphasis was placed on table service and food etiquette. The girls also studied self improvement, manners, hair and nail care, makeup, proper dress, and ways of walking gracefully.

Harvey Girls began work in coffee shops. After gaining experience in basic service, they were promoted to the dining rooms. Lillian recalls it was much like graduation from junior high to high school when she was first allowed to serve in a dining room.

"At every Harvey House, there was always a dormitory next to the restaurant," she said. "Times were different then; we appreciated having a housemother. We even had a wardrobe mistress who inspected our appearance before we went on the floor each day."

The most experienced and capable waitresses were moved to resort hotels and Lillian soon graduated to El Tovar near Grand Canyon. She was even selected to serve one summer on a Harvey cruise ship that took passengers from Florida to Cuba.

Lillian remembers the special Harvey House silver that was moved from place to place for very special occasions. "There was enough for eight to ten pieces at each place setting," she recalled. "We had to know how to set up quickly for elegant parties, then pack that silver away so that it could be used again somewhere else."

When she married a Fred Harvey cook at El Tovar, she was no longer allowed to work. Besides, she had almost reached the mandatory retirement age of thirty-five. Lillian returned to her home in Tucumcari where she kept books and worked in other restaurants before taking the reins at the Blue Swallow. But those Arizona days with Fred Harvey Houses in Ash Fork, Winslow, and at Grand Canyon continue to hold special memories for Lillian Redman.

LILLIAN REDMAN'S NEW MEXICO BREAD PUDDING (CAPIROTADA)

1½ CUPS BROWN SUGAR
1½ CUPS WATER
1 STICK CINNAMON
1 WHOLE CLOVE
2 TABLESPOONS BUTTER OR MARGARINE
3 CUPS BREAD CUBES (OR LEFTOVER CAKE ROLLS OR DOUGHNUTS)
½ POUND LONGHORN CHEESE, GRATED
1 CUP RAISINS
½ CUP NUTS (PECANS, PINONS, OR PEANUTS)
⅓ CUP BRANDY OR ORANGE JUICE

BOIL BROWN SUGAR, WATER, CINNAMON, AND CLOVE gently for about 15 minutes. Add butter or margarine. Meanwhile, lightly toast bread and cut into cubes. Remove cinnamon and clove from syrup. Butter an 8 x 8 baking dish and fill with bread, cheese, raisins, and nuts.

Leave in layers or toss lightly together. Pour the brandy or orange juice into syrup then dribble evenly over the bread mixture. Bake uncovered in a preheated 350° oven for about 30 minutes. Pudding should be softly set but not dried out. *8 servings.*

Down the street from the Blue Swallow Motel, another Route 66 classic sits comfortably under a giant sombrero on the corner of Tucumcari Boulevard and 1st Street. La Cita was originally on the north side of the highway but an early owner decided a towering, brightly painted sombrero would attract more customers, so the move was made. La Cita is a Route 66 prototype that has survived despite several owners and a history as varied as the highway out front. Letica Montoya manages the cafe today and his wife does most of the cooking.

Inside, the two dining rooms are decorated with an ever changing rainbow of bright paintings, Mexican memorabilia, and lush greenery. Authentic New Mexican fare includes Mrs. Montoya's open faced enchiladas and her piping hot chili.

Del's Restaurant is another Tucumcari classic that has been a part of Route 66 history since the 1940s when Del and his wife, Wilma, bought their first Route 66 eating place. Originally located further down Tucumcari Boulevard, Del moved to the far westside location to expand and entice the increasing Route 66 traffic. Del's has changed hands and been remodeled many times during its fifty-plus years, but succeeding owners have kept the original name. Fred and Zula Barnett own the popular cafe that is capably managed by Lavone Bond. Bond says this good chili con queso has been served for years at the restaurant.

DEL'S CHILI CON QUESO

¼ CUP CHOPPED ONION
2 TEASPOONS VEGETABLE OIL
1 CAN (16 OUNCES) STEWED TOMATOES
1 CUP CANNED GREEN CHILIES
1½ TEASPOON GARLIC POWDER
1½ TEASPOONS OREGANO
1 POUND VELVEETA CHEESE, CUBED
MILK TO MAKE DESIRED CONSISTENCY

SAUTÉ ONIONS IN OIL UNTIL THEY ARE TRANSLUCENT. Strain off fat and add tomatoes, chilies, and seasonings. Simmer mixture 20 to 30 minutes. Add cheese a little at a time, stirring constantly to blend. Thin with milk to desired consistency. *4¼ cups.*

Del also owned the Tower Restaurant, a favorite tourist stop that is gone today. The three-storied affair had a deck on the second level and a private dining room above that. Food was carried from one floor to the next by elevator and guests could sit outside and enjoy the view of Tucumcari Mountain in fine weather.

One unusual Tucumcari cafe owner inspired a 1940s hit song that was recorded by pop singer Dorothy Shay. "Two Gun Harry from Tucumcari" climbed to the top of the charts for a short time after it was distributed by Columbia Records.

Harry Garrison owned Harry's Lunch, a post-World War II version of a fast food outlet. Flamboyant, colorful, and never at a loss for words, Harry was Tucumcari's self-appointed ambassador to the world. His cafe was across from the railroad station where Harry met arriving passengers in Western garb, complete with his twin pearl-handled six-guns. When Dorothy Shay stopped in Tucumcari for lunch one day, Garrison escorted her to his cafe. She later wrote the song about falling in love with a cowboy from Tucumcari.

The payoff for Harry's burger and fry shop resulted in many travelers pulling off Route 66 with a feeling they already knew something about the town. They had just traveled cross-country listening to music describing a bowlegged, gun-totin' cowboy and his lovesick girlfriend.

Dean's Cafe can still be found on old Route 66 on the west edge of town, but Blake's, Ayer's and the Pow Pow Restaurant only conjure up memories for travelers. Tucumcari's Randle Hotel Coffee Shop was also considered an excellent place to stop during the 1930s and early 1940s. The coffee shop wasn't large, but it offered air conditioning, a prime drawing card for weary travelers.

" The Waffle House, Tucumcari. AAA headquarters, a good place to eat, home cooking, regular meals, shortorders, always open."

(Old Arizona, N.M. guide)

Heading west from Tucumcari, travelers leave the Staked Plain for Pecos River Country. Grassland and mesas give way to boulders and steep bluffs. It is easiest to take the interstate along here.

Montoya, Newkirk, and Cuervo remain as minuscule roadside settlements just west of Tucumcari. Richardson's Store has been the center of community life in Montoya for years, but all that remains of Cuervo is a few abandoned buildings and a lonely cemetery.

The Club Cafe, a Santa Rosa Route 66 landmark since 1935, closed its doors for a final time in August of 1992. This internationally acclaimed slice of Americana was born during the Dust Bowl and Great Depression and grew to prosper during the heady days when America's love affair with cross-country travel reached a peak along Route 66.

Ron Chavez has been the driving force behind the cafe for the last eighteen years. In fact, he got his first job shining shoes and peddling papers in front of the cafe soon after World War II.

Like many food businesses along Route 66, the Club Cafe finally had to bow to changes in American travel habits. The interstate highway bypassed downtown Santa Rosa, fast food chains appeared at the off-ramps, and the general economy slowed.

As a result, one of Route 66's most enthusiastic entrepreneurs has tightened his belt and set his sights in a new direction. Chavez will concentrate on his fledgling business featuring mail order Old Santa Fe salsa roja,

enchilada sauce, tortilla mix and several other New Mexico items. Already, his loyal customers have begun to order, then re-order, direct from the "Chili People of New Mexico." Now, people across the country have a source for Ron Chavez authentic, time-tested, traditional recipes that can be prepared under his guidance. "They'll get the real thing, New Mexico red chili — the pod, not the soup.

They'll get chili with flavor, not just heat," he beams.

Needless to say, Chavez is an authority on the New Mexico red chili. His ideas and plans for the future flow as smoothly as his conversation. "The first thing people who don't understand chili want to do is have it fiery," Chavez says. "In our New Mexico tradition, yes, it has to have a kick, but the flavor must be there to enjoy. To truly savor chili, you must experience the aroma, the bouquet, the toasty flavor. It's like a fine wine, a wonderful experience for people who have never really tasted it before."

Chavez learned the restaurant business from the ground up, working as a dishwasher and busboy at the Club Cafe before he learned how to cook. "Phil Craig and Floyd Shaw owned the place back then," he said. "Phil took me aside and showed me how to bake sour dough biscuits and cinnamon rolls."

Chavez and his staff prepared all kinds of food at the Club Cafe. "Every morning in our kitchens everthing was cooked fresh. The biscuits and cinnamon rolls, the spareribs, and the carne adovada. What a great aroma!"

Chavez' eyes sparkled when he talked about the Club Cafe sourdough biscuits. "Our starter has been sitting there for over thirty years. It just keeps working and working, and we keep adding, and it keeps working. It's one of my prize possessions. You can't find better biscuits anywhere."

Perhaps sales of Old Santa Fe products will generate enough business so that someday the Club Cafe can reopen and travelers can once again savor the sourdough biscuits and other good food that made the Club Cafe a Route 66 classic.

CLUB CAFE SALSA

6 WHOLE CHILI PEQUIN
1 CAN (8 OUNCES) TOMATO SAUCE
5 JALAPEÑOS, SEEDED AND DEVEINED
PINCH OF OREGANO
¼ TEASPOON GARLIC POWDER OR 1 SMALL CLOVE GARLIC
1 TEASPOON SALT
½ TEASPOON BLACK PEPPER
1 CAN (28 OUNCES) OF WHOLE TOMATOES
1 MEDIUM ONION, CUT INTO LARGE PIECES

PLACE CHILI PEQUIN, tomato sauce, jalapeños, oregano, garlic, salt and pepper in blender or food processor. Pulse 10-15 seconds to blend. Add tomatoes and onion. Blend to a coarse texture. Let salsa stand in the refrigerator for at least an hour, but preferably longer. Serve with chips or use to enhance your other favorite dishes! *2 cups fresh salsa.*

CLUB CAFE TACO FILLING

1 GRATED POTATO, FRIED
1 POUND MEDIUM-FINE LEAN GROUND BEEF
¼ TEASPOON GARLIC POWDER
1 TEASPOON BLACK PEPPER
PINCH OF OREGANO
1 TEASPOON GROUND RED CHILI
½ CUP GRATED LONGHORN CHEESE
CHOPPED TOMATOES
SHREDDED LETTUCE
6 TO 8 TACO SHELLS

FRY THE POTATO. BROWN AND DRAIN MEAT. Add garlic powder, pepper, oregano, chili, and potato. Stir to blend. (The potato holds the meat mixture together.)

Place a spoonful or two in each taco shell and sprinkle with cheese. If desired, place in oven or microwave to melt cheese. Top with tomatoes and lettuce. *6 to 8 large tacos.*

Ron offers this traditional guide for making a perfect enchilada:

1. Fry two corn tortillas in moderately hot vegetable oil, softly! Drain the tortillas between two paper towels. Set aside.

2. Lay one tortilla on a plate. Sprinkle it with a thick bed of grated cheese (Longhorn or any Cheddar) and chopped onions (optional), and lay the second tortilla on top. Now add a small amount of water to chili sauce, stir to blend, and heat the sauce in a microwave or on stove top until warm (not hot), and stir well until creamy and smooth. Pour the chili sauce over the stacked, filled tortillas until chili sauce covers tortillas completely. Sprinkle more grated cheese atop chili, heat (1½ minutes in microwave oven) and serve with lettuce and diced tomatoes on the side.

OPTIONAL

3. Enhance a can of refried beans by adding five teaspoons Chavez red chili sauce and grated cheese. Heat the mixture in a microwave oven and serve with enchilada.

4. Top enchilada with sour cream to taste, or an egg if desired, after it comes out of the oven.

5. Add finely shredded roast beef, chicken, or turkey to cheese filling to enhance the enchilada "eating celebration."

6. Serve original New Mexican Salsa Roja with corn chips as an excellent appetizer while enchilada is being prepared. The salsa smooths the palate much like a glass of wine.

el farol

Travelers have a choice soon after leaving Santa Rosa. The original 1926 route heads northwest through Dilia, Romero (later Romeroville), Bernal, Rowe, Pecos, and Glorieta. The spectacular drive is a memorable experience.

In 1937, the jog to Santa Fe was eliminated. Instead, the highway continued west through Buford, (now Moriarty) toward Albuquerque. Route 66 became a shorter and easier drive.

The 1926 version of Route 66 wound into Santa Fe on College Street, now called Old Santa Fe Trail. Santa Fe, established in 1610, is the oldest European settled community west of the Mississippi and a capital for more than three hundred years. The city formed the end of the famed Camino Real linking Santa Fe and Mexico City. Years later, it became the terminus of the famed Santa Fe Trail.

Santa Fe is a city that caters to its citizens and visitors with an unbelievable number of outstanding restaurants. There is unique history along with delicious food at almost every stop. As you enter Santa Fe, turn right on Canyon Road to El Farol, a

Spanish restaurant for over twenty years. The building is estimated to be 250 years old and within recent memory has been a private residence, a barbershop, an eating place, and a neighborhood bar.

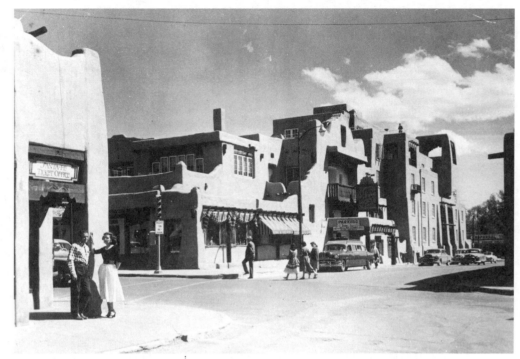

Manager Ned Laventall says repair and minor remodeling has been attempted, but the two-foot-thick adobe walls move and breathe and defy maintenance. Several years ago, a trap door basement was discovered and a number of artifacts found there were moved to the state museum. Old murals on the walls are by an early Santa Fe artist, Alfred Morang.

El Farol's is in a rapidly changing neighborhood. Many of the native residents have sold to art dealers who do a thriving business along Old Canyon Road. A meal at El Farol, or next door at owner David Salazar's Canyon Road Cafe, is memorable. Ned Laventall is chef/manager at both places.

El Nido, a "local's choice" for over sixty years, also offers distinctive Santa Fe dining satisfaction with a big serving of history.

Back at the Plaza, the La Fonda Hotel awaits your pleasure.

When Santa Fe was founded in 1610, old records show the town already had a fonda, or inn. The trading party that opened the Santa Fe Trail in 1821 found an adobe fonda occupying the corner where the La Fonda is located today. This early fonda became the destination of trappers, mountain men, soldiers, gamblers, and opportunists who all contributed to Santa Fe's prosperity. The present-day La Fonda was built in 1920 on the site that was literally "at the end of the Santa Fe trail."

When the 1920 La Fonda business venture failed in 1925, the hotel was sold to the Atchison, Topeka, and Santa Fe Railroad, who leased it to Fred Harvey. For more than forty years, the La Fonda was a proud cornerstone of the Harvey chain. The La Fonda is a part of Historic Hotels of America and is a Registered National Historic Landmark. In 1991, it was recognized as one of the ten best places to stay in the United States. Guests at the La Fonda can choose from La Plazuela, the enclosed skylit courtyard restaurant, the Bell Tower Bar, or the La Fiesta Lounge. The margarita recipe at the La Fonda remains a closely guarded secret, but the executive chef, Lela Cross, shares these favorites.

LA FONDA BLACK BEAN SOUP

⅛ CUP OLIVE OIL
⅛ POUND BACON, DICED
⅛ POUND SMOKED HAM, CUT INTO 2-INCH PIECES
1 MEDIUM ONION, CHOPPED
2 CLOVES GARLIC, MINCED AND PRESSED
2 STALKS CELERY, CHOPPED
1½ CUPS DRIED BLACK BEANS
2½ TEASPOONS DRIED GROUND RED CHILI
4 CUPS WATER
1 TABLESPOON BEEF BASE
1 TEASPOON CHOPPED CILANTRO
¼ CUP SHERRY
SALT AND PEPPER TO TASTE
SOUR CREAM, GUACAMOLE, CHOPPED GREEN ONION

HEAT OIL IN LARGE PAN. Add bacon, ham, onions, garlic and celery. Brown slowly until soft. Meanwhile, clean beans, drain. Add to vegetable mixture with dried chili, water and beef base. Bring to boil, reduce heat, cover and simmer 2½ - 3 hours. Add extra water as necessary. Skim fat occasionally from top of soup. In a food processor or blender, puree mixture until smooth. Refrigerate until next day.

Remove from refrigerator when ready to serve. Add sherry, cilantro, salt, and pepper to taste. Serve warm. Garnish with dollops of sour cream and guacamole and sprinkle with chopped green onion. *6 to 8 servings*

LA FONDA FRENCH TOAST

3 SLICES BREAD, EACH CUT ¾ INCH THICK
2 EGGS
½ CUP WHIPPING CREAM
PINCH OF SALT
2 TO 3 TABLESPOONS VEGETABLE SHORTENING
CONFECTIONERS' SUGAR
APPLESAUCE, HONEY, SYRUP, OR JAM

TRIM CRUSTS FROM BREAD. Cut each slice in half to form triangle. Whisk together the eggs, cream, and salt. Soak bread in egg and cream mixture.

Meanwhile, heat shortening in skillet. Fry bread, being careful not to crowd, turning to cook on both sides. Transfer to clean towel to absorb grease. Place on baking sheet to allow to puff up in preheated 400° oven for 3 to 5 minutes. Sprinkle with confectioners' sugar and serve immediately with applesauce, honey, syrup, or jam. *1 to 2 servings.*

LA FONDA FLAN

2 CUPS SUGAR
9 EGGS
6 CUPS EVAPORATED MILK (FOUR 12-OUNCE CANS)
2 TABLESPOONS VANILLA
½ TEASPOON NUTMEG
½ TEASPOON CINNAMON
1 TABLESPOON SUGAR

MEASURE SUGAR INTO A DEEP PAN. Place over heat and stir constantly with a wooden spoon. Melt sugar until caramelized and golden brown. Remove from heat and pour into individual bowls or a large pan just so it coats the inside.

While sugar is being prepared, beat eggs with milk, vanilla, nutmeg, cinnamon, and sugar. Pour carefully into containers. Place flan in a large flat pan with an inch of water. Bake in a preheated 350° oven for 1 hour and 10 minutes. When cooled and ready to serve, turn over onto plate. Before serving add fresh whipping cream for garnish if desired. *Eighteen ½-cup servings.*

On the west side of the plaza is the Plaza Cafe that opened its doors in 1918 as the Star Cafe, then became the Capital Cafe, and finally the Plaza in 1942. Some fine early day photographs decorate the walls and the food is good.

The Pink Adobe Restaurant, on Old Santa Fe Trail, was opened by Rosalea Murphy in the summer of 1944. Rosalea, who came to Santa Fe from her native New Orleans by way of San Antonio, opened the restaurant at the suggestion of friends who enjoyed her cooking.

She vowed to use only the finest and freshest ingredients and almost overnight, her apple pie and French onion soup won customers and fame. Rosalea combines the best of Creole French with Spanish and Native American cuisine. She was the first restaurant owner in Santa Fe to serve seafood.

The Pink Adobe is located in one of the earliest settlements of European origin in the United States and sits across the street from San Miguel Chapel and within sight of the oldest house in the city.

The restaurant has expanded to four dining rooms with the Dragon Lounge across the patio. The original menu has increased to include a wide variety of esoteric foods. All the recipes have been created by Rosalea herself. A Pink Adobe menu dated 1951 lists onion soup with French bread and garlic butter for fifty cents and this classic apple pie at twenty-five cents a slice, à la mode for thirty-five cents.

PINK ADOBE FRENCH APPLE PIE

CRUST

2 CUPS FLOUR
¾ CUP LARD
1 TEASPOON SALT
6 TO 7 TABLESPOONS COLD WATER

FILLING

1 POUND FRESH APPLES OR 1 CAN (16 OUNCES) APPLES, PEELED AND SLICED
2 TABLESPOONS FRESH LEMON JUICE
½ TEASPOON GROUND NUTMEG
½ TEASPOON GROUND CINNAMON
½ CUP WHITE SUGAR
¼ CUP SEEDLESS RAISINS
1 CUP BROWN SUGAR
2 TABLESPOONS FLOUR
2 TABLESPOONS BUTTER
½ CUP SHELLED PECANS
¼ CUP MILK

HARD SAUCE

½ CUP BUTTER
1½ CUPS POWDERED SUGAR
1 TABLESPOON WATER
1 TEASPOON BRANDY OR RUM

PREPARE THE CRUST BY WORKING THE FLOUR, lard, and salt together with your fingers until crumbly. Add water until dough holds together. Divide into two equal balls. On a floured pastry cloth, roll out one ball thin enough to line a 9-inch pie tin. Roll out second ball in same manner for top crust.

Prepare the filling by tossing the apples with lemon juice, nutmeg, and cinnamon. Line the crust with the apple mixture. Spread white sugar and raisins evenly over the apples.

Mix the brown sugar, flour, and butter in a bowl. When blended, spread over the contents of the pie tin and sprinkle with pecans. Add most of the milk and cover with the top crust. Prick top with fork and brush the rest of the milk on the pastry.

Bake for 10 minutes in a preheated 450° oven, then reduce heat to 350° and bake another 30 minutes. To prepare the hard sauce, cream the butter until light. Beat in the sugar and add water. Beat in the liquor and serve over each slice of pie. *8 servings.*

Between the Old Plaza and St. Francis Cathedral, The Shed serves lunch in cozy, thick-walled adobe rooms decorated with unique artifacts and original paintings. The restaurant was once part of the eighteen-room home of Governor Bradford Prince, whose family resided there until 1940. The King of Spain originally gave this property to Captain Diego Arias De Quiros in 1692 in recognition of his services in the reconquest.

Thornton and Polly Carswell opened the original Shed on July 4, 1952. They had renovated an old barn in the area referred to as "Burro Alley" where natives once tied animals while they made the rounds of local cantinas. The restored Shed could accommodate twenty-two people. The "shedburger" they created for the original menu remains a cornerstone item today, even after a 1960 move to the present location where Northern New Mexico cuisine is featured.

The Carswells' son, Courtney, and his wife Linnea, now operate the restaurant which has expanded to four dining rooms and a patio. Consuela Peña, the head cook, has been at The Shed since it opened in 1952, and continues to supervise preparation of first-class Northern New Mexico style food. Yellow corn tortillas may be substituted for the Shed Tacos if blue corn tortillas aren't available.

SHED STYLE TACOS

I POUND LEAN GROUND BEEF
I CUP HOMEMADE CHILI SAUCE
(OR CANNED ENCHILADA SAUCE)
12 BLUE CORN TORTILLAS
COOKING OIL
CHOPPED LETTUCE
CHOPPED ONIONS
CHOPPED TOMATOES
I POUND GRATED LONGHORN CHEESE

BROWN THE GROUND BEEF IN A HEAVY SKILLET and drain off all the grease. Mix with chili sauce and keep warm in skillet. Fry tortillas quickly in a little hot oil until they are soft and limp. Drain. Allow two to a plate and place 2 tablespoons of the hot meat mixture on each tortilla. Add spoonfuls of the chopped lettuce, onions, tomatoes, and cheese. Fold tortillas over and sprinkle with more grated cheese. Place tacos in preheated 425° oven until the cheese melts, about 5 minutes or less. *6 servings.*

Another of the best in Santa Fe is La Tertulia, offering the finest in regional cuisine as well as a recreation of the Spanish national treasure, paella. When Willie and June Ortiz opened La Tertulia in 1972, they selected a menu of native New Mexican dishes perfected from recipes that have been in Willie's family for generations. Willie supervises the kitchen while the Ortiz's daughter, Joy, keeps an eye on the dining rooms, assuring personal attention for all the guests.

La Tertulia sits on the famous Camino Real, "The Royal Highway." It was formerly a rambling adobe convent associated with the historic Guadalupe Church across the street. Its oldest rooms, estimated at 150 years, predate the convent, which existed from the early 1920s. Several noted Santa Fe families have made the splendid residence their home.

Dinner at La Tertulia might begin with tostadas and salsa followed by guacamole salad. Then diners have a choice of posole with accompanying garnishes or tacos, enchiladas, beans, and Spanish rice. Or perhaps they will choose a chalupa or a green chili enchilada topped with an egg, New Mexico style. With the dinner come feather light sopaipillas with honey butter and Willie Ortiz's special sangria.

Posole, or hominy, can be prepared with dried, frozen, or fresh hominy (corn). It is cooked until the kernels are soft and seasoned with pork, garlic, oregano, chili peppers, and onion. Popular accompaniments include lemon or lime wedges, fresh lettuce, tomatoes, radishes, and perhaps some cheese.

This recipe, shared by Willie Ortiz, has been cut to a family-size portion. Posole freezes well so any extra can be saved easily.

LA TERTULIA POSOLE

1 BAG (1 POUND SIZE) DRIED POSOLE
1 HEAD FRESH GARLIC
1 PINCH OREGANO
½ POUND LEAN PORK, CUT IN BITE-SIZED PIECES
½ CUP CHOPPED ONION
WATER FOR COOKING
SALT, PEPPER, AND CHILI PEPPERS TO TASTE

WASH POSOLE IN HOT WATER AND PLACE IN LARGE PAN. Add minced fresh garlic, oregano, pork, onion, and enough water to cover. Bring to a boil, then simmer in a covered container until posole is soft, about 3 to 3½ hours. Add water as needed to barely cover posole. Add salt, pepper, and chili peppers to taste after corn is soft. *6 to 8 servings.*

LA TERTULIA GUACAMOLE

1 RIPE AVOCADO
¼ TEASPOON GARLIC SALT

PEEL AND MASH THE RIPE AVOCADO. Mix in the garlic salt. Serve immediately on lettuce with crisp tostadas.

Travelers on Old Route 66 leave Santa Fe on Cerrillos Road, named for the Cerrillos Hills where some of the oldest mines in the country once drew men seeking their fortunes in turquoise and gold.

Original Highway 66 south of Santa Fe was a treacherous road. Winnie Steele remembers riding with her school superintendent down La Bahada Hill headed toward Albuquerque in 1927. There were twenty-one hairpin curves to be negotiated in his Model T Ford. Reverse was used for braking all the way. Near the base of the hill, they stopped at the Santa Domingo Indian Trading Post to get hold of their nerves again.

To find the Santa Domingo Trading Post today, take Exit 259 off I-25 and drive about five miles west. Fred Thompson has managed this outpost in time for over 40 years. His 5,000-page guest book dates back into history and the front windows are filled with newspaper stories about famous guests. There's a rusting Frazer imbedded in sand out front and an old-fashioned pop cooler inside, along with enough unique merchandise to keep the most intrepid garage sale enthusiast busy for hours.

Return to the interstate for the short drive to Algodones, where old 66 picks up again all the way to Albuquerque. You can't miss Carman's Purple Pullman, even though abandoned — it's the brightest spot leaving town.

In December of 1933, the Twenty-First Amendment ended prohibition. That same year in Bernalillo, Felix Silva, Sr., opened Silva's Saloon with the third liquor license issued in New Mexico. On old, old Highway 66, Silva's Saloon was the first bar in Bernalillo and remains the oldest bar in the state still operating with the original owners.

After Silva purchased the saloon, he had just enough money left to purchase $50 worth of stock to supply the big oval bar. Friends and neighborhood patrons began bringing him odd bits of memorabilia to adorn the bare walls. The collection grew and soon covered every inch of space, so he began hanging the accumulation from the ceiling.

Silva's employees refer to today's compilation as an upside down landfill. This astonishing hoard is made up of hundreds of new and used hats, lanterns, tools, jugs, knives, calendars, and all kinds of cookware. Someone has added a U.S. Cavalry saddle, a grape crusher and a 15-gallon whiskey still. Behind the bar is a fine collection of Elvis dolls and several hundred archaic liquor bottles. An appropriate sign on one wall reminds customers, "Don't Sit on the Heater."

Felix Silva, Jr., runs the family bar today. Felix Sr., now an octogenarian, still works several hours each day. Silva's Saloon is a seasoned piece of all-American history.

SILVA'S SALOON MARGARITA

RIM A 5-OUNCE GLASS WITH SALT. Pour 1⅓ ounces Cuervo Tequila and ⅓ ounce Triple Sec in glass. Fill glass with Tavern Sweet-Sour Mix. Enjoy!

Bernalillo is also home to Abuelita's New Mexican Kitchen and the Prairie Star, an elegant continental restaurant located off Jemez Dam Road. A breathtaking view of the Sandia mountains offers an unexpected bonus. In the early evening, the sun is in just the right spot to turn the Sandia mountains red. Perhaps this is why the name was chosen since Sandia means "watermelon" in Spanish.

Travelers may choose to enter Albuquerque from the west instead of taking the early, longer route through Santa Fe. To do this, simply follow I-40 from Santa Rosa and head toward Cline's Corner.

Cline's Corner is a giant tourist trap in the dessert at I-40 and State Highway 285. It was named for Roy Cline who began his fledgling business in 1933, just as Route 66 was being graded for paving. The highway alignment moved three times and Roy followed the moves, finally owning all four corners where U.S. 66 and 285 crossed. Roy operated his station and cafe until 1963. By then, Cline's Corner was on Interstate 40 and had become a recognized name to travelers.

Roy Cline, Jr., called the area the coldest, meanest, windiest place on Highway 66. He credited the free Conoco road maps given to travelers as the best publicity his family ever had. Highway signs did the rest.

Absentee owners have collected a wide assortment of odds and ends from the Orient to sell with the buffalo horns, cactus honey, and velvet paintings of the New Mexico landscape. Perhaps Moriarty, where a real sense of Old 66 is still alive, would be a more authentic stop.

Land along here is high-plateau country with the elevation almost 7,000 feet. Cattle and sheep roam nearby slopes and travelers get a big dose of limitless space before finally beginning a drop into the fertile Estancia valley area where cedar, juniper, and pinon thrive in the high desert climate.

At Exit 203 on I-40 take a quick detour for a better view of the ghostly remains of the Longhorn

Ranch Indian Trading Post. The Longhorn started as a tiny cafe with a few stools and grew to a full-service hotel and restaurant, coffee shop, and cocktail lounge. The old slogan, "Where the West Stops to Rest" is still visible although the paint is fading fast. To encourage travelers to stop, the owners sometimes had an employee drive a brightly painted stagecoach along the side of the road. Cowhands decked in Stetson hats were available for pictures and most had wild west stories to tell. What's left of the Longhorn is crumbling among shoulder-high weeds.

The Estancia Valley has always been the center of New Mexico's pinto bean industry. When the first crops were planted over 75 years ago, bean warehouses sprang up around Moriarty and Edgewood. But

1949 was the last year for a big crop in the valley. Drought forced growers out of business and in the 1950s much of the land went into the soil bank. Wind and dust had won a battle.

Pinto beans are grown on a much smaller scale in the Estancia Valley today. At the Moriarty Museum, an antique bean-cleaning machine reminds folks how the beans were put through rollers to crush clods and tumbled over screens to remove any remaining trash before being sacked in 100-pound bags for shipment.

Moriarty is host each October to the National Pinto Bean Fiesta and Cook-off. The all-day affair at the city park on Historic Route 66 attracts some 1500 hardy folks. Here is a one of the 1991 winning recipes. The candy is exceptionally good! For ease of preparation, it can be made successfully using a food processor.

THE SPIRIT OF THE OLD WEST STILL LIVES AT
The Longhorn Ranch

Real Concord Stagecoach used to Haul Mail and Passengers in the days of Buffalo Bill

TERRY GENGER'S PINTO BEAN FIESTA FUDGE

First Place, Specialty Division, 1991 Pinto Bean Fiesta and Cook-off

1 CUP WARM COOKED PINTO BEANS
¾ CUP MELTED BUTTER
1 CUP COCOA
1 TABLESPOON VANILLA
2 POUNDS POWDERED SUGAR
1 CUP CHOPPED PECANS

MASH OR SIEVE BEANS. Add melted butter, cocoa, and vanilla. Mix thoroughly. Stir in powdered sugar gradually. Add nuts and press mixture into a 9 x 13 buttered pan. Store in refrigerator until ready to serve.

Moriarty is home to two Route 66 vintage eating places, Blackie's Restaurant, once the Route 66 bus stop, and El Comedor De Anayas, built in 1953 by Lauriano and Filandro Anaya. El Comedor is often referred to as a "watering hole" for politicians. It is said that much more of central New Mexican business is settled over coffee at El Comedor than in the offices of any of the city or county administrators in the area.

The popular restaurant has been in the Anaya family for four generations. Ralph, Gabe and Mike Anaya, along with Mike's son Steve, run the restaurant today. El Comedor offers authentic New Mexican cuisine.

Old Highway 66 continues through Moriarty to Sedillo Hill where Comer's Truck Stop once did a thriving business. Near Edgewood, the Cherry Hill Cider Stand has also disappeared. Travelers in the 1940s made the little stand a regular stop for its ten-cent glasses of refreshment.

Highway 66 dipped and twisted its narrow way through the mouth of Tijeras Canyon where travelers were drawn to Manny Goodman's Covered Wagon Trading Post before entering Albuquerque. Manny fronted his building with a massive concrete and wooden covered wagon pulled by a pair of papier-mâché oxen. He also planted six-foot-tall jack rabbits, palomino horses, and other critters around the parking area. When the intersection was demolished to clear a path for I-40, the menagerie headed into the sunset and Goodman moved farther down Route 66 to set up a new Covered Wagon store in Albuquerque's Old Town district.

Albuquerque's Central Avenue is a seventeen-mile stretch of original Route 66 that slices through the center of this lovely city. Albuquerque spreads gracefully beneath the Sandia Mountains and across the broad Rio Grande Valley.

Much of the neon and glitz from Route 66 days remain on Central Avenue with many vintage motor courts and eating places still evident. A Main Street revitalization program has upgraded the old Nob Hill area where the De Anza Motel remains a classic from the 1940s. The adjoining Turquoise Restaurant has closed.

Scalo's still serves good Italian cuisine and Baca's Mexican Restaurant offers a wide menu at Clem Baca's large white stucco location. Baca's has served the public in two other locations along historic Route 66 since first opening in 1949. Such notables as Mikhail Baryshnikov, Mel Torme, Juliet Proust, and Anthony Quinn have enjoyed Baca's delicious food.

Several examples of pure Spanish Pueblo Revival style architecture remain in Albuquerque. The old

Monte Vista Fire Station is a perfect example.

The fire station, completed in 1936, was built on the east edge of Albuquerque by the WPA as an "anti-depression transfusion." E. H. Blumenthal, Albuquerque's award winning city architect, designed the fire station with a third-floor tower to offer a protective view of the city and provide a shaft where hoses could be hung to dry. The station features hollow block construction covered by stucco and was originally designed to house five men and a pumper truck. It was used by the city until the early 1970s.

A variety of businesses occupied the location until Kerry Rayner and his partners bought the old station, made extensive repairs, and opened as an up-scale restaurant in 1985. Many features from the station were retained in the renovation including the original brass pole, high ceilings, and reel-opening construction of the engine door. The Monte Vista Fire Station is on the National Registry of Historic Places.

The restaurant interior is comfortably appointed in sand, dusty rose, and turquoise. An open-air second-floor patio bar, complete with a corner fireplace, offers a breathtaking view of the Sandia mountains, and in warm weather, guests can choose tables on the flagstone patio out front. The Monte Vista Fire Station offers a gourmet experience in a setting unique to Historic Route 66.

Award-winning chef Rosa Rajkovic has created an ever-changing menu of American cuisine.

MONTE VISTA FIRE STATION TOMATILLO-JICAMA SALAD WITH CILANTRO

12 TOMATILLOS, QUARTERED AND CHOPPED
1 JICAMA, SLICED AND JULIENNED
1 SMALL RED ONION, VERY THINLY SLICED
2 TO 3 SERRANOS (JALAPEÑOS)
½ CUP FRESH CILANTRO CHOPPED
1 TABLESPOON OLIVE OIL
2 TABLESPOONS ORANGE JUICE
1 TEASPOON CHAMPAGNE VINEGAR
1 TABLESPOON LIME JUICE
¼ TEASPOON SALT

COMBINE TOMATILLOS, jícama, onion, serranos, and cilantro. Toss lightly to mix. Prepare dressing by combining olive oil, orange juice, vinegar, lime juice, and salt. Shake vigorously. Pour over salad just before serving. *8 servings.*

Across from the University of New Mexico campus, the Frontier Restaurant does a thriving business. Cinnamon rolls are turned out in quantity here. Fifty-pound bags of flour form the basis of each recipe and the popular rolls are made fresh several times a day. Tortillas are also prepared in-house and sell as fast as the rolls.

Tom Willis opened The 66 Diner on Central Avenue where a vintage Phillips 66 gas station once stood. Tom is an enthusiastic member of the New Mexico Route 66 Association and has certainly done his part to revitalize a vanishing part of American history. The building was redesigned in the "trolly car mode" with plenty of neon and glass brick. Tom painted his restaurant white and filled the bright

interior with turquoise vinyl booths and a dozen framed photographs of Route 66 classic locations done by photographer Terrence Moore. An antique Seeburg jukebox cranks out old tunes and nostalgic aromas drift from the kitchen. The diner attracts an eclectic crowd of hungry folks who thrive on good home cooking with a chaser of history. The blue plate special is usually Betty Jo's meatloaf and the popular green-chili cheeseburger is dished out in record numbers. *Albuquerque Monthly Magazine* named the diner's milkshakes the best in town, but its prize trademark is the Route 66 Pileup, a breakfast combo of pan-fried potatoes, bacon, cheese, chili, tortillas, and two eggs.

ROUTE 66 PILEUP

SPREAD A CUP of freshly prepared cubed cottage fries on the plate. Top with two slices of crisply fried bacon and fresh chopped green chili. Add melted cheddar cheese and two eggs, cooked to order. Top with red or green chili sauce and serve hot. *Serves one.*

Cafe Oceana

Across the street from the 66 Diner is another Willis restaurant, Cafe Oceana. The unique cafe was once the Mercantile Company Store, built in 1928 when the state of New Mexico was only 16 years old. The exterior walls, original hardwood floor, and pressed tin ceiling still exist although several businesses have come and gone. In 1982, Willis and his partner, Dale Harris, remodeled the historic building and began serving Albuquerque residents quality seafood dishes. Cajun-style favorites, soup, seafood salads, and creative Southwestern specialties keep the daily blackboard filled with dining pleasure.

Large windows and overhead skylights create an airy feeling and the decor provides a comfortable touch.

CAFE OCEANA MEDITERRANEAN STYLE FLOUNDER

2 POUNDS FRESH FLOUNDER FILLETS
SALT AND FRESH PEPPER TO TASTE
¼ CUP WHITE WINE
3 TABLESPOONS EXTRA VIRGIN OLIVE OIL
6 CLOVES GARLIC, MINCED
4 ROMA TOMATOES, COURSELY CHOPPED
½ CUP WINE
10 CALAMATA OLIVES
1 ½ TABLESPOONS FRESH SQUEEZED LEMON JUICE
2 TABLESPOONS FRESH BASIL LEAVES, CHOPPED

SALT AND PEPPER THE FLOUNDER FILLETS LIGHTLY. Roll the fillets in pinwheel fashion and place in a shallow baking dish. Pour the white wine over fish and drizzle with one tablespoon of the olive oil. Bake covered for 18 minutes in a preheated 350° oven.

In a medium sauté pan, heat remaining olive oil over high heat and add garlic. Cook for 1 minute but do not brown garlic. Add the tomatoes and cook 2 minutes more, stirring often. Add the wine and olives and continue to cook for 2 minutes. Add lemon juice and basil and remove from heat. Remove fish to heated serving plates and spoon sauce generously over fish. *4 servings.*

Nearer downtown Albuquerque, the famous Alvarado Hotel, one of the last mission revival style Harvey Houses, vanished under urban demolition in 1970. The historic hotel opened in 1902 and served presidents, governors and other dignitaries with style and grace rarely seen in the West.

Just two blocks off Historic 66 at 403 2nd Street is an Albuquerque institution, the M & J Restaurant and Sanitary Tortilla Factory. This unique mom-and-pop business began in 1975 when Jake Montoya decided he and his wife, Beatrice, should go into business for themselves. Bea was working as a waitress at Baca's at the time. She remembers how frightened she was of his idea. "I asked him how we could do it and he said, 'Easy, we'll just lease a building,' and he did!" she said.

Jake and Bea started their tiny cafe with $15 in the cash register. Their first customer gave Bea a $20 bill and she had to borrow money for the change. "I said to myself we would never make it, I almost cried that first day, but I saw hope in his eyes, and I knew we had to try," she recalls. Their first cafe was a tiny place with only nine stools that averaged $26 a day in profits. "But after a year we bought it out," she said. The Montoyas have lasted and their business has grown through what Bea calls strong will, determination, plenty of hard work, and good food. Many of their fourteen employees have been with them since they began.

All the food is made at their restaurant under the watchful eye of the owners. Their daughter, Eileen, works with them now and Bea says it is all worth the effort because of Eileen and their grandson, Daniel.

In back of the restaurant the Montoyas supervise the making of 16,000 tortillas each morning. Most are sold commercially and Jake and Bea reserve the remainder for their own customers. Yellow and blue corn tortillas, as well as difficult-to-make red chili tortillas, follow a similar process. No artificial colors or preservatives are used. The famous blue corn tortillas come from native New Mexican blue corn. The corn is first cooked with lime to loosen the skins of the kernels, then cooled and run through what Bea believes to be one of the oldest stone grinders still in use. From there the resulting masa goes to the spreader and cutter and is finally cooked three times at high temperature before being packaged for distribution. The Montoyas have another machine they couldn't part with: it peels and seeds chilies, turning out the pulp so necessary for the red and green chili sauce that makes New Mexican food distinctive.

Bea is a bubbling, vivacious ball of fire. She is a judge for the American Chili Cook-off held each year in Albuquerque and her official apron hangs with other mementoes on walls covered with awards and letters from satisfied customers. Amidst all the hustle and bustle, Bea still keeps a small candlelit spot nearby, where she can retreat occasionally from her hectic pace to say a prayer and give thanks.

In 1991 the Montoyas enlarged their restaurant to seat 180. It is now open evenings on weekends and daily for lunch. The M & J Restaurant has received national and international recognition for good food.

Jake says he measures by sight but agreed to share his technique for preparation of Carne Adovada, the basis for their award-winning "5 Hongo Burrito." Years ago, when they first won the award for having the "A-1 Champion Burrito in Albuquerque," many new customers found the restaurant. Their friends continue to eat regularly with Bea and Jake.

Jake's 5 Hongo Burrito is made with a flour tortilla, warmed and wrapped around Carne Adovada and covered with red or green chili sauce.

M & J RESTAURANT
CARNE ADOVADA

3 POUNDS BONELESS CUSHION PORK
2 PINTS RED CHILI SAUCE
WATER TO THIN AS NEEDED
3 TABLESPOON SALT
3 TABLESPOONS GRANULATED GARLIC
¼ TEASPOON OREGANO
1½ TEASPOONS WHOLE COMINO SEEDS
12 FLOUR TORTILLAS

DICE THE RAW PORK INTO BITE SIZED PIECES. Boil for at least one hour or until meat is very tender and fat has been cooked away. To two pints of red chili sauce, add salt, garlic, oregano, and comino seeds. Drain water from the pork and cover with chili sauce. Continue cooking for another 30 minutes. Serve the meat and sauce rolled in a flour tortilla and covered with additional red or green chili sauce. *12 burritos.*

Near the center of town, the Downtown 66 Station has become a popular gathering place for musicians, artists, poets, and those who enjoy the creativity of sound. Open-mike jams on Friday and Saturday nights draw an enthusiastic crowd.

The upstairs location gives the impression of an unfinished loft and Ron Camden, the owner, has covered the walls and ceiling with vintage signs from beverage manufacturers and old service stations.

Ron is especially proud of a framed photograph taken on Central Avenue years ago that shows crossroad signs for Route 66 and Highway 85. The north-south route

follows El Camino Real, the first road established by Europeans in what is now the United States.

Ron is an enthusiastic Route 66 supporter and his menu reflects a variety of "road dishes," many with prices ending with ".66."

DOWNTOWN 66 STATION HUBCAPS

A MODEL T REGULAR: Cover one flat, crispy flour tortilla with beans, cheese, lettuce, tomato and red or green chili or salsa. For an additional 66 cents each, add GTO - guacamole, Cadillac - carne adovada, Bently - beef strips, Rambler - chicken, Buick - BBQ beef.

DOWNTOWN 66 STATION CAPPUCCINO SHAKE

CHILL A CUP OF ESPRESSO and stir in an equal amount of either a chocolate or vanilla milkshake. Serve in a large chilled glass.

The KiMo Theater, in downtown Albuquerque, is a distinctive New Mexican revival building dating from 1927. The theater is a classic in the same mode as the Coleman Theater in Miami, Oklahoma, and the California Theater in San Bernardino. All are vintage works of art. Diagonally across the street from the KiMo is Lindy's, where cooks since 1929 have been ladling out "the best chili in town." The restaurant's original name, Coney Island Cafe, was inspired by the Coney Island in New York. Lindy's is the oldest restaurant in town doing business at the same location. It still serves its local version of the famous chili hot dog. Narke Vatoseow has called Lindy's home for over thirty-five years. Now his son, Steve, does much of the cooking but Narke still gets to work by five o'clock each morning.

Outside, the old cafe signals its age, but inside, the color of soft sunshine provides a warm atmosphere. The owner/bosses and their employees know most of the customers. Many have been coming in for years.

Customers at the counter visit comfortably and a home-like atmosphere pervades the historic site. Notables have also found the restaurant through the years. Muhammad Ali once ate with Narke and more recently, Victoria Principal filmed a portion of a TV movie at the site.

Steve says he still makes the same great Red Chili that has been served for years at Lindy's.

LINDY'S RED CHILI

2½ POUNDS COARSELY GROUND BEEF
I MEDIUM ONION, DICED
2 TABLESPOONS BLACK PEPPER OR TO TASTE
2 TABLESPOONS GARLIC POWDER
2 TABLESPOONS CUMIN
2 TABLESPOONS OREGANO
½ CUP PAPRIKA
I TABLESPOON SALT
½ CUP CHILI POWDER OR TO TASTE
2 CUPS WATER
I CUP FLOUR
ADDITIONAL WATER AS NEEDED

COOK MEAT AND ADD REMAINING INGREDIENTS except flour. Combine flour with water to make a roux. Add to meat mixture until desired thickness occurs. Let simmer until flour is cooked, at least half an hour. Serve hot. *12 to 14 servings.*

Old Town in Albuquerque is a trip into time, a paradise for shoppers, and an opportunity to sample some of the best of New Mexican cuisine. Several unique restaurants are located in and around Old Town, including Monroe's and the High Noon. Both offer a big dose of history with their outstanding food.

La Placita has been a vital part of Old Town for more than fifty years. The restaurant is located in a hacienda built in 1706 by the wealthy Armijo family. Virtually unchanged through the years, it was constructed originally with foot-thick walls and deep-set windows.

The hacienda was a center of social and political activity, especially during the life of Don Amborsio Armijo, who often entertained extravagantly. When his daughter, Teresa, was married in 1872, he built a second floor to the house and had a walnut staircase designed the length of Teresa's wedding train. The staircase is still intact and the second floor houses a gallery.

La Placita today has six dining rooms that seat 250. The restaurant houses an exceptional collection of regional art. The kitchens at La Placita continue to turn out famous chili rellenos, tacos, enchiladas, and sopaipillas as they have for years.

Elmer and Rosa Lea Elliott took over the restaurant in 1950 and their son and daughter-in-law run the historic site today.

Here is La Placita's sopaipilla recipe. To recreate the big, puffy sopaipillas the Elliotts serve, be sure to roll the dough thin enough and to cook the sopaipillas in oil that is sufficiently hot.

LA PLACITA SOPAIPILLA MIX

4 CUPS FLOUR
¾ TEASPOON SALT
2 TEASPOONS BAKING POWDER
I TABLESPOON SHORTENING
I CUP WARM WATER, APPROXIMATELY
SHORTENING OR OIL FOR FRYING

THOROUGHLY MIX DRY INGREDIENTS, then add shortening and blend. Slowly add about one cup of water and knead until smooth. Dough should be near the consistency of pie dough. Cover dough and let rest for about an hour.

To cook, roll dough very thin, about ½₂ of an inch, then cut into rectangular strips about 3 x 4 inches. Cook in deep fat at about 400° as doughnuts are cooked, immersing and turning until golden brown. Serve hot with honey.

The Elliotts owned an historic Route 66 restaurant nearer downtown from 1941 to 1959. Their Court Cafe catered to the traveling public and was a "Chicken in the Rough" franchise. Next door was the popular Court Bakery.

"In Albuquerque, it's the Court Cafe - 109-111 North 4th Street - that serves your every whim - metropolitan service at popular prices - private booths and counter - wash rooms - maps."

(Old Travelmat, Inc. advertisement)

Liiberty Cafe- 105 West Central, Albuquerque, "The home of good eats," where the choicest foods are served, we specialize in steaks and sea foods, tourists welcome.

(Old New Mexico, Arizona guide)

On 4th Street, where Route 66 entered Albuquerque from Santa Fe until 1937, Sadie's Cocinita and Lounge serves enthusiastic diners in a new adobe building that is typically New Mexican in decor with soft sand colors, skylights, high ceilings and softened lines. A large mural on the south wall of the main dining room depicts the restaurant's original site.

Sadie Koury started her restaurant business in the early 1950s near 2nd and Osuna. The original cafe had nine stools and often there was standing room only.

When Sadie retired in 1975, her sister Betty Jo and her husband, Bob Stafford, took over Sadie's. Many of Sadie's original recipes are still used. The food is authentic and good.

For another unique New Mexico experience, stop at Albuquerque's Indian Pueblo Cultural Center on 12th Street. The center's restaurant serves up buffalo burgers, rabbit stew, and enchiladas made from a choice of deer, elk, beef, or buffalo. The buffalo meat is said to be 70 percent leaner than beef. All the game is shipped in from Colorado and recipes are authentic. The restaurant is usually open from 7:30 a.m. to 3:30 p.m. daily.

At the vintage Casa Grande Restaurant, across the street from the old El Vado Motel, breakfast is served anytime. For regulars, that means huevos rancheros, chili omelets, eggs, or waffles. The long lunch and dinner menu includes Mexican dishes and a wide variety of gringo entrees. The Casa Grande once included a hotel, bar, and gas station as part of a Route 66 complex.

Travelers have a choice when leaving Albuquerque. Old Route 66 heads directly west but the original 1926 alignment drops south to Los Lunas.

Los Lunas is a fascinating village 20 miles south of Albuquerque. Back in 1692, Domingo de Luna arrived in the area with a huge land grant from the King of Spain. In nearby Valencia County, Don Pedro Otero came to the area under similar circumstances. Both men made fortunes on sheep and became powerful in political and social circles. Their families joined through two marriages and united the families into the Luna-Otero dynasty.

In 1880, the Santa Fe Railroad asked for a right of way through the 35,000 acre Luna ranch. In return, the railroad agreed to build a new home for Don Antonio Jose Luna and his family. The mansion's Southern colonial style architecture was inspired by several Luna family trips to the south. Materials were shipped from all over the world, but local adobe made up the basic structure and a Southern colonial mansion appeared on the Rio Grande.

The home soon passed into the hands of Solomon Luna and then to his nephew, Don Eduardo Otero, in the early 1900s. During this time, the solarium and front portico were added and the home was surrounded with elaborate ironwork fencing. Eduardo's wife, Josefita, cared for the magnificent gardens and painted lovely murals on the solarium walls. Otero wool, produced on their vast holdings until the 1930s, was considered some of the finest in the nation.

The depression, the government's breaking up of huge land grant holdings, and Don Eduardo's interest in politics rather than ranching all contributed to family members spreading out and taking up other occupations. In 1949, Ted Otero sold the Luna mansion. It had several owners before Earl Whitmore and his three partners purchased it with plans for a unique eating place in mind.

The Luna Mansion was renovated and opened in 1977 as a National Historic Landmark and elegant restaurant. The new owners have preserved the history and family stories to share with patrons.

The New Mexico state constitution was formulated in the front parlor of the mansion. A rare photograph of all the signers of that constitution is now hanging in the bar. The old home has first floor walls that are three feet thick, made from adobe bricks that were dug from land behind the mansion. The rose marble fireplace in the parlor came from Italy and has been valued at over $12,000 by appraisers. An elegant glass transom, several silver wall sconces, and some intricately carved brass and porcelain door hinges and knobs remain from the original home. Fixtures in the bar came from the Alvarado Hotel in Albuquerque.

It is thought that both Santa Fe and the tiny community of Los Lunas became stops on original Route 66 because Don Eduardo Otero, who lived in the mansion at the time, insisted that the highway come through the capital and his home or not be built through the state. After his death in the mid-30s, the road was finally straightened.

Don't miss this wonderful piece of history along original Route 66. There are many more tales to discover, including those of the mansion ghost, Josefita, who continues to make her presence felt among employees and guests.

LUNA MANSION GREEN CHILI CHICKEN SOUP

1 QUART CHICKEN STOCK
1 QUART HEAVY WHIPPING CREAM
2½ CUPS HOT GREEN CHILI
4 CUPS DICED, COOKED CHICKEN MEAT
2 TABLESPOONS CUMIN
SALT AND PEPPER TO TASTE

BRING CHICKEN STOCK AND WHIPPING CREAM TO A BOIL. Reduce heat and simmer. Add green chili, chicken meat and cumin. Simmer until all ingredients are thoroughly blended. Season with salt and pepper. *15-18 6-ounce servings.*

Across the street from the Luna Mansion is another restaurant in historic yet simple surroundings. Teofilo's Restaurant has been open since 1985 in the Wittwer House, the former home of Los Lunas doctor, W.F. Wittwer.

It seems that in 1899, young Dr. Wittwer's train was stopped in Los Lunas as he headed for a promising career in El Paso. Citizens, recognizing a need for his services, offered Dr. Wittwer $50 a month to remain as the community physician. He stayed for sixty-five years. The house was built for the doctor and his wife in 1913, on land purchased from the Solomon Luna estate. It is registered as a state landmark and has been restored to its original style. Authentic New Mexican cuisine is served.

Travelers choosing the direct route west from Albuquerque cross the Rio Grande on the Old Town Bridge, pass a nondescript area clogged with small businesses, and climb out of the Rio Grande Valley toward Nine-Mile Hill and the high plateaus.

To the west, old 66 becomes a frontage road and disappears into the vast desert. From Laguna to Grants, the old road is New Mexico 124. Near the village of Paraje is the turnoff to the Sky City of Acoma, the oldest Indian pueblo in America, located on a mesa some twelve miles south of the highway.

Budville is an all-but-gone village twenty-three miles east of Grants. Continuing on the old loop, travelers drive into Cubero where the Villa De Cubero Tourist Courts and Cafe, built in 1937, stands abandoned. The Gunn family once ran the adobe cafe and specialized in succulent lamb. A general store and gas station remain open across the highway. Travelers who stay on the interstate will pass Santa Maria de Acoma in McCartys, a sunbaked community southeast of Grants where a lovely old Catholic church sits solidly against a mesa wall. There are ancient lava flows along here, giving the area the name of "Malpais," or evil country.

Original Highway 66 follows six miles of Santa Fe Avenue in Grants, a "bust and starve" community that is home to the only uranium mining museum in the world. The community is a starting point for tours to surrounding pueblos and natural wonders.

Back in 1881, the Atlantic and Pacific Railroad pushed west from Albuquerque. By the next year, a post office was established and Grants Station was born. During the building process, some 4,000 men and 2,000 mules worked in the area.

When Bud and Shirley Rieck opened their Grants Station Restaurant, they wanted to incorporate the city's railroad history, but never dreamed of collecting the mementoes they have amassed today. Their collection began even before Bud purchased an old Santa Fe caboose from a nearby coal line. "It was all a lark," he said, "I wasn't even sure what I would do with it." Their son, an architect, encouraged them to make the caboose a part of the restaurant.

Santa Fe employees found ties for Rieck from an abandoned siding and a section crew helped lay the track and put the car in place. The brightly painted caboose sits next to Grants Station today, a well-preserved piece of railroading history that is often used for special parties. Most of the memorabilia in the restaurant has been given to the Riecks by railroad enthusiasts. Their most famous contributor is Michael Gross from "Family Ties," who eats at Grants Station when he comes through town.

The Riecks serve good New Mexico dishes as well as traditional fare.

GRANTS STATION GREEN CHILI

1¼ POUNDS LEAN GROUND BEEF
1 CUP FLOUR
2 CUPS CANNED TOMATOES, WITH LIQUID
2 TABLESPOONS GARLIC SALT
3 WHOLE CANNED JALAPEÑO PEPPERS, OR TO TASTE
1¼ POUNDS FROZEN OR CANNED HOT GREEN CHILIES
2 QUARTS WATER

BROWN MEAT AND STIR IN FLOUR. Meanwhile, combine tomatoes, garlic salt, and jalapeños in blender. Add to meat mixture. Puree green chilies in blender or food processor and stir into mixture. Add half the water and simmer until desired thickness is achieved, adding remaining water as needed. The longer the chili simmers, the thicker it will get. *3 quarts.*

The Monte Carlo Restaurant is the oldest eating establishment still in existence in Grants. Eskie Mazon built the landmark restaurant in 1947. He had owned the C & B Cafe before moving to his newer and bigger location.

Eskie built apartments on the second floor and rented them to teachers and mining personnel who needed a place to live during Grants' boom years. When Santa Fe Avenue was widened in 1955, ten feet along the front of the Monte Carlo had to be cut off. Eskie says Grants and the Monte Carlo have never been the same.

Eskie's son, Jerry, took over when he retired, and in 1989, the Monte Carlo was bought by his daughter-in-law, Maria Mazon, and sisters, Merla Olguin, Dorella Zenz, and Flora Schuck. Recognized in the *New Mexico Magazine* for some of the best salsa in the state, they prepare recipes that have been handed down in their family for generations. The salsa remains a secret but they share their recipe here for Chilis Rellenos. To make a delicious variation called Chilis Rellenos Del Mar, they stuff the tender green chilies with cheese, bay shrimp and crabmeat.

MONTE CARLO CAFE CHILIS RELLENOS

BATTER

1 CUP ALL-PURPOSE FLOUR
1 TEASPOON BAKING POWDER
½ TEASPOON SALT
¾ CUP CORN MEAL
1 CUP MILK
2 EGGS, SLIGHTLY BEATEN

CHILIS

12 LARGE GREEN CHILIES WITH STEMS, PARCHED, PEELED, AND SEEDED (OR THREE 4 OUNCE CANS OF WHOLE GREEN CHILIS)
1 POUND MONTEREY JACK OR LONGHORN CHEESE, CUT IN STRIPS
RED OR GREEN CHILI SAUCE

GARNISH

TOMATO WEDGES
SHREDDED LETTUCE

COMBINE FLOUR WITH BAKING POWDER, salt, and corn meal. Blend milk with eggs and combine with dry ingredients. Stir to a smooth batter, adding a little extra milk if necessary so that batter will cling to chilies. Set batter aside.

Open small slit in each chili below the stem and remove seeds. Fill each chili with cheese, using care to avoid breaking chili. Dip stuffed chili into batter using a large spoon. Fry in hot fat (420°) in an electric skillet until batter is golden brown, about 4 to 5 minutes. Drain on absorbent paper. Serve with chili sauce and garnish with lettuce and tomatoes. *12 chilies, 6 servings.*

Grants - Orange Front Soda Shop - Sanitary fountain service, electric sandwich equipment, Kodak supplies, sundries, Navajo rugs, curios, all tourist needs.
(old Arizona, New Mexico guide)
Thoreau, Crown Point Trading Co., Oldest trading post in this district, curios, operating Red Arrow Cottage Camp, Navajo rugs, Indian jewelry, tourists supplies.
(Old Arizona, N.M. guide)

Carrot fields covered the land between Grants and Bluewater after World War II. Now that the railroaders, miners, and farmers have left, Grants has settled down as a quiet tourist center.

About six miles west of Thoreau, the highway crosses the Continental Divide. At 7,275 feet, the Divide is the highest point on the entire length of Route 66. At one time, the Top O'The World Hotel and Cafe served tourists. Today, trading posts, a gas station, saloon, and gift shop greet tourists who stop to record their presence on camera and stretch their legs before hitting the highway again.

Nearby Fort Wingate has been a military reservation since Civil War days. From Wingate, travelers drive into the breathtaking red sandstone cliffs on the outskirts of Gallup. Zuni, Hopi, and

Navajo artisans trade and sell their fine arts and crafts around Gallup. The huge Navajo reservation that surrounds the city is the largest in America.

The doors to Gallup's fabled El Navajo Hotel closed to the public on May 11, 1957, and a wrecking ball leveled the hotel. This Fred Harvey masterpiece featured some of the country's best pueblo architecture and had been a classic stop since 1923.

Another old classic, the El Rancho Hotel, has been completely resurrected by Armand Ortega, a well-known community leader and Indian trader.

Formally opened December 17, 1937, the El Rancho has been a gathering place for the rich and famous for much of its life. The rustic two-story open lobby features a circular staircase, heavy beams, finely crafted Navajo rugs, and mounted trophy heads.

Autographed photos of many of the stars who have stayed at the hotel are interspersed with native art on the balcony walls. The hotel guest list reflects the many classic films made in the area.

Stop at the El Rancho to absorb a giant dose of history.

Have a meal in the comfort of the dining room decorated in Spanish/Indian motifs, and enjoy the unique menu, designed to honor the famous personalities who have dined in the hotel. Omelets are always on the breakfast menu. They come large and fluffy, filled with onions, bell peppers, ham, and cheese. Those accustomed to the New Mexican cuisine top the omelets with red chili.

Later in the day, meals often begin with baskets of tortilla chips and fresh tomato salsa.

ROUTE 66 SALSA

2 CLOVES GARLIC
2 TO 3 FRESH JALAPEÑO PEPPERS, OR TO TASTE
6 TO 8 GREEN ONIONS, CHOPPED
4 TO 5 SPRIGS PARSLEY OR CILANTRO
5 RIPE TOMATOES, PEELED
½ TEASPOON SALT, OR TO TASTE

DROP GARLIC CLOVES INTO FOOD PROCESSOR TO MINCE. Add seeded peppers, onions, and parsley and pulse until finely chopped but not pureed. Add tomatoes and process until tomatoes are blended but slightly chunky. Add salt. Thin with a little tomato sauce if desired.

Manhattan Cafe, Gallup, all American, regular meals, short orders, 24 hour service, special attention to tourists, come as you are, next to corner of 3rd and Coal.

(Old Arizona, N.M. guide)

Earl's Family Restaurant does a thriving business at 1400 East 66 Avenue. Earl Nelson, a Cherokee Indian from Oklahoma, opened his first restaurant in Gallup in 1947, calling it Earl's Park and Eat. "Earl's Park and Eat was so far out on the east side of town that Earl had to carry all the water for the cafe for quite a while," recalls Sharon Richards, who went to work for Earl in 1969. She and her husband, Maurice, bought the restaurant when Earl retired in 1974. In 1982, Sharon built a small restaurant beside Earl's, calling it Earl's Too. In December, 1990, Sharon and her family opened a new Earl's Family Restaurant and closed the two smaller eating places.

Sharon's sister, Ruth Scrimshaw, shares these recipes that have been in the family for years and are always on the menu.

EARL'S RESTAURANT SANTA FE CHICKEN SOUP

6 CUPS WATER
2 CUPS CRUSHED TOMATOES
¼ CUP CHICKEN BASE
2 CUPS PINTO BEANS, COOKED
2 CUPS CHOPPED MILD GREEN CHILIES, CANNED
¾ CUP CHOPPED COOKED CHICKEN
1 CAN (13½ OUNCES) TOMATO JUICE
⅓ TEASPOON BLACK PEPPER
SALT TO TASTE

COMBINE ALL INGREDIENTS and cook slowly for 2 hours.
3 quarts.

EARL'S CHOCOLATE CAKE

CAKE

2 CUPS SUGAR
½ CUP COCOA
2 CUPS FLOUR
2 TEASPOONS BAKING SODA
1 TEASPOON BAKING POWDER
1 CUP VEGETABLE OIL
1 CUP BUTTERMILK
2 TEASPOONS VANILLA
1 CUP WATER
2 EGGS, BEATEN

CHOCOLATE FROSTING

1 STICK MARGARINE
1 BOX (1 POUND) POWDERED SUGAR
2 TEASPOONS VANILLA
½ CUP COCOA
HALF AND HALF
½ CUP CHOPPED ENGLISH WALNUTS

COMBINE SUGAR, COCOA, FLOUR, BAKING SODA, and baking powder in a large bowl, stirring rapidly with a fork to blend. Combine vegetable oil, buttermilk, vanilla, water, and eggs in a separate bowl. Add liquid ingredients to dry ingredients gradually, beating to blend well. Pour into a greased 9 x 13-inch cake pan. Bake in a preheated oven at 350° for 25 to 30 minutes.

To make the frosting, melt margarine, stir in sugar, vanilla, cocoa and enough half and half to make spreading consistency. Sprinkle chopped nuts on top.
15 pieces.

In the center of the oldest historic section of Gallup and across from the depot is the Eagle Cafe, owned by Norman and Maryann Nomoto. A stop at the Eagle is a rewarding trip back in time. In 1919, the Taira family opened Kitchen's Cafe in the same location. Today's Eagle Cafe has the original porcelain-topped counter and tin ceiling that was used in Kitchen's. The beveled mirrors and neon signs have been there as long as Nomoto can remember. The building itself is almost a hundred years old. Kitchen's Opera House, once the social center of Gallup, stands empty above the cafe. The old stairway, sealed behind the cafe wall, hides ghosts from a different era.

Nomoto's grandparents bought the Eagle Cafe in

1945. They sold to Nomoto's uncle Tatsukawa. Now Norman and Maryann are third generation owners.

Nomoto says lamb stew is the most popular item on the menu, especially with his Navajo customers. The recipe was originally served by his grandmother, who made it without a written recipe. It took Nomoto and his cooks several months to reproduce the stew and he still can't write down exact proportions. "We just begin with forty pounds of lamb plate each day and boil it first to reduce the fat. Then we add vegetables — carrots, onions, celery, and tomato — along with seasonings, to the diced meat," he says. "We're still learning. It gets better all the time."

Nomoto works long hours and has a growing list of regular clients. He says business is especially good the first part of each month when his Indian customers are in town. During August Ceremonial time, there is never a moment to rest.

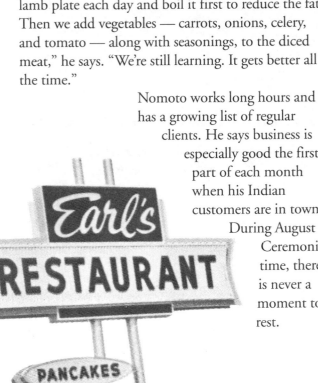

Stop at the Eagle, have dinner with Norman and Maryann, and enjoy the feel of this true Route 66 classic. Spanish Sauce is served with several dishes at the Eagle. Norman particularly recommends it over meat loaf.

EAGLE CAFE SPANISH SAUCE

½ YELLOW ONION, FINELY CHOPPED
2 STALKS CELERY, FINELY CHOPPED
3 TOMATILLOS, FINELY CHOPPED
1 TABLESPOON COOKING OIL
2 TABLESPOONS CHICKEN BASE
3½ CUPS WATER
¼ CUP LEMON JUICE
¼ CUP ORANGE JUICE
1 TEASPOON CHILI PEQUIN
1 CAN (8 OUNCES) WHOLE TOMATOES
CORNSTARCH TO THICKEN (OPTIONAL)

Sauté onion, celery, and tomatillos in a tablespoon of cooking oil until soft. Combine chicken base with water, lemon and orange juices, chili pequín, and canned whole tomato. Stir and heat, adding sautéed vegetables. Cook slowly for 15 minutes. If a thicker sauce is desired, blend a teaspoon or more of cornstarch with ¼ cup of water, add to the sauce, and heat through. *5 cups.*

Next door to the Eagle, Richardson's Trading Company and Cash Pawn, Inc. has been in business since 1913. The atmosphere inside reflects an earlier generation when Navajo families spent an entire day trading wool, blankets, and jewelry for food and clothing.

Gallup is known for its Navajo tacos. At the Ranch Kitchen, considered the home of this world-famous dish, Alice Joe has dished out her classic version for over twenty-five years. Earl Vance is the original owner and John Jewett has taken over management since Vance's retirement. Indian and Mexican arts and crafts provide a decorative theme at this vintage Route 66 eating place at 3001 W. Highway 66. The gift shops offer the distinctive massive silver work of the Navajo and the delicate turquoise mosaic jewelry of the Zuni. Here is Alice Joe's recipe for Navajo fry bread.

RANCH KITCHEN NAVAJO FRY BREAD

4 CUPS FLOUR
3 TEASPOONS BAKING POWDER
1 TEASPOON SALT
1¼ CUPS LUKEWARM WATER
2 POUNDS SHORTENING FOR FRYING

SIFT DRY INGREDIENTS TOGETHER. Add lukewarm water and knead dough for about 5 minutes. Cover with a towel and let rise 15 minutes. Heat about 2 pounds of shortening in a heavy skillet to 375 to 400°. Pinch off small portions of dough and roll out thin rounds 4 inches in diameter. Poke a small hole in the center to allow grease to escape. Drop rounds gently into hot fat and allow to brown. This takes only a few seconds. Turn over, and allow other side to brown. Remove from fat and drain on paper towels. Serve with butter and honey or use as a base for Navajo Taco. To make the Navajo tacos, top fry bread with chili, shredded lettuce, chopped onions, tomatoes and grated cheese. *Sixteen 4-inch rounds.*

During the second week of August, the annual Gallup Inter-Tribal Indian Ceremonial is held in Red Rock State Park. Tribes from throughout North America participate in four days of rodeo, tribal dances, and exhibits of the finest Indian arts and crafts in the country. Native American foods can be sampled on the park grounds throughout the ceremonial. The same park is host to a Southwest Food Fest in October. Area restaurants serve their specialties and recipes from local cooks are prepared and judged. Navajo Tacos are always available.

This Navajo Taco Chili recipe is shared by the Gallup Tourist Bureau.

GALLUP NAVAJO TACO CHILI

1½ POUNDS GROUND ROUND
1 POUND DICED LEAN PORK
1 CAN (8 OUNCES) DICED TOMATOES
14 OUNCES FROZEN DICED GREEN CHILIS
1 CUP COOKED PINTO BEANS OR LARGE CAN REFRIED BEANS
SALT AND GARLIC POWDER TO TASTE

BROWN MEATS SEPARATELY. Combine all ingredients together and add enough water to cover. Simmer for 1 to 1½ hours, adding a little water as needed. Let cool before refrigerating unless mixture is to be used right away. This chili can be frozen to be used at a later date.

To make Navajo Tacos, put chili mixture on fry bread. Top with diced onions, chopped tomatoes, shredded lettuce, and grated cheese.

Other long-time Gallup restaurants include Panz Alegra, the Butcher Shop, La Barraca Family Restaurant, and Virgie's. Pedro's Mexican Restaurant is a local favorite just a block off Route 66.

The final 16-mile stretch of New Mexico Route 66 continues west into Mentmore on state highway 118. Stop for the view along here — it's worth every minute! Watch a sunrise or a sunset, and breathe deeply in the wide open spaces. There is no ceiling over New Mexico! At Manuelito, cross under I-40 to the south side. Arizona is only a few miles to the west.

ARIZONA

ARIZONA. The high mesa country of Arizona lies basking in the sun for most of each year. Route 66 covers this dramatically beautiful desert plateau for 376 miles before crossing the Colorado River into California.

Much of the early Arizona Route 66 highway hype can still be found just inside the state line at Yellowhorse Trading Post, Ortega's, and the two-story concrete Tee Pee Restaurant.

To step back into another world, turn north at Chambers for a visit to the Hubbell Trading Post National Historic Site. Much of the merchandise is similar to what has been sold there since Lorenzo Hubbell founded it in 1876. Nearby Navajo and Hopi residents still buy and trade for supplies at the post and visitors will find a wide selection of hand crafted rugs, jewelry, and kachinas.

At the Petrified Forest National Park and Painted Desert, two parks in one cover 93,533 acres. There are at least six separate forests of giant stone trees among the multicolored rocks and hills. The restaurant at the park entrance is operated by the Fred Harvey Company, a subsidiary of Amfac, Inc.

The story of Fred Harvey is indelibly linked with Americans on the move, first by rail and later by automobile along Route 66.

On nineteeth-century railroads, it was common for passengers to carry their own shoebox lunches. Home-prepared food was preferable to taking a chance at unreliable and often dirty stops.

Fred Harvey saw his opportunity. He proposed the management of eating places all along the Santa Fe line and railroad owners liked his plans. His first restaurant was opened in 1876 on the second floor of a wooden railroad station in Topeka, Kansas.

The impact was spectacular. Fred Harvey restaurants quickly expanded to Winslow, Williams, and Ash Fork in Arizona, Albuquerque in New Mexico, and San Bernardino, Needles, and Barstow

in California. In each spot, Harvey provided culture and refinement alien to most of the rough-and-tumble population.

In Holbrook, one of Fred Harvey's earliest restaurants was housed in several old boxcars on a rail siding. Holbrook was changed forever by the arrival of trains, but the city still retains much of its dusty Old West flavor.

Holbrook's historic Navajo County Court House, built in 1898, has become a quality museum and tourist information center. The stop is worthwhile if only to see the original one-piece jail that was used until 1976.

Route 66 winds into Holbrook on Navajo Boulevard and makes a left turn onto Hopi Drive where Campbell's Coffee House once stood. The coffee house was a high school favorite that served great "son-of-a-gun stew." When the location became the Automat Cafeteria and Bus Stop, its owners advertised the first eating establishment of this kind in Arizona. Today, Aguilera's Restaurant occupies the corner.

Just down the street, at Joe and Aggie's Cafe, travelers can dine at a family-owned eatery that began in 1946 when Joe and Aggie Montano opened Joe's Cafe in old Holbrook. They moved to the present location, once the home of the Cactus Cafe, in 1965.

Joe and Aggie's daughter, Alice Gallegos, runs the cafe today, along with her husband, Stanley, and their son, Troy. It's the oldest restaurant in town still in business, perhaps because they continue to use Aggie's good Mexican and American recipes and maintain a warm and friendly atmosphere. "When we first moved in here, traffic out front was terrible," Alice remembers. "When those truckers put on their brakes to make the turn at the corner, they made so much black smoke that we would have to come in early to scrub the soot off our tables every morning."

Alice says she makes red and green chili sauce "pretty hot." She remembers one Easterner who came in and boasted that he had never found any chili sauce too hot for his taste. Alice brought out some of her best and he took a mouthful. When he could finally speak again, he admitted he had met his match.

Alice points out that New Mexico and Arizona

natives have grown up with the chili tradition and appreciate the taste that may be more slowly acquired by others.

To reinforce that all her food is not hot, Alice shares these easy directions for making cheese crisps.

JOE AND AGGIE'S CHEESE CRISPS

DEEP FRY A LARGE FRESH FLOUR TORTILLA UNTIL CRISP. Sprinkle well with grated Longhorn cheese. Place tortilla on tray in 350° oven just long enough to melt the cheese. As soon as the tortilla is removed, cut in wedges to serve. Top with chili sauce to make a Green or Red Crisp if desired.

Across the street from Joe and Aggie's Cafe, Julien's Roadrunner makes a good stop for Indian art. Take time for a visit.

Sim Yee's Sundown Cafe is another longtime Holbrook eating place that features good Chinese American food. The Roadrunner Cafe on Navajo Boulevard offers a wide menu with plenty of stick-to-the-ribs dishes.

During the 1930s and 1940s, Holbrook's Green Lantern offered some of the finest food found in this part of Arizona. Indian decor enhanced the comfortable dining room where homemade pastries and desserts were featured daily. Anna Scorse was the proprietress and for years she served breakfasts for a quarter and lovely dinners from fifty cents to a dollar.

For those seeking an upscale dining experience today, try the Butterfield Stage Company, an eating and drinking establishment owned by

CACTUS CAFE, 120 W. HOPI DR., HOLBROOK, ARIZ.
FIRST IN QUALITY AND SERVICE

Dusan and Violeta Pesut.

This exceptional restaurant has been enlarged and remodeled on the site of Holbrook's old Motaurant Dining Room. It holds singular appeal for those in search of the American rustic Wild West fable.

Pesut, a personable young native of Yugoslavia, has spared no expense in decorating the 10,000 square-foot restaurant that provides seating for up to 500 in its innovative dining rooms and bar. Although the actual Butterfield Stage Line ran far to the south of Holbrook, the restaurant captures a piece of history from the time of that famous transcontinental route.

An antique stagecoach sits atop the restaurant roof and life-sized mannequins of Wyatt Earp and Mae West greet visitors in the foyer. Each private booth focuses on a different "bad guy" from Western history and customized dishes speak to the quality service. Music from the 1940s and 1950s provides background with just the right nostalgic touch.

Pesut says he has always liked stories of the American West and wants his restaurant to reflect the unique ambiance of the area. "Europeans who come over here want to see things like the Grand Canyon and Tombstone," Pesut says. "We offer them a one-of-a-kind place where they can have a good time. I don't think they will forget us." Steaks and seafood are featured on the menu and the restaurant offers an extensive list of drinks. The skillful Navajo head cook who has worked at the restaurant for years prepares most of the dishes without the hindrance of written recipes, relying on experience and native skill.

The restaurant has been praised for quality

food and service in the *Washington Post* and *Los Angeles Times* and is a stop for Maupintours and other cross-country groups.

Wild West drink favorites at the Butterfield Stage come with appealing titles like the Lawman's Bullet and the Gun Runner. Here are the makings for a few others.

"CLAMITY" JANE

CLAMITY'S FAVORITE WAY TO COOL DOWN was with the refreshing fruit-filled taste of Smirnoff Vodka, Hiram Walker Peach Schnapps, and orange juice served over ice.

JUDGE ROY BEAN

AFTER ANOTHER HANG'N', the Judge always liked to relax with one of his favorite margaritas, a "lively" mixture of Jose Cuervo Tequila, Hiram Walker Triple Sec, Contreau, and citrus juices blended or on the rocks.

PONY EXPRESS-O

THIS ONE WILL MAKE YOU WANT TO GET ON YOUR HORSE and git-e-up: Espresso combined with Kahlua, Bailey's Irish Cream, and Grand Marnier.

Travelers will find another highway institution just a block from the Butterfield Stage Company. The Wig Wam Motel has been renovated and landscaped and once again invites enthusiastic children and their nostalgic parents to stop and spend the night in a tee pee. The Wig Wam is an inviting throwback to the heyday of Route 66.

"Holbrook, Rees Cafe, 24 hour service, regular meals, short orders, American owned and operated, cleanliness is our motto."

(Vintage Arizona/New Mexico Highway map)

Magnificent red cliffs and proud mesas adorn the skyline as travelers head west. At Joseph City, founded by the Mormons in 1876, the Western Hat Cafe stands behind boarded windows but the Cook Shack and Pacific Cafe have disappeared.

Five miles west of Joseph City, the Jack Rabbit Trading Post is doing business as it has since 1949. Highway signs still proclaim "Here It Is," and a freshly painted second-generation giant jack rabbit sits out front. Sweet cherry cider is for sale to soothe those with attacks of nostalgia.

Winslow is a Route 66 community that is proud of its past while planning enthusiastically for the future. The historic Beale Road passed through Winslow. Lt. Beale surveyed along the 35th parallel in Arizona back in 1857. One objective was to test the theory of using camels for desert transportation. The National Old Trails Highway followed much of the Beale Wagon Road. In 1926, the Old Trails Highway became U.S. Route 66.

SAN PASQUAL, THE PATRON SAINT OF COOKING

Winslow's excellent Old Trails Museum tells the story.

Fred Harvey's La Posada Hotel stands graciously next to the railroad in Winslow. Tommy Thompson at the Chamber of Commerce and Janice Griffith at the Old Trails Museum expect that a community offer to restore La Posada will soon result in an agreement with the Santa Fe to return the magnificent old hotel to the city as a tourist attraction.

Fred Harvey brought his genteel service to Winslow in 1877, but it was 1929 before the

60,000-square-foot La Posada was built as the most elegant hotel in the Harvey chain. Architect Mary Colter considered the project, which cost over a million dollars, her favorite. Along with La Posada, Hopi House, Hermit's Rest, and Phantom Ranch at Grand Canyon survive today as tributes to her talent.

If optimistic railroad executives could have seen the coming depression, La Posada would probably have never been built. But it survived through the hard years as a desert resort for wealthy winter guests like Charles Lindbergh and Gene Autry.

The dining room was best known for the heavy gold table linens that set off the hotel china, crystal, and silver. Arched windows looked out on gardens of lush flowers. An informal lunchroom seated 120 and was decorated in Spanish tile. The kitchen at La Posada was all electric and there was even a room where kitchen refuse was frozen to prevent odors and flies.

During World War II, more troops were fed and quartered at La Posada than at any other Fred Harvey stop. With the crowds, service had to be streamlined and many of the Harvey standards were relaxed. The first paper napkins appeared. When railroad traffic gave way to automobiles and airplanes, business dwindled and this once elegant hotel closed for good in 1957.

Today's classic in Winslow is the Falcon Restaurant that opened July 9, 1955. Owners Jim, George, and Pete Kretsedemas came from Greece by way of Alabama and joined an uncle in the Winslow business. For nearly forty years, these community-minded brothers have provided fine home-style meals to thousands of travelers and generations of local families. Their banquet room hosts local civic clubs and has seen countless state officials and a fair share of Hollywood celebrities including Joel McCrea, Richard Burton, and Fess Parker.

Back in 1953 Route 66 traffic was so heavy that Winslow became the first Arizona community to establish one-way highway traffic. Third Street carried the load west and original Highway 66, 2nd Street, became the eastern route. The Falcon is strategically located between the two.

"When we first began, I couldn't believe the highway traffic! People used to wait in line to get in here," Pete says. "I never realized how much we missed Route 66 customers until a few years ago when people began coming back searching for places they remembered on the old road. Now we have a lot of senior citizens and some of the younger generation who get a big kick out of finding places like ours."

Pete says it's actually shorter to drive through Winslow than it is to take the bypass that curves to the north, hiding much of the city.

When La Posada closed in 1957, the liquor license became available from The Bull Ring, La Posada's lounge. So the brothers applied and eventually added their own cocktail lounge next to the restaurant. Bull Ring furnishings came with the license so the Falcon Lounge still uses the original cash register from the old hotel. The lady bartender at La Posada came to work at the Falcon for another twenty-five years. Pete, Jim, and George remain among the few original restaurant owners on the historic highway and their enthusiasm for Winslow and Highway 66 is contagious. Pete says people are looking for America and realize more and more that the place to find it is off the expressway.

FALCON RESTAURANT BARBECUE SAUCE

Place the following ingredients in a 10-gallon pot:

4 MEDIUM ONIONS, FINELY CHOPPED
4 HEADS FRESH GARLIC, MINCED
2 CUPS FRESH SQUEEZED LEMON JUICE
4 CUPS SALAD VINEGAR
4 CUPS GRANULATED WHITE SUGAR
2 POUNDS BROWN SUGAR
2 CUPS PREPARED MUSTARD
2 CUPS WORCESTERSHIRE SAUCE
18 TABLESPOONS CHILI POWDER
12 TABLESPOONS GROUND CUMIN
2 TABLESPOONS GROUND THYME
2 TABLESPOONS GROUND OREGANO
3 TABLESPOONS CAYENNE PEPPER
6 TABLESPOONS BARBECUE SPICE
6 TABLESPOONS HOT DRY MUSTARD
3 TABLESPOONS SALT
1 TABLESPOON PEPPER
1 #10 CAN TOMATO PUREE
6 #5 CANS TOMATO JUICE
2 #10 CANS CATSUP

STIR TO MIX WELL. Bring sauce to boil then simmer for 1½ hours, adding a small amount of water as needed. Remove from heat and allow to cool. Store in smaller containers in refrigerator until needed. *8 gallons.*

FALCON RESTAURANT RICE PUDDING

2 CUPS WATER
¼ TEASPOON SALT
½ CUP RICE
2 CUPS MILK
½ CUP SUGAR
2 EGGS, BEATEN WELL
1½ TEASPOONS VANILLA
¼ CUP RAISINS (OPTIONAL)
SPRINKLE OF CINNAMON AND SUGAR

MEASURE WATER AND SALT INTO A SAUCEPAN, cover, and bring to a boil. Add rice and cook until water is absorbed and rice is soft. Heat milk and add to rice; stir in sugar. Beat eggs and stir in a little of the warm milk mixture. Add eggs to rice. Bring mixture to a slow boil while stirring constantly. Remove from heat immediately. Do not overcook. Stir in raisins if desired. Pour pudding into a 9 x 9 pan or individual dessert dishes and sprinkle with cinnamon and sugar to prevent a skin from forming on top. Chill and serve. *6 to 8 servings.*

Winslow is also home to two tiny remnants from the 1940s rarely found today — Valentine Diners. The prefabricated diners were built in Wichita, Kansas, after World War II and were numbered and leased across the country to meet the postwar demand for fast food.

National Cafe

Made of aluminum, the diners were built in seven or nine stool sizes. They were leased complete with stainless fixtures behind the counter and a payment box next to the door where the lease-holder could deposit the first fifty cents he made each day as rental money. Once a month, the Valentine man came by, unlocked the deposit box and took out the daily envelopes of cash. If the manager was short, the tiny restaurant was quickly closed.

On 2nd Street, across the street from La Posada, is Irene's. The tiny diner is still painted with the original red stripe on a white background typical of all Valentine Diners. Irene Archibeque, who runs the cafe, says she was a child when the diner was moved to Winslow in 1947. She and her friends watched as it was set into place. Irene's was called the Highway

Diner back then and did a thriving business with Route 66 and railroad customers.

Leon Dodd's One Spot Grill, at 114 East 3rd Street, has been painted grey. This old Valentine Diner was originally called the Birth Place Diner because it is located on the site of Winslow's first dwelling. Thelma Holloway was the first manager of the tiny eatery that once had a miniature stork perched on top in honor of the historic location.

The old Grand Cafe is gone today. In its place is the 2 Star Cafe. Felix Baca, owner of nearby Anasazi Gifts, says the best Chinese food in Winslow can be found at the 2 Star.

Winslow's classic National Cafe opened in the 1930s at 118 E. 2nd and served thousands of Route 66 customers through the 1960s. Harry Lee, the proprietor, kept the restaurant open 24 hours a day. Janice Griffith remembers the National as a high school hangout where young people inhaled huge plates of their favorite french fries with gravy.

Winslow also offers several other eating places with a touch of Route 66 history, including Joe's Cafe and the Entré Restaurant, both specializing in Chinese food, and the Brown Mug that serves good Mexican dishes.

Two Guns has faded into the desert. There's no one there at all. Older area residents tell of the time when the town consisted of three saloons and six houses of ill

repute. The land has recently been sold. Perhaps a new Two Guns will thrive again with tourist dollars.

Twin Arrows Trading Post, 20 miles east of Flagstaff, offers a small diner that was originally another part of the Valentine chain. Modifications hide its history but the owners supply a creative menu with offerings like jack rabbit ears and buzzard eggs.

Winona was made famous by song and was home to one of the first tourist courts on Route 66. Today, a surviving gas station and nearby house are for sale. Follow the old road through Townsend into Flagstaff or continue into the city on the interstate.

Thanks to Martin Zanzucchi and a group of enthusiastic Route 66 supporters, Santa Fe Avenue has been renamed Historic Route 66 in Flagstaff.

On the east side of town, Miz Zip's Cafe welcomes her regulars and an assortment of cross-country travelers as it has for almost thirty-five years. The big sign out front sports a perky little lady in glasses and the comfortable cafe behind the sign caters to a crowd that calls Miz Zip's their second home. It's a place where small-town ambiance is still alive and well, where folks feel comfortable and welcome. Four generations make up the Miz Zip story. Mom and Pop Lockhart started Miz Zip's along with her son and his wife, Bob and Norma Leonard in the late 1950s. Bob and Norma's son and daughter-in-law run the cafe today along with their daughter, Lauri.

In 1957, Route 66 was a two-lane street and the restaurant was considered "way out of town." A big plate of pancakes and syrup with a cup of coffee cost fifty cents and eggs, cooked to order, were fifteen cents each. "Not much has changed through the years but the prices" says Judy Leonard, who operates the restaurant today with her husband Craig.

"Colleen Schutte still bakes pies like she has since 1960, and a lot of other help has been with us for years." Many of the customers are regulars, too. Elton Turner, Jerry Brooks, and Don Nichols average twenty-five years of good eating with Miz Zip. Bill Drye, a Flagstaff old-timer, used to come by to reminisce about his memories of Pancho Villa.

During the 1950s and 1960s, drivers in the Great American Car Classic Run made the restaurant a regular stop. Vintage photographs line the walls of the little restaurant along with memorabilia from bygone days. Milkshakes are still made the old fashioned way and hash browns are made from scratch.

Many of the pie recipes came from Lila Lockhart's early kitchen. Stop awhile with Miz Zip. Judy and Craig Leonard will make you feel right at home.

MIZ ZIP'S COCONUT PIE

2 CUPS MILK
⅓ CUP SUGAR
1½ TABLESPOONS CORNSTARCH
2 TEASPOONS FLOUR
½ TEASPOON SALT
2 EGGS, SEPARATED
½ CUP COCONUT
1 TEASPOON VANILLA
2 TABLESPOONS SUGAR
1 SHALLOW 9-INCH BAKED PIE SHELL

MEASURE MILK INTO A HEAVY SAUCEPAN and heat to scalding point. Combine sugar, cornstarch, flour, and salt and add to the milk, whisking constantly. Continue heating until mixture begins to thicken. Beat egg yolks until smooth and golden. Whisk yolks into slightly cooled milk mixture after it has thickened. Continue cooking for just a few minutes.

Remove from heat and add vanilla and all but one tablespoon of the coconut. Pour mixture into pie shell. Meanwhile, beat egg whites until frothy. Add sugar and continue beating until stiff. Cover pie with egg whites and top with remaining coconut. Bake pie in preheated 425° oven until browned, about 10 to 15 minutes. *One 9-inch pie.*

MIZ ZIP'S BLUE CHEESE DRESSING

½ CUP CRUMBLED BLUE CHEESE
¼ CUP DILL PICKLE JUICE
¾ TEASPOON GARLIC SALT
1 SHAKE TABASCO SAUCE
1½ CUPS SOUR CREAM
1 CUP MAYONNAISE

COMBINE CHEESE, PICKLE JUICE, GARLIC SALT and Tabasco. Beat until smooth using electric mixer. Add sour cream and mayonnaise and continue beating until well blended. *3 cups dressing.*

Flagstaff's Museum Club, built by Dean Eldredge in 1918, originally housed his trading post and over eighty taxidermy mounts he had prepared. Eldredge constructed the huge log cabin around five live trees in the midst of a ponderosa pine forest several miles east of town. Today, those same pines, complete with branches, mark the four corners and center of the Museum Club's dance floor. The original inverted forked trunk of a ponderosa pine forms the entrance. The club was transformed from a taxidermy shop to a roadhouse in 1936 and received one of Coconino County's earliest post-prohibition liquor licenses. Locals affectionately call it the Zoo Club because of its years as a dead animal museum. Such Music greats as Willie Nelson, Waylon Jennings, and Bob Wills have appeared at the club.

Current owners Martin and Stacie Zanzucchi continue to restore and add to the contents of the unique building. In 1982 they added a 120-year old gilded and mirrored mahogany bar to enhance the Western atmosphere.

Lore surrounds the Zoo Club and ghosts galore haunt the place. "If atmosphere were measured like applause, the Zoo Club would send the needle off the scale," says writer Robert Baird. "The Museum Club is the kind of place people in Ohio imagine when they think of the Wild West."

A recent popular automotive magazine ranked the Museum Club among ten best American roadhouses. Don't miss this Route 66 classic.

MUSEUM CLUB NEON MOON

¾ OUNCE CAPTAIN MORGAN'S SPICED RUM
¾ OUNCE VODKA
½ OUNCE BLUE CURACAO

POUR ALL INGREDIENTS OVER ICE IN A TALL GLASS:
Fill the remainder of the glass with ½ orange juice and ½ pineapple juice. Garnish with an orange slice.

MUSEUM CLUB RED NECK

½ OUNCE SLOE GIN
½ OUNCE SOUTHERN COMFORT
½ OUNCE AMARETTO
½ OUNCE VODKA

POUR THE INGREDIENTS OVER ICE IN A TALL GLASS. Fill the remainder of the glass with orange juice.

The Kachina Downtown has been on the Flagstaff restaurant circuit for only seven years, but Frank Garcia opened his original Kachina at 2220 East Highway 66 during the heyday of Route 66. His cook for many years was known only as "Okie." Garcia retired only to discover he wasn't ready to quit work, so he reopened his original Kachina. His son-in-law, Randy King, is the chef/manager downtown.

In the heart of old Flagstaff, Fred Wong and his wife manage the Grand Canyon Cafe begun by Fred's father Albert Wong in the 1940s. The Grand Canyon is the cafe that has been in Flagstaff longer than any other with original family owners. Wong prepares Cantonese style food, but is best known for his chicken-fried steak. Albert Wong and his brothers did a thriving business in the heyday of Route 66. Many of the cafe guests were travelers returning from Las Vegas where they received silver dollars at the gambling tables. They paid for their meals in the heavy money and Fred remembers the older Wongs carrying weighty bags to the bank, wishing all the way that their customers would use paper currency.

GRAND CANYON CAFE CHICKEN-FRIED STEAK

BEGIN WITH FRESH CHOICE STEAKS. Dip the steaks in flour, then milk, and then cracker meal. Lightly salt and pepper. Fry in vegetable oil until tender.

Granny's Closet in Flagstaff captures the nostalgia of an earlier day in a comfortable atmosphere created by dark wood and subdued lighting. The decor might best be described as Southwest Victorian.

In 1974, the children of Frank and Sally Zanzucchi bought a Route 66 favorite, the Lumberjack Cafe. They named their new venture Granny's Closet in honor of their grandmother, Mrs. Ermelinda "Granny" Zanzucchi. The 20-foot Lumberjacks that stood at either corner of the original restaurant were donated to Northern Arizona University and now stand at the university's Skydome.

The restaurant has been enlarged and remodeled through the years and the best of American and Italian cuisine is served. Frank and Sally Zanzucchi operate Granny's today with several of their children.

They do much of the cooking themselves and use many recipes from "Granny" Zanzucchi's extensive collection.

"Both of Frank's parents were Italian immigrants," Sally says. "He came over before the turn of the century and she followed in 1912. They moved to Flagstaff and opened the Flagstaff Dairy in 1929. It was a family institution for 50 years. We're old-timers around here." Individual loaves of freshly baked bread have become a restaurant trademark, as have the deep-dish apple pies that are made in five-inch pie tins.

GRANNY'S CLOSET DEEP-DISH APPLE PIE

I #10 CAN APPLES, CANNED IN WATER
4 CUPS SUGAR
I TEASPOON SALT
I TABLESPOON CLOVES
2 TEASPOONS CINNAMON
¼ CUP LEMON JUICE
¼ CUP FLOUR
12 DEEP-DISH PIE CRUSTS

DRAIN APPLES AND COMBINE WITH SUGAR, spices, lemon juice and flour. Divide into deep dish crusts, top with circles of pie dough. Seal, cut air vents, and place on trays to bake in preheated 400° oven for 45 minutes.

DEEP DISH PIE CRUST

8 CUPS FLOUR
4 CUPS VEGETABLE SHORTENING
I TABLESPOON SALT
2 CUPS COLD WATER, APPROXIMATELY

BLEND SHORTENING INTO FLOUR WITH PASTRY BLENDER. Add salt and barely enough water to hold together. Handle carefully. Roll pastry into 12 circles to fit 5-inch deep-dish pie tins.

Save remainder of dough to roll and top pies. *Twelve 5-inch deep-dish pies.*

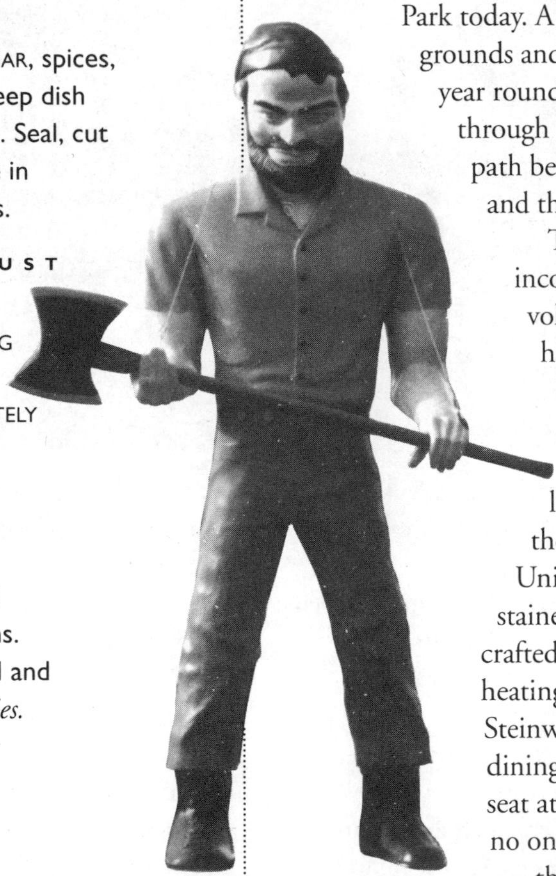

The Riordan Mansion in Flagstaff was built in 1904 by Michael and Timothy Riordan, prominent pioneer owners of the Arizona Lumber and Timber Company. After marrying two sisters, they built the 13,000-square-foot home and raised their families in spacious comfort. The unique structure had two nearly identical components connected by a common gallery.

Located next to the Northern Arizona University campus, the complex is an Arizona State Park today. A visitor's center is on the grounds and guided tours are available year round. When Route 66 came through Flagstaff, the highway cut a path between the brothers' home and the location of their mill.

The mansion's rustic exterior incorporates log-slab siding and volcanic stone arches with hand-split wooden shingles. The interior has forty rooms and much of it has been restored to reflect the lifestyle of the family during the early part of this century. Unique features include the stained glass windows, hand-crafted furniture, an unusual heating system, and a superb Steinway grand piano. One of the dining room tables was crafted to seat at least ten and designed so that no one could sit at the head or foot — the large table is pointed at both ends.

The kitchen contains an original iron cook stove and the families' turn-of-the-century cookware and dishes are on display.

Here is one of Caroline Riordan's cookie recipes, selected from her original collection.

RIORDAN MANSION OATMEAL COOKIES

¾ CUP BUTTER

1 CUP BROWN SUGAR

1 TABLESPOON MILK

2 EGGS

½ CUP CHOPPED RAISINS

2 CUPS OATMEAL

1 CUP FLOUR

½ TEASPOON SODA

½ CUP CHOPPED WALNUTS

CREAM BUTTER AND ADD BROWN SUGAR. Mix well. Stir in milk and eggs and beat thoroughly. Add remaining ingredients and stir to combine. Bake in preheated 375° oven for 10 minutes. *55 cookies.*

Grand Canyon can be reached from either Flagstaff or Williams. The classic trip today is by way of a 1910 steam locomotive that departs from the once-bustling Williams Depot and Fray Marcos Hotel each morning.

Commercial development at the Grand Canyon began in 1903 when the Santa Fe began construction of El Tovar. It was called the most expensive log hostelry in America and cost $250,000.

Fred Harvey

In 1919, when Grand Canyon became a National Park, the Fred Harvey Company became the official concessionaire. The hotel has always been the pride of the Fred Harvey system. The hotel is built of native stones and pine logs from far-away Oregon, and the interior is mainly peeled slab, rough wood, and tinted plaster. Charles Whittlesey designed El Tovar like a large country club-house with a rambling three- and four-story design containing nearly a hundred bedrooms.

Early guests were expected to dress formally for dinner, which was served in the nearly 90-foot-long dining room. Expertly uniformed Harvey waitresses served gourmet meals with impeccable service.

During those early years, railroad tank cars brought fresh water to the hotel from Del Rio, 120 miles away. Fresh fruits and vegetables were grown on the premises and the hotel even had its own dairy.

Through the years, El Tovar has been renovated, with the strict requirements of comfort and service to guests kept to mind. Those enjoying a stop at the hotel will leave with a never-to-be- forgotten experience. At the Fred Harvey Museum at Bright Angel Lodge, menus, pictures, stories, and examples of elegant Fred Harvey dinnerware and silver are all on display.

Frederick Henry Harvey was born in London in 1835 and emigrated at age fifteen to work in a New York restaurant for $2 a week. Harvey, more than any other person, has been credited with bringing civilization to the West. He provided all his customers the ultimate in service, including Irish

EL TOVAR

Fred Harvey
On the South Rim
Of the Grand Canyon

Tonight's Favorite

Chilled Fruit Supreme

Mountain Trout Saute Amandine

Julienne Potatoes
Canyon Salad Bowl

| Rolls | 3.25 | Beverage |

Cocktails

Manhattan	.70	Martini	.70
Gourmet Martini—Made with			
Imported Gin and Vermouth			.80
King Size Manhattan			1.00
King Size Martini			1.00

APPETIZERS

Jumbo Shrimp Cocktail .75   Fruit Au Kirsch .50
Tomato or Grapefruit Juice .25
Bismark Herring .50   Chopped Chicken Livers .60
Assorted Relish Tray .40
Antipasto .40   Cottage Cheese Mexical .30
Anchovy Canapes .45
Tomato Maderline on the Rocks .35

DINNER

(Tour 1-A Holders Are Entitled To Complete Du Jour Dinner)

Fruit Cocktail   Shrimp Cocktail (50c extra)   Chilled Tomato or Grapefruit Juice
    Chopped Chicken Livers   Melon Wedge (in season)   Bismark Herring
                                             or
          New England Clam Chowder   Chilled Consomme

ENTREES

	Entree	Special
FILET OF SOLE with Lemon Butter	2.25	1.75
ROAST SPRING CHICKEN with Wild Rice	3.00	2.50
FISHERMAN'S PLATTER with Fried Shrimp, Scallops and Halibut Steak served with a Special Sauce	2.85	2.35
BRAISED SWISS STEAK with Mushroom Gravy	3.25	2.75
ROAST ENGLISH ROUND OF BEEF Au Jus	3.50	3.00
BROILED LAMB CHOPS au Cresson with Chutney	3.95	3.45

(Entree Special Includes Vegetable, Potato, Roll & Butter)

Buttered Peas   Brussels Sprouts   Baked Potato   Lyonnaise Potatoes
          Tossed Green Salad, Choice of Dressing

DESSERTS

Hot Apple Pie with Cheddar Cheese   Layer Cake
    Berry   or   Cream Pie   Pudding
          Strawberry Sundae   Chocolate Sundae   Orange or Lime Sherbet
          Chocolate, Vanilla or Special Ice Cream   Swiss, Cheddar or Blue Cheese
    Beverage   Rolls

Steaks, Chops and Specialties

Harvey House Sirloin Butt Steak		3.50	Breaded Veal Cutlet, Milanaise		2.20
Broiled New York Sirloin Steak		4.00	Fried Deep Sea Scallops, Tartar		2.30
Filet Mignon, Mushrooms		3.95	Louisiana Shrimp Platter		2.75
Broiled Rib Lamb Chops		3.45	Pan Fried Mountain Trout		3.00
Broiled Center Cut Pork Chops		2.25	Fluffy Three Egg Omelette		2.00
Broiled Chopped Beef Steak		2.25	Broiled Baby Lobster Tails		3.25

Served with Baked or French Fried Potatoes, Tossed Green Salad, Rolls and Butter

Desserts

Snowball Sundae .45   Chocolate or Butterscotch Sundae .35
          Old Fashioned Strawberry Shortcake .50   Melon in Season .45
    Fresh Berries in Season .55   Assorted Pies .25   Layer Cake .25
Cheese, Assorted .50   Fruit Jello .20   Pudding .25
    Chocolate, Vanilla or Butter Pecan Ice Cream .25   Orange or Lime Sherbet .25

BEVERAGES: Coffee, Cup .15   Tea, Pot .25   Milk .15   Iced Coffee .15   Iced Tea .15
          Sanka .25   Postum, Pot .25

table linen from Belfast, Sheffield silver, and the best of food —unheard-of luxuries on the Great Plains. He delighted in serving quail and antelope killed along the route. He paid local boys $1.50 a dozen for prairie chicken and $.75 a dozen for quail. Upon Fred Harvey's death in 1901, the business passed to his oldest son Ford, who headed it until his death in 1928, when his youngest son, Byron, took over. Byron Harvey, Jr., followed his father and two grandsons, Daggett and Stewart Harvey, followed Byron, Jr. The Fred Harvey tradition at Grand Canyon is maintained today by Amfac, Inc. El Tovar's executive chef, Estebán Colon, shares this delicious recipe.

El Tovar Chicken and Shrimp Curry

1 TABLESPOON OLIVE OIL

1 TEASPOON CORIANDER SEEDS, TOASTED 5 MINUTES IN
DRY SKILLET

½ TEASPOON WHITE PEPPERCORNS

2 WHOLE CLOVES

¼ TEASPOON RED PEPPER FLAKES

1 TABLESPOON CUMIN SEEDS

2 TABLESPOONS CURRY POWDER

1 TABLESPOON CHOPPED FRESH GINGER

½ CLOVE GARLIC

⅛ WHOLE NUTMEG

1 TABLESPOON KOSHER SALT

1 QUART CHICKEN STOCK

1 CUP DRY WHITE WINE

2 CUPS HEAVY CREAM

4 TABLESPOONS LIGHTLY SALTED BUTTER

¼ CUP ALL-PURPOSE FLOUR

¼ CUP CLARIFIED BUTTER

4 WHOLE BONELESS CHICKEN BREASTS (8 OUNCES EACH),
CUT IN 1½ BY ¼ INCH STRIPS

1½ POUNDS MEDIUM SHRIMP, PEELED AND DEVEINED

HEAT THE OIL IN A SKILLET and add the coriander seeds, peppercorns, cloves, red pepper flakes, and cumin seeds. Stir to avoid burning. Add curry powder, tossing to blend. Place in spice mill or coffee grinder with the ginger, garlic, nutmeg and salt. Grind to a powder and set aside.

In a deep saucepan, boil the stock and wine together until reduced to 2 cups. In a separate pan, reduce the cream to one cup.

In a clean pan, melt the butter. Add flour and cook, stirring for two minutes without letting the mixture brown. Add the prepared curry mixture and the reduced stock and cream. Bring to boil over medium heat, stirring constantly. When sauce is thick and smooth, strain through a fine sieve into a clean saucepan.

Heat two tablespoons clarified butter into a large skillet and in it sauté the chicken, tossing until seared on all sides. Heat the remaining two tablespoons clarified butter in another skillet; sauté the shrimp for one minute. Add the shrimp to the chicken and sauté together for 2 to 3 minutes, stirring. Spoon the sauce over the shrimp and chicken mixture. Bring to boil while stirring.

Serve curry with steamed rice and Peach Chutney.
8 to 10 servings.

Williams, more than almost any other community on Route 66, seems to cling comfortably to the past. The small community was the last town to be bypassed as Route 66 came to an end. On October 13, 1984, the markers were moved and cross-country travelers could finally take a completely sterile route from Lake Michigan to the Pacific.

Six blocks of Williams' downtown business section is listed in the National Register of Historic Places. This section of "America's Main Street" takes visitors comfortably back to an earlier time and serves as an Arizona cousin to the popular TV community of Cicely, Alaska. Only the moose is missing. An Arizona deer or antelope could easily become a substitute.

At Old Smokey's Pancake House and Restaurant, good breakfasts are turned out wholesale every morning. The little restaurant maintains a rustic, mountain atmosphere with knotty pine walls and yellow gingham curtains at the windows. Jean and

Lyndol Barrett have run the busy restaurant for eight years, but it was originally owned by Rod Graves, who started it in 1945 along with Rod's Steak House down the street.

At Old Smokey's, eight varieties of homemade bread come out of the ovens every morning. Donna Stecher, one of the friendly waitresses, often has her good homemade candy for sale, too.

Down the street, the Little Fat Lady Cafe and Little Fat Lady II, are capably managed by Lucia Kreutzer who says her husband gave her the name when they were first married. Lucia doesn't have time to fit the image today — she is too busy. After 21 years as postmistress in nearby Ash Fork, Lucia has retired to manage her two cafes.

The original Little Fat Lady Cafe is in a corner building on Bill Williams Avenue dating from 1928. It was once home to Arnold's Cafe and later to Bowden's. After World War II, the place became a bus stop. Lucia's newer location has taken the place of the Coffee Pot Cafe.

The walls at the Little Fat Lady Cafe are lined with over a hundred photographs of singers and movie stars that Lucia's son has collected for her. An old-fashioned glass jar sits next to the cash register filled with giant-sized chocolate chip cookies. On the back wall, through the clear windows of an old-fashioned refrigerator unit, meringue pies wait briefly for takers.

Lucia specializes in American and Mexican dishes and serves some of the biggest cinnamon rolls in captivity. Daily specials are always available from five o'clock to ten o'clock p.m. and include such hearty temptations as "All you can eat" barbeque beef ribs," served with soup or salad, a choice of potato, vegetable, and garlic toast, all for $6.95. The atmosphere in both Little Fat Lady locations is relaxed and friendly. Waitresses are used to answering travel questions and making visitors feel right at home. Lucia says chili is always ready on the stove and shares these directions for brewing up her popular version.

LITTLE FAT LADY GREEN CHILI

DICE EQUAL PORTIONS OF PORK AND BEEF and fry separately in a large pan. Drain off any excess fat.

Combine the meat and add a little water, beef base, onion salt, garlic salt, and Lowery's seasoning salt. Simmer meat mixture until it is well done. Blend a can of whole tomatoes in the food processor or blender and add to the meat along with a can of Ortega or El Paso chilies. Simmer to blend flavors. Meanwhile, combine a small amount of flour and water and pulse in the blender until smooth. Add to chili mixture and continue simmering until flour has cooked. Add additional water if needed.

Rod's Steak House was established in Williams by Rod Graves and his wife in 1945. Graves initiated a tradition of quality food very quickly. Duncan Hines began recommending the restaurant by 1947.

The steak house trademark became the Bar Mary Jane brand that Graves used on his Hereford Ranch east of Williams. The distinctive brand came from the name of a friend and is still used on all the restaurant's advertising.

Today, Stella and Lawrence Sanchez own and operate the popular dinner spot that continues to be recognized for excellence in the *Mobil Guide* and *100 Best Restaurants in Arizona*.

The Sanchezes have continued to update the

restaurant while keeping the original appeal established by Graves so many years ago. "A lot of people eat with us who remember eating here as children or when they were on their honeymoon," says Mrs. Sanchez. "They are amazed to find us still in business and pleased that we have kept the same atmosphere."

Rod's Steak House is a long, narrow, rather unpretentious building that stretches for a block between Bill Williams and Railroad Avenues. With the kitchen in the center and dining areas on both streets, the restaurant makes the most of Williams' one-way traffic. The atmosphere is casual and comfortable and Mrs. Graves occasionally comes by to visit with customers and reminisce about the busy Route 66 days.

Ernest Lopez is head cook at Rod's Steak House. He originated this popular chowder that is one of the most requested recipes served at the restaurant.

ROD'S STEAK HOUSE MEXICORN CHOWDER

1 MEDIUM CHOPPED ONION
1 CHOPPED RED BELL PEPPER
1 CHOPPED GREEN BELL PEPPER
1 CAN DICED GREEN CHILI (ABOUT 6 TO 8 CHILIES)
4 CHOPPED ZUCCHINI
1 STICK BUTTER OR MARGARINE
2 TABLESPOONS FLOUR
1 CAN (8 OUNCES) CONDENSED MILK
3 CANS (11 OUNCES) MEXICORN, DRAINED
1 POUND GROUND SIRLOIN
SALT AND PEPPER TO TASTE
DASH CAYENNE PEPPER
1 POUND GRATED LONGHORN CHEESE

LITTLE TOWN

I Like To Live In A Little Town
Where The Trees Meet Across The
Street.

Where You Wave Your Hand And
Say "Hello"
To Everyone You Meet.

I Like To Stand F[...]
Outside The Gr[...]sip
And Listen To T[...]
Of
The Folks That [...]

For Life Is Int[...]
With The Frie[...]
Know,

And We Hear Their Joys And
Sorrows,
As We Daily Come And Go.

Sauté onion, pepper, chilies, and zucchini in butter or margarine. Add flour, milk, and Mexicorn. Sauté ground beef and drain any fat. Add to soup mixture and simmer for about 10 minutes. Add salt, pepper and cayenne. Simmer soup for another 20 minutes, then add grated cheese and allow to melt before serving. *12 to 14 servings.*

The Escalante Hotel opened around 1905 in Ash Fork, but there had already been Fred Harvey service in this railroad center for ten years. Harvey worked out an amazing system. At the last telegraph stop before a Harvey depot, the conductor would wire ahead with the number of customers. Then, at the edge of the yard, he would blow his horn, giving the chef time for last minute preparation. At the platform, a smiling porter would meet the customers with a brass gong and lead the way to the dining room. Harvey Girls would take over and offer the traditional impeccable service.

Today, Ash Fork looks like the flagstone capitol of the nation. The early railroading bustle has faded away and the community offers little more than memories for passing motorists. For hungry travelers, the Bull Pen Restaurant at Ted's Truck Center turns out food that will fill you up, guaranteed. Take a drive through town and imagine what this area was like just after the turn of the century.

Just past Ashfork at Crookton Road, drivers can access the longest existing section of Historic 66 in the country. The old road is well preserved and makes a relaxing drive through high desert ranch land, ancient volcanic outcroppings, and magnificent canyons. The highway continues through Seligman, Kingman, and Oatman to Topock for more than 180 miles.

Seligman is home to a Route 66 legend, Delgadillo's Snow Cap. Northern Arizona's most famous drive-in is operated by Juan Delgadillo and is located on the east side of town.

Drivers can't miss it. Juan's dry sense of humor and delightful collection of road memorabilia make the visit pure delight.

He and his wife, Mary, have run the Snow Cap for 40 years. It's a modest stand by drive-in standards, with doors on either side making it easy for customers to come in and order. But be advised, Juan has placed door knobs on the left and right of each door. The knob on the side with the hinges is "just for practice" Juan says.

Those ordering coffee receive a standard reply, "Today's coffee or yesterday's?" Juan offers mustard in a squeeze bottle stuffed with yellow cord. When he squeezes it toward a hamburger, the cord flies out. "Want a napkin with that?" and he will pull up a handful of crumpled but clean paper napkins. "They're only slightly used," he quips.

Juan serves standard quick-stop fare: malts, shakes, sundaes, hamburgers, "dead chicken," and cheeseburgers with cheese. He says he has never heard of a cheeseburger without cheese and dead chicken means just that — chicken nuggets or a chicken sandwich.

In front of the brightly decorated restaurant is a 1936 Silver Streak Chevrolet. From inside, Juan can turn on its musical horn to play "Yellow Rose of Texas" and more. He swears the car is air-conditioned and comes complete, decked with plastic flowers and a Christmas tree, ready for the town's annual Christmas parade or any other special event.

Juan's son has helped him with remodeling to display more of his collection and has recently repainted signs on the outhouse in back of the Snow Cap. May the visitor beware — enough said.

Juan's brother, Angel Delgadillo, can be found nearby at his barber shop and pool hall that also doubles as Seligman's Chamber of Commerce. Angel is the driving force behind Route 66 in Arizona and the founder of the state organization. His enthusiasm is contagious. Stop to pick up one of the excellent Arizona Route 66 Association tour maps or some other memorabilia and visit a while with Angel or his wife, Vilma.

On the west side of town, the Copper Cart serves hungry travelers "the best coffee in town" and prepares folks to set out west on the longest and best preserved stretch of Route 66 still in existence.

This section of road offers gentle grades and curves that make an easy drive. The area is filled with scenery only appreciated by those who take time to enjoy the countryside. Count the antelope grazing near the road or stop to watch the antics of prairie dogs as you head toward Kingman.

The Grand Canyon Cavern makes an interesting stop. The cave is twenty-one stories down by elevator and was discovered in 1927 when a young wood cutter nearly fell into the cavern. A nearby restaurant will fill you up after the trip.

Peach Springs once supported several cafes, including the Quamacho. Today the town of 800 is a trading center and headquarters for the Haulapai Indian Reservation that covers nearly a million acres next to the Colorado River.

A few miles down the road, stop to have a cup of coffee with Mildred Barker at the Frontier Cafe and Motel, Truxton. Mildred and her husband moved to the area over twenty years ago by way of two other Route 66 communities, Sayre, Oklahoma, and Grants, New Mexico. Mildred says Alice Wright built the original cafe years ago. "The story goes that Alice inherited some money in Los Angeles. A fortune teller told her to go 400 miles from Los Angeles and build a cafe," Mildred said. "So she got here to Truxton and stopped."

Alice's husband built the big sign out front and a traveling painter added the long-armed man that directs folks indoors. Mildred has had his image retouched and the friendly sign continues to lure folks to the good home cooking inside.

Mildred serves plain food, well prepared. Chili and beef stew are best sellers and cornbread is the standard accompaniment with either order. Here is her guide for preparing stew.

FRONTIER CAFE BEEF STEW

FOR A FAMILY-SIZED STEW, begin with about 1½ pounds of stew meat. Pressure cook the meat until tender.

Add diced potatoes, carrots, onions, celery, cabbage and a can of crushed tomatoes. Then add water to cover and some beef base for flavoring. Salt and pepper to taste and cook slowly until the vegetables are done. Serve with homemade cornbread.

The remains of Crozier, Valentine, and Hackberry break the descending drive into Kingman. This is powerful country with an ever-changing panorama of the Black Mountains in the distance. Highway 66 leads straight into Kingman. Army surveyor Edward F. Beale came through the Kingman area on his trip across Arizona with a caravan of camels to test their military use. Today Beale Street parallels Andy Devine Boulevard through the center of the city.

In 1937, the Lockwood Cafe in Kingman became one of the first franchised restaurants in the country when they added "Chicken in the Rough" to their menu. The concept snapped fingers at the Fred Harvey tradition of linen tablecloths and napkins. The dining style that involved devouring a hearty chicken meal in public without benefit of knife or fork inevitably overcame the more formal approach. When the cigar-smoking, golf-playing chicken trademark went up outside the Lockwood, "Chicken in the Rough" became an instant hit.

In the late 1930s, the Kit Carson Guest House, Santa Claus Inn, was opened a mile-and-a-half out of town. The small air-conditioned restaurant served a big farm breakfast for 75 cents. Santa Claus Acres was a new concept with novel buildings. The Santa Claus Inn specialized in Chicken à la North Pole and Rum Pie à la Kris Kringle. By the early 1950s, the Santa Claus Inn had taken a new holiday name, The Christmas Tree Inn, and Duncan Hines still considered it one of the best eating places along Highway 66 in Arizona. Today, two uniquely upscale restaurants offer Kingman diners quality service and outstanding food.

The House of Chan at 960 W. Beal is operated by Mary and Tommy Chan. Mary is a member of a six-generation Kingman family. Her great-grandfather, Lum Wo Chun, one of Kingman's earliest residents, came to Mohave County in 1884 to open a restaurant. Mary's father Charlie Lum was a prominent businessman and civic leader in Kingman who worked as a young man in his father's cafe, the White House, and later purchased and operated his own Kingman business, the Jade Restaurant. He also owned several other local businesses, including a Kentucky Fried Chicken franchise. Charlie Lum's formula for success was common sense, honesty, personality, and hard work. He always emphasized the hard work. When he opened the Jade in 1951, he often worked fifteen to twenty hours a day. The restaurant was the only one serving Chinese food in Kingman at the time and Charlie prospered. As a result, he returned much to Kingman and imparted a love for his community and a valuable work ethic to his daughter, Mary. He has retired and is living in Hawaii today. Mary met her husband Tommy Chan while he was working for her father at the Jade Restaurant. For several years, the young couple operated Kingman's Holiday House Restaurant.

House of Chan is located on the site of an old

Phillips 66 gas station. A piece of the parking lot out front is original concrete from the station. The menu includes some of the best Cantonese cuisine along Route 66 as well as charcoal broiled steaks and seafood dishes.

HOUSE OF CHAN SHRIMP EGG FOO YOUNG

3 EGGS
1 CUP FRESH CHOPPED COOKED SHRIMP
½ CUP CHOPPED ONIONS
½ CUP CHOPPED CELERY
½ CUP CHOPPED CANNED WATER CHESTNUTS
¼ TEASPOON SUGAR
¼ TEASPOON SALT
¼ TEASPOON PEPPER
¼ CUP VEGETABLE OIL

BEAT EGGS IN A MEDIUM-SIZED BOWL. Add all remaining ingredients except oil and mix well. Heat oil in skillet. Shape mixture into patties by dropping 1 heaping tablespoon of mixture into hot oil. Cook until lightly browned. Serve with any favorite gravy.

Note: Cooked chicken or mushrooms may be used in place of shrimp if desired. *10 to 12 patties.*

HOUSE OF CHAN CHINESE NOODLE SALAD DELIGHT

1 SMALL HEAD CABBAGE
1 GREEN ONION
½ CUP SLICED ALMONDS
3 TABLESPOONS SESAME SEEDS
1 PACKAGE (3 OUNCES) ORIENTAL FLAVOR SOUP MIX NOODLES

DRESSING

⅓ CUP SUGAR
⅓ CUP VINEGAR
1 CUP OIL
1 TEASPOON SALT
⅛ TEASPOON PEPPER
PACKET OF SEASONINGS FROM ORIENTAL NOODLE SOUP

CHOP CABBAGE AND ONIONS. Toast almonds and sesame seeds. Break up noodles with your hands. Combine ingredients and toss lightly to mix. Combine dressing ingredients and shake vigorously. Pour over salad. *10 to 12 servings.*

The 4th Street Social Club, Restaurant and Dinner House is a historic "must stop" in Kingman. Located in an 1899 building on the site of Lum Sing Yow's White House Cafe and the Kingman Drug Company, the restaurant has been carefully remodeled to reflect a charming turn-of-the-century eating establishment. The feel of another era has been captured in the lace curtains, stained glass, beveled mirrors and oak tables. A variety of dining chairs, collected individually to reflect a wide range of early period furniture, adds to the charm of the rooms. Antique chandeliers hang from the original pressed tin ceiling providing a kaleidoscope of light and the subdued green and white background contributes to a feeling of comfort and hospitality.

The soda fountain at the 4th Street Social Club was salvaged from a 1940 aircraft carrier and the drugstore counter is authentic, complete with old seats and original tile. The Social Club has been placed on the National Register of Historic Places and has won the Arizona Governor's Award for Historical Preservation.

Ron Robinson, Jr., and his wife Sue own this lovely establishment and Ron is chef.

4TH STREET SOCIAL CLUB BLACK BEAN CHILI

(NOT FOR THE FAINT OF HEART)

4 CUPS BLACK BEANS
2 TABLESPOONS CUMIN SEED
2 TABLESPOONS OREGANO
2 LARGE FINELY CHOPPED YELLOW ONIONS OR TO TASTE
1½ CUPS FINELY CHOPPED GREEN BELL PEPPERS
2 CLOVES GARLIC, MINCED
½ CUP OLIVE OIL, OR OTHER LOW-CHOLESTEROL OIL
1 TEASPOON SALT
3 CUPS CANNED CRUSHED WHOLE TOMATOES
8 SPRIGS FRESH CILANTRO
¾ CUP FINELY CHOPPED JALAPEÑO CHILES, OR TO TASTE

SORT AND CLEAN BEANS. Rinse well. Place beans in large pot and cover with several inches of water. Cover and bring to boil. Reduce heat and cook for 1¾ hours or until beans are tender. Add more water as needed to keep beans covered. Reserve 1 cup cooking water, then strain beans. Set aside. Place cumin seed and oregano in a small pan and bake in a 325° oven for 10 to 12 minutes until the fragrance is toasty.

Sauté onions, green peppers, and garlic in oil along with the cumin, oregano, and salt for 10 minutes or until onions are soft. Add tomatoes, cilantro, and chiles to the beans along with sautéed onion mixture. Simmer for 15 minutes to blend flavors.

Serve portions of 1¼ cups hot chili in a preheated bowl. Garnish with grated cheese and/or diced onions and fresh chopped cilantro to taste. This recipe freezes well. *8 generous servings.*

4TH STREET SOCIAL CLUB CANADIAN PIKE FLORENTINE

1 PIKE FILET, 7 TO 8 OUNCES*
½ CUP DRY WHITE WINE
¼ CUP BUTTER
JUICE OF ½ LEMON
4 OUNCES FRESH SPINACH
4 SLICES BACON CUT INTO 8 PIECES
¼ CUP FINELY GRATED JACK CHEESE
¼ CUP FINELY GRATED CHEDDAR CHEESE
1 CLOVE GARLIC, DICED
SALT AND PEPPER TO TASTE

HOLLANDAISE SAUCE

½ CUP BUTTER
4 EGG YOLKS, WELL BEATEN
2 TABLESPOONS LEMON JUICE
⅛ TEASPOON SALT AND PINCH OF WHITE PEPPER

PREHEAT OVEN TO 375°. Skin filet and cut in half to make two very thin fillets. In small pan, cook bacon until crispy and drain off fat. Add spinach and ¼ cup white wine and cook until spinach is tender. Drain. Place half of spinach mixture on each filet. Top with cheeses, then carefully roll each filet. Melt butter in a pan and add remaining white wine and garlic. Place rolls in pan, sprinkle with salt and pepper, and bake in preheated oven for 10 to 15 minutes or until fish is flaky. While fish is cooking make hollandaise sauce. Melt 2 tablespoons butter in top of a double boiler, then gradually pour butter into beaten egg yolks, stirring constantly. Return yolks to pan and place pan over hot water in double boiler again. Add remaining butter by tablespoons, stirring after each tablespoon until melted. Remove sauce from heat and stir in lemon juice, salt and pepper.

Place a little sauce on plate, place filet rolls on sauce and spoon more sauce on top. Enjoy!
White fish, such as sea bass or fresh water bass, may be substituted. 1 serving.

The Candyman, a relatively new resident on 4th Street, offers irresistible delights displayed in old-fashioned counters. Don't even try to resist your favorites. Places like this are almost impossible to find today.

The Historic Beale Hotel on Andy Devine Boulevard was once managed by this native son's father; and the old Santa Fe depot, built in Mission Revival-style, is a reminder of the city's railroading past. Jerry Richard, an avid Route 66 supporter and past president of the Arizona Route 66 Association, operates the local Quality Inn Motel and Route 66 Distillery. Motel guests can enjoy continental breakfasts at the Distillery and browse through one of the best collections of Route 66 memorabilia found anywhere. Arizona's Route 66 office is located at the Chamber of Commerce office in Kingman. The city's excellent museum is in the same block. Take time to visit both.

More and more old road enthusiasts are leaving Kingman on the corkscrew Route 66 road to Oatman. The drive should be taken slowly to absorb the spectacular scenery and Wild-West history.

Soon after the turn of the century, miners began to tear fortunes in gold from the ground around this area. Now, long-deserted mine shafts, stopes, and outbuildings are barricaded with barbed wire and "Keep Out" signs.

The remains of an old Route 66 filling station can be found about a mile before Ed's Camp comes into view. Fire agate claims can be picked up at Ed's.

You can't miss the blasted remains of Goldroad. The townsite, razed to escape taxes in 1949, was one of the first mining communities in the Black Mountains. Gold was found there in 1864.

Oatman sprang into being when nearly 8,000 miners, bartenders, cooks, assayers, and shopkeepers came in search of the $36 million in gold eventually mined from the area. By the late 1930s, the mines had petered out and Oatman rapidly declined.

A hardy group of desert-loving folks kept the town alive until tourists rediscovered the wealth in this rough wilderness. The community has come quickly back to life with a giant dose of history, some local residents to add color, and a small flock of

WELCOME TO THE "OATMAN HOTEL"
Breakfast   4.95
6 oz Steak, 2 eggs, hash brown, tst,
2 eggs, hash browns, toast
2.00
—Omelets—
Cheese omelet 2.50   Ortega 2.95
Chili cheese   2.95   Spanish 3.50
Bacon & cheese 2.95 Denver 3.50
Ham & cheese   3.50
Breakfast Burrito 2.50
Breakfast Muffin   2.25
Pancakes   2.00
Silver dollar pancakes 2.00
Pigs in a blanket   2.50
French Toast   2.00
—OVER—

hungry burros who roam the streets. Arts and crafts shops and plenty of good food complete the picture.

The two-story Oatman Hotel, where in 1939, Clark Gable and Carole Lombard spent a night on their honeymoon, now serves as the town's museum. At the bar/restaurant, on the main floor, dinner can be ordered at noon from a menu hand-printed on a paper bag.

Angie Moylan is one of the cooks at the Oatman. She says Burro Biscuits were on the menu there for years. This breakfast feast began with grilled English muffins topped with eggs cooked over easy. Cheese was melted on top and the biscuits always came with a side order of ham, bacon, or sausage.

Hot chicken wings are Angie's own creation. She rolls the chicken wings in a mixture of flour, black and white pepper, cayenne, and garlic salt before frying them up by the platterful.

The bar's walls and ceiling are covered with signed dollar bills. Scotch Haley, a friendly young bartender, says they amount to around $2,000. As Scotch tells it, the bills were collected through the years since no one was ever turned away while digging for "that lucky strike." Miners would just sign a bill and tack it up, promising to come back and pay up completely when they could.

The Oatman Hotel is Mohave

County's only two-story adobe building and is listed on the National Register of Historic Buildings.

Across the street at the Silver Creek Saloon and Steak House, Peggy Putnam presides over an establishment that was built with 8 x 8 beams from the old Victoria Mine. The beams were all under ground before 1900.

Peggy has lived around Oatman for over 30 years and is delighted with the increased tourist traffic. She has plenty of customers to enjoy her good cooking.

The saloon and steak house is dark with a low ceiling above the bar. Pictures of clients line one wall and the atmosphere is casual. A band entertains on weekends from noon till 6 p.m. Most tourists leave town by sundown since there aren't many accommodations and the road isn't exactly the best, either direction.

Peggy has been serving her own popular version of fry bread for years. Here are her directions.

SILVER CREEK SALOON MEXICAN WOODEN INDIANS

BEGIN WITH A RECIPE OF SWEET YEAST BREAD DOUGH. Make as usual and allow to rise a second time. Store in refrigerator until needed. Cook lean beef roast overnight or until very tender. Shred and season with salt, cayenne pepper, and spicy salsa that contains onion. For each Mexican Wooden Indian, roll out a piece of the bread dough ½-inch thick and 8 x 8 inches square. Place several tablespoons of beef filling in center of dough along with some Jack and Cheddar cheese. Seal dough by rolling it and pinching the ends so that the meat filling can't escape. It looks similar to a small rolling pin.

Carefully lower the dough into preheated fryer of vegetable shortening set at 350°. Cook for 3 to 4 minutes or until golden brown. To make sure the meat mixture is hot, put into microwave for another minute. Cut dough diagonally into 3 pieces and serve on a large platter surrounded with a bed of lettuce and diced tomatoes. Top with more salsa and sour cream if desired. *2 to 3 servings.*

Leave Oatman on the well-marked road down to Golden Shores and Topock. The old Route 66 river bridge across the Colorado River now supports a pipeline. Take the interstate into California.

CALIFORNIA

CALIFORNIA. Needles is a Mojave
Desert oasis that bakes under the
blistering sun most of the year. Bare
brown mountains form a jagged
rim to one side, while the
nearby Colorado River offers a
lifeline of water. Those who
love the desert find beauty in
every direction.

When I-40 replaced Route 66,
there were nineteen cafes in Needles to
serve the town's 5,000 residents and the
traveling public. Today, tourists come to enjoy
the river and dry climate and Needles continues
much as it did before the time of the interstate.
The 66 Burger Hut has been feeding hungry
roadies for over thirty-five years at the corner of
Broadway and D Street. The only thing new is the

name. Route 66 enthusiasts will remember the location as Irene's Tacos, Burritos and Hamburgers. A palm tree pierces the front awning where the owners cut a hole as the tree headed skyward. The small pink stucco drive-in offers no inside seating but customers at the windows don't seem to mind. Danny Bradshaw owns this drive-in classic today. Irene, or Rene to her friends, has been head cook on the day shift for over thirty years. Her sister Rita has been cooking at night for almost as long. Rene says it is the only place in town serving vegetarian food. "All the recipes served here are original," she said. In addition to regular orders for hamburgers, burritos, and tacos, Rene says she gets lots of orders for her Super Chimichangas.

66 BURGER HUT SUPER CHIMICHANGA

BEGIN WITH A 10-INCH FLOUR TORTILLA. Fill it with seasoned ground beef and cheese. Roll and fold the ends, much like an envelope. Secure the tortilla with toothpicks. Deep fry the chimichanga until lightly golden. Serve in a rectangular paper tray topped with refried beans, cheese, diced lettuce, and chopped tomatoes. Add sour cream and avocado if desired.

One of Needles' best kept secrets is a Mexican restaurant located in a tiny yellow building just a block off Broadway called the Rio Vista Cafe. Pete and Sophie, who run the place, keep the door locked much of the time, but just knock and you'll be made welcome. They are usually open for business from two o'clock. until seven o'clock p.m. each day, and they serve some of the tastiest Mexican food on the road.

At the Hungry Bear Cafe, owner Bob Dressel will share his enthusiasm for the old road along with his extensive collection of model cars, displayed in the back dining room. Bob has also assembled an excellent selection of posters and signs from the 1950s.

Bill McDonald turns out great pastry in the kitchen and the other friendly folks at the Hungry Bear will make you feel welcome. The cafe, established in 1965, can be found on the west side of Needles at 1906 W. Broadway.

El Garces was the Fred Harvey lunchroom in Needles. For years the restaurant never closed, offering air-conditioned service to desert-weary travelers who had 290 miles to face before reaching Los Angeles. Today it stands abandoned.

Traveling west from Needles, the old, old Route 66 alignment heads toward Goffs, population, 37. Goffs Country Store and Kitchen is a community center for a far-flung crowd of regulars. The first Saturday of every month the chairs and tables are pushed back for a country-and-western dance. The sign advertising the festivities says, "Real Americana - Real Pick and Fiddle."

During the week, neighbors stop by to catch up on local news over a beer or a cup of coffee. Bill DeWitt, a regular at the kitchen, says the best food on the desert can be found right here.

The Goffs Schoolhouse, built in 1914 and abandoned in 1937 after Highway 66 was realigned, has been reopened as a museum and is being restored. Dennis Casebier, chairman of the Friends of the Mojave Road, lives nearby and is a wealth of information on the desert.

To follow Historic Route 66, take the National Trails Highway from Goffs to Essex, then for another seventy-five miles to Ludlow. It's a quiet drive that gives an opportunity to appreciate the desert.

Essex, 16 miles southwest of Goffs, has a school and post office. Tracie's Cafe, in front of a giant car graveyard on the east edge of town, sports a badly faded wooden sign out front that offers food, sodas, pool, and games. In the dirty window is a placard: Closed. On the west edge of the tiny community, the old sign for Tony's Coffee Shop and Motel has finally

melted back onto the desert floor.

At Chambless Camp, Gus Lizalde is repairing and rebuilding a once-abandoned Route 66 stop with all the enthusiasm of a young entrepreneur.

Gus employs a young cook who prepares some of the best Mexican food you'll find on the road. The location is set across from the jagged Marble Mountains. Out back is a camp for Cadiz migrant workers who come in to harvest the grapes and lemons that are raised a few miles to the south.

Gus has plans for continued renovation, a small tourist court, and eventual recognition and appreciation from travelers for the good food he plans to continue serving. There is nothing pretentious here, but your stop will be rewarded with a warm welcome and a full stomach. Chambless Camp is a throwback to what Route 66 was all about.

CHAMBLESS CAMP SALSA

1 LARGE ONION, FINELY DICED
3 TOMATOES, DICED MEDIUM FINE
2 FRESH YELLOW CHILIES, MINCED
(ABOUT 2½ INCHES LONG)
3 TABLESPOONS CILANTRO, FINELY CHOPPED
DASH OF GARLIC POWDER
SALT TO TASTE

COMBINE ONION, TOMATOES, YELLOW CHILIES, and cilantro. Stir lightly to blend flavors. Add garlic powder and salt. Store in refrigerator until served. *2 cups salsa.*

CHAMBLESS CAMP GUACAMOLE

3 RIPE HAAS AVOCADOS
1 TABLESPOON WARM WATER
1 SMALL TOMATO, FINELY DICED
1 SMALL ONION, FINELY DICED
PINCH OF SALT

SPOON OUT AVOCADO PULP AND MASH. Add water to pulp and blend until soft and smooth. Stir in tomato and onion. Salt to taste. *2 ½ cups guacamole.*

On the west edge of the tiny community, the old Chambless Road Runner Cafe stands abandoned. The big faded sign can still be read, but looks as though it may not last much longer. Gus hopes to build a big sign of his own to replace the road runner landmark. With his plans and enthusiasm, the sign will be in place before long.

Herman "Buster" Burris has lived and worked in Amboy for 54 years. In fact, he owns everything in this community of twenty-seven people except the school. He remembers when his small desert oasis had a thriving population of some 500 hardy folks.

Buster's flourishing garage, cafe, and motel lost highway customers overnight when the interstate took the place of Route 66 in 1974. Roy's Motel and Cafe (named for his father-in-law) got pretty quiet, but Buster hung on because he loves the desert.

For several years, Buster tried to sell his seventy-three acre town, lock, stock and barrel. He and his wife even appeared on the popular "What's My Line" show. They stumped the panel, including their favorite star, Betty White, and took home a $2,000 prize when no one could guess they had put a whole town on the market.

But Burris says his ship is about to come in again. Or maybe it's his train. A consortium called Rail Cycle hopes to soon bring Southern California garbage via Santa Fe trains to a landfill eight miles from Amboy. At an age well past that when most men retire, Burris looks to the future because of trash. "We'll all benefit by it," he said. "Right now, I could use help and the more likely we get more people here to work at the trash site, the more people will come in and I'll be able to get that help."

Help is what Burris's wife wants, too. She wants them to be able to take off in their camper to see some of the country, even tour Europe. "But Buster has made friends from all over the world. They expect him to be here when they come through, and he loves this desert," she says.

The comfortable restaurant behind the gas pumps is a time-honored stop for travelers who prefer Route 66 to the hectic pace of the truckers on the interstate.

This chili recipe came from Burris' ex-mother-in-law and has been used at Roy's Cafe for years. Mrs. Burris insists the cooks follow it exactly.

ROY'S CAFE CHILI

20 POUNDS CHILI MEAT
2 #10 CANS TOMATO SAUCE
12 TABLESPOONS CHILI POWDER
6 TABLESPOONS CRUSHED CHILI
2 TABLESPOONS BLACK PEPPER
4 TABLESPOONS SALT
3 TABLESPOONS GARLIC
2 TEASPOONS OREGANO
2 TEASPOONS COMINOS (CUMIN)
15 TABLESPOONS PAPRIKA
8 CUPS DICED FRESH ONION
BEANS TO ADD LATER

PLACE THE MEAT IN A LARGE ROASTER in a preheated 450° oven to brown. Stir frequently until done. Add remaining ingredients and set oven at 375°. Cover and bake the chili for 3 hours in the oven. Freeze chili in blocks to be thawed and served later. Keep a fresh pot of beans on the stove to add to the chili just before serving.

Eight miles west of Amboy, the ghost town of Bagdad had several hundred turn-of-the-century residents. Bagdad was named for the Middle Eastern Capital in the late 1800s when the community was a mining and railroad center. Today, the only residents are assorted lizards, scorpions, snakes, and pack rats, hardy survivors of the driest spot on Route 66.

A "Bagdad" sign along the main line of the Santa Fe track is all that remains of the community where the last post office and school closed in 1923. A Harvey House Restaurant was established in Bagdad in 1887 but no one seems to remember when it finally closed.

The Bagdad Cafe is what most Route 66 travelers remember. Alice Lawrence owned the little cafe that was the only place for miles around with a dance floor and juke box. Folks with overheated cars ate at the Bagdad while their engines cooled and men from the mining camps and railroad were the regular customers.

The tiny town served as inspiration for a 1988 movie and subsequent short-lived television program, "Bagdad Cafe." Nineteen episodes were produced before the show was cancelled in 1990.

The interstate bypassed Bagdad but the community had died years before. The cafe, depot, and few remaining structures have disappeared under vandals' hands or melted into the hot desert floor. Today, only those who know where to look can find a few broken foundations and the shattered glass that once housed the hopes and dreams of early desert citizens.

At the A-frame Ludlow Coffee Shop, the aroma of good food drifts around the building and travelers know satisfying food will soon be served up in quantity. Ginnie Knoll and her family have operated the restaurant for a quarter of a century. Many Ludlow travelers are repeat customers who know they can expect quality at this small desert stop. John Knoll, Ginnie's brother-in-law, says the community grew up to serve the miners and railroad employees in the desert. The Knolls' family-operated businesses didn't change much because of I-40 since Ludlow is located where the interstate and Historic 66 (the National Trails

Highway) meet. With Needles 100 miles behind and Barstow fifty miles ahead, those needing help have kept Ludlow in business through the years. Heat takes its toll on travelers in the summertime and the Knolls and their employees are quick to recognize symptoms of heat stress, heart attacks, and other ailments. Help can be summoned quickly.

"The other problem we deal with frequently is lost family members. Parents drive off without their children and spouses leave their mates behind," Knoll says. One man in a camper drove all the way to Boron where a highway patrolman flagged him down and asked if he would like to find a wife. "I've got all the wife I need," he answered, before he was told that she had been left in the cafe restroom back in Ludlow.

The small wood frame home that was Mrs. Millet's Cafe during the 1930s still stands at the old Highway 66 intersection in Dagget. Mrs. Millet served travelers all they could eat for $1 a plate in the 1930s. The frame house with the unusual curved roof can't be missed. It is sadly in need of repair, but brings back many desert memories for those who once traveled this section of the historic route.

Across the Santa Fe tracks, the old Stone Hotel is being restored as a museum. Travelers can also turn off Historic 66 here for a six mile trip to Calico, a ghost town that has been refurbished to thrive again on tourist dollars.

Travelers who are searching for authentic movie history will find the Bagdad Cafe from 1989 film fame in Newberry Springs. The little cafe was called the Sidewinder then, but owner Dick Devlin has changed the cafe name to match all the publicity.

Krystyna Bingham, one of Devlin's friendly waitresses, says the cafe has been in Newberry Springs "forever." The location was originally a barn and eventually became a bar before Devlin took it over in 1977. Devlin has a good collection of old movie snapshots and memorabilia on the walls. The well-worn menus list specialties of buffalo burgers and stew. This is the same Dick Devlin who in the 1950s owned Shanty Devlin's on Route 66 in Cucamonga.

In Barstow, Route 66 enthusiasts return to I-15 to continue the trip over El Cajon Pass to San Bernardino.

Barstow's Casa Del Desierto Hotel and Restaurant is a stop filled with history. The Fred Harvey structure was built around 1910 by the Santa Fe Railroad. The very elegant Spanish/Mediterranean renaissance design featured tapestry brick and gray stone trimming with a red tile roof and arcade balconies on both floors. The restaurant was one of Fred Harvey's best. Barstow was the junction of all the Santa Fe lines from Southern California, San Francisco and the San Joaquin Valley. Casa Del Desierto was built on the "wrong side of the tracks," and for years there wasn't a bridge for Barstow citizens to get to the building without stair-stepping almost a quarter mile of rails.

Today, through efforts of the city, the vintage depot has had a facelift. Casa Del Desierto is a "must" stop in the desert. A coffee shop and dining room are in place again, there are waiting rooms for bus and train travelers and a well-stocked gift shop. The Western American Railway Museum is an added drawing card.

Other hotels in Barstow during the peak railroad years included the Beacon, Melrose, Drumm, Jordan,

2672   CASA DEL DESIERTO, SANTA FE HOTEL, BARSTOW, CALIF.

and Ray. During the late 1930s and early 1940s, the Beacon Coffee Shop was considered one of the best places to eat for miles. Air-conditioned, trim, clean, and offering excellent service and food, it was as popular with locals as with travelers.

Although off the Route 66 alignment, Idle Spurs makes a memorable eating stop in this desert community today. The restaurant offers an upscale dining experience where quality food and service is a habit.

Barstow's El Rancho Cafe and Motel has been a Route 66 landmark since the 1950s. Constructed partially from railroad ties, with stonework done by Navajo Indian craftsmen, the El Rancho was built to last. It remains busy today. The Village Cafe is another vintage eating place many travelers remember as a haven from the desert heat.

The highway curves southwest out of Barstow and heads toward the San Gabriel Mountains, passing through Lenwood, Hodge, Helendale, Oro Grande, and Victorville.

Victorville is a resort and farming center where many early-day westerns were filmed. The city is home to the Dale Evans and Roy Rogers Museum. A vintage 66 iron bridge crosses the Mojave River here. Joe's Cafe, topped with a giant baseball bat, has served customers for years on the north side of town.

About five miles south of town is a bit of 66 glitz transplanted from another time by Miles Mahan. A 20-foot high wooden hula girl stands paralyzed in the desert wind above an outdoor museum that includes at least a dozen bottle trees and a graveyard of old signs, trashy treasures, and discarded bits of wood covered with Mahan's distinct poetry. Here is a step into another world, an opportunity to meet a real live roadside attraction, and a reminder of fascinations that once dotted much of the old road. Newton's the Outpost was established on Route 66 at Highway 395 back in 1928. The original cafe and station has become the Outpost Wedding Chapel and a newer Outpost Cafe was built in 1964 when Route 66 became I-15.

Cajon Pass, the "Gateway to Southern California," has been used for almost 150 years. The San Bernardino Mountains form a breathtaking backdrop as drivers head toward Santa Monica and

the Pacific Rim. The Summit Inn can be found at the top of the pass on old 66 at the Oak Hill Road exit.

San Bernardino has been host to an Orange Festival every year since 1911. Old Route 66 through the city was once lined with juice stands and many travelers consider the orange juice stands among their most cherished Route 66 memories.

Will Rogers made his last public appearance in San Bernardino's California Theater in 1935. The theater, at 562 W. 4th, was built in 1928 by architect John Paxton Perrine. Designed with the art deco exterior so popular in that era, it has been restored and now features shows that reflect the golden past of Southern California.

Ray Kroc was a fifty-two-year old salesman for his Multimixer milk-shake machine when he called on Mac and Dick McDonald in San Bernardino one day in 1954. Kroc was fascinated with the sales techniques used at the McDonalds Drive-In. He watched and learned as customers lined up to buy hamburgers, fries, and milk shakes.

Kroc flew back to Chicago from that trip with a freshly signed contract allowing him to begin a

restaurant venture that ultimately changed America's eating habits.

Today, an old-fashioned arch stands on the corner of 14th and North E where the San Bernardino Civic Light Opera Association has their offices. A plaque commemorates that first McDonald's. The original building was razed years ago.

Across the street, a mom-and-pop Monster Burger Stand dishes out giant 8-inch hamburgers on homemade buns.

Back in 1949, the Mitla Cafe at 602 Mt. Vernon Avenue was recognized by Duncan Hines as having outstanding Spanish food. Hines praised the wide variety that included tacos, enchiladas, tostadas, tamales, chili con carne, chilies rellenos, and combination plates with fried beans and cheese.

The Mitla still operates in San Bernardino as does the vintage Mina's Cafe. Try either for a memorable experience.

The old Morgan's Cafeteria at 1049 6th Street is gone today but was considered the finest cafeteria in the area during the 1940s and 1950s.

From San Bernardino, continue west along Foothill Boulevard, a 60 mile trip to the ocean's edge. The old road took several circuitous routes through Los Angeles and its suburbs. Foothill, Huntington, Alosta, and Santa Monica boulevards are the easiest to follow today. Historic 66 signs are well placed in most of the metropolitan communities but traffic congestion can be a problem for the faint of heart. This is another time to forget being a road purist and explore and enjoy each distinct community as it comes along. The Wig-Wam Motel in Rialto barely survives as a seedy remain from the glamour

days of Route 66. Today's self-evident highway sign reads, "Do it in a teepee." Perhaps some entrepreneur will someday restore this old road classic.

Fontana is home to Bono's Restaurant and Deli where a true Grand Duchess of the highway has presided since 1936. The restaurant is a bit of inland valley history with roots in Sicily and a dream of the California grapes.

Mrs. Bono, who says her first name and age are not important, came to the valley in the 1920s with her husband and his parents to become vinyard owners.

Fontana wasn't a city yet and for miles, all one could see were vines interspersed with occasional groves of citrus fruit. Route 66 was a dusty path between the vines.

"Back then, it was pretty hard," she recalls. "My children would come home from school and say they needed a nickel for the cafeteria and I didn't have any nickels to give them. So I told my husband I'd do anything to help, I would stay out in the hot sun and wind and rain to make a few nickels."

So the Bonos set up a few tables and some umbrellas and she began her fledgling business. "This was Route 66 out here," she pointed; "the Greyhound buses used to stop and the children were in school and the men out in the fields and you can imagine the rush."

Orange juice sold at "ten cents for all you can drink." She also sold lemons for a nickel a dozen and grapes to those who wanted to make their own wine.

"My father-in-law used to go to Tama Trading in Los Angeles once a month to buy spaghetti and olive oil and tomatoes and things like that," she said. "I'd tell him, instead of buying half a case of tomatoes, buy a whole case, and instead of just a little spaghetti, double the order." She sold the extra in her little shed and soon began making Italian sausage. A small winery was the next addition.

"There was no living in grapes," she says. "The men would pick our grapes and store them under a shed by the railroad." Then they had to sleep there at night to prevent theft. The early morning freight train would stop for the grapes and her father-in-law would race to San Bernardino and catch the passenger train to Chicago or wherever the load was headed, unload the grapes, sell them, and return home. The years just before World War II were especially hard. Grapes sold for $7 a ton. "And there were always problems," she said. "Bugs, moles, or grasshoppers ate them and there was always sulfuring and weeding and keeping the equipment in shape."

"Our minds were made up though; our three children were going to college," she said. So the fields and the business were left to their parents. In 1957, the Bonos added the restaurant to their market and fruit stand.

Joe Bono has come home to run the business with his mother today. He left his law practice and job as a Deputy District Attorney to return to the land where he was born. "I love my mother, and family is important," he said. "I can always go back to practicing law."

Mrs. Bono says she makes spaghetti as it has been prepared for generations. "First, I brown the garlic in olive oil then add my homemade sausage and cook it slowly until done. I drain off the fat and always use Di Napoli crushed Italian-style peeled tomatoes in heavy puree. While the sauce is heating, I boil Costa spaghetti in lightly salted water and drain it when it's done. Then I pour the sauce over the spaghetti to serve. It's really very simple."

Joe says the old days on Route 66 are long gone. But folks eating at Bono's Restaurant in Fontana can recapture a little of the independent, entrepreneurial spirit in this authentic Italian restaurant, run by a strong, vivacious lady who has been serving Route 66 customers longer than anyone else on the historic road!

Fontana was home during the 1930s and 1940s to the Fontana Inn, set in the midst of a lovely garden plot where guests were invited to pick flowers. Meals were served much like those in a fine home. Chicken and steaks were the specialty and all the vegetables came fresh from the growers.

Rancho Cucamonga, in the "Valley of the Vines," was the center of early California wine production. The Mission Fathers of San Gabriel brought the first grape cuttings to the area in the late 1700s to provide juice for their sacramental wines. The plants formed the basis for a vineyard and winery that Tiburcio Tapia established in 1839. His winery was the first in California, and the second in the nation. By 1860, Thomas Winery owner John Rains had made his newly named winery the largest in the state. The winery's two 1400-gallon oak aging casks were not coopered locally but came around the Horn on a clipper ship.

Thomas Winery's production was enjoyed by Route 66 travelers until it closed. The Cucamonga Rancho Winery (Thomas Vineyards) was designated as a California Registered Historical Landmark in 1951.

Today the winery is the cornerstone of the Thomas Winery Plaza shopping center. A corrugated tin building containing the circa-1856 brick still is home to a gift shop. And the main adobe building houses a restaurant and museum filled with winery artifacts. A special section of the museum houses the California Route 66 Territory Visitors Bureau where information and maps are available to visitors.

Less than a block away, a fledgling Route 66 Cafe specializes in breakfasts and offers "good food and hospitality just like travelers enjoyed when the famous Highway 66 stretched across our country."

Within a mile, the remains of the historic Virginia Dare Winery have become part of another shopping center at Haven Avenue and Foothills Blvd.

In the late 1950s, at Foothill and Archibald Avenue in Cucamonga, Shanty Devlin's beer bar averaged sales of 110 kegs of beer a month. Shanty's was famous for good fellowship and fun, but even more, for the peanuts on the bar and peanut shells all over the floor.

Each October, Rancho Cucamonga hosts an Annual Grape Harvest Festival at the regional park. Thousands of guests flock to the celebration to enjoy food and sample wine provided by local vendors. A highlight of the festival is the Annual Grape Stomp where the public gets to jump in vats of juicy grapes and compete for prizes.

Near Archibald Avenue, the 1944 building that housed Dolly's Diner stands in disrepair behind boarded windows. Even the old sign is gone. Nearby, several service stations and relics of tourist courts from the same period can still be identified.

The Sycamore Inn of Rancho Cucamonga makes a nostalgic stop for those interested in Western history. The inn is located on the site of a tiny pioneer tavern and trailside inn that "Uncle Billy" Rubottom opened in the Gold Rush days of 1848. Once a stop for the famed Butterfield stage, the old inn was on the San Bernardino/Los Angeles road long before Route 66 came along. It was once a house of ill repute, and there are many stories that surround the inn, including the one about José Ramon Carillo, who died there in 1864 after being ambushed and shot on the road.

On the corner of the Sycamore Inn parking lot, a four-foot-high stone Oso Bear stands guard above a plaque that shares some of the area history.

Today, Sycamore Inn has been remodeled and redecorated to serve customers in an atmosphere of low light, dark red carpets, exposed wood beams, and cushioned chairs. The original stone fireplace is surrounded by tables covered with white cloths and friendly hospitality characterizes the inn. The Sycamore Inn nestles in the cool shade among some of California's largest sycamore trees and has been recognized in state and national guides for quality food and service.

Located across Foothills Boulevard, the Magic Lamp Inn is a brick and tile Route 66 vintage restaurant run by Tony Vernola. With oriental overtones, the building must have been constructed with Aladdin in mind.

The Buffalo Inn, "since 1929," is home to the Buffalo Burger as well as other casual favorites. A big wooden sign with a carved buffalo hangs out front and the coldest beer in town is served inside. A favorite with nearby Claremont college students for years, The Buffalo Inn is also a Route 66 classic.

Griswold's Hotel, Theater and Dining Center in Claremont all began back in 1909 when retired professor George Carter Griswold decided to prepare his mother's orange marmalade recipe to sell from his kitchen.

By 1915 Mr. Griswold had added candied fruit

to the business, built his first factory, and created new techniques that are still used in the candy industry today. In addition to marmalade, he produced candied figs, apricots, dates, orange peel, and watermelon rind.

Griswold built a series of stone cellars for storage and served hundreds of Route 66 tourists who stopped to tour and sample his quality products.

He sold the candy business in 1946 but retained his home on Foothill Boulevard, where he turned the front rooms into a gift shop that he operated until his death at age ninety-two.

Meanwhile, Alton and Betty Sanford bought his candy business, and capitalizing on the cellars, established Griswold's Stone Cellar where they sold jams and candies. To augment their income, they sold gallons of fresh orange juice to Route 66 tourists. They soon added a gift shop and hired a Swedish baker. Their baker suggested they use one of the cellars for a smorgasbord. The idea was so successful, they sold the candy business and concentrated on good food.

The smorgasbord soon outgrew the cellars, so they bought the Oxford Inn, diagonally across the street from the cellar location. This is the present site of the Griswold complex.

Griswold's Smorgasbord is the cornerstone for businesses that include a luxury hotel complex and the Candlelight Pavilion, a regionally famous dinner theater. The nearby old Claremont High School building has been renovated as part of the Griswold complex and houses gift shops, art galleries, and restaurants. All this from orange marmalade — a Route 66 American dream come true!

GRISWOLD'S MEXICAN-STYLE SQUASH

½ CUP ONION, FINELY CHOPPED
1 MEDIUM TOMATO, CHOPPED
1 TEASPOON VEGETABLE OIL
1 CLOVE GARLIC, MINCED
4 MEDIUM ZUCCHINI, DICED (ABOUT 7 TO 8 CUPS)
1 CUP DICED BREAD CUBES
2 TABLESPOONS WATER
SALT AND PEPPER TO TASTE
1 CUP GRATED CHEDDAR CHEESE

Sauté onion and tomato in vegetable oil until onion is golden. Add garlic, zucchini, bread cubes, water and seasoning. Simmer until just tender. Place vegetable mixture in 1 quart casserole, drain any excess liquid, and top with cheese. Heat in oven or microwave until cheese melts. *8 servings.*

GRISWOLD'S BRAN MUFFINS

MUFFIN SPREAD

¼ CUP BUTTER OR MARGARINE
6 TABLESPOONS BROWN SUGAR
6 TABLESPOONS GRANULATED SUGAR
2 TABLESPOONS HONEY
1 TABLESPOON WATER

MUFFIN BATTER

½ CUP WHOLE WHEAT FLOUR
¾ CUP CAKE FLOUR
6 TABLESPOONS SUGAR
½ TEASPOON SALT
½ TEASPOON CINNAMON
½ TEASPOON SODA
½ CUP RAISINS
2 EGGS
¼ CUP HONEY
¼ CUP OIL
¼ CUP CRUSHED PINEAPPLE, DRAINED
3 CUPS WHOLE BRAN CEREAL
1½ CUPS BUTTERMILK

CREAM BUTTER. GRADUALLY BEAT IN SUGARS. Blend in honey and water and whip until fluffy. Coat muffin pans liberally and evenly with mixture, using about 1½ teaspoons per tin.

Now prepare the batter. Combine flours, sugar, salt, cinnamon, and soda. Stir in raisins, eggs, honey, oil and pineapple. Add bran and buttermilk and mix until batter is smooth. Fill coated muffin tins ¾ full. Bake in preheated 400° oven for 18 to 20 minutes. Remove from tins immediately by turning upside down on cooling racks. *24 muffins.*

Today, Route 66 through Glendora is Alosta Avenue. For an interesting stop, turn north to the city's center on Glendora Avenue. It's an eight-block storybook setting right out of Alice in Wonderland. Perfectly trimmed trees and orderly shops line the clean street where old buildings haven't changed; they've just been spruced up.

Make your first stop at the corner of Foothill Boulevard and Glendora Avenue where Fenderbenders offers eats and drink in a bright red and white atmosphere right out of the 50s. Then take a walking tour of the circa-1925 buildings to see what a community can do to revitalize its image.

Azusa is the site of an early McDonalds, one of the few that survived modernization. It was built in 1954 before Ray Kroc took over the organization. The building lies deserted and abandoned where Route 66 curves from Alosta Boulevard onto Foothills. Just down the street, an attendant at a non-franchise fast food stand says he regularly points out his once-famous neighbor to tourists while they munch hamburgers and fries.

In Duarte, the Blvd. Cafe was operated by the Tomasian family for forty-three years. The original sign was only large enough to accommodate an abbreviation and by the time the Tomasians got around to changing it, folks had gotten used to the unusual name.

When the city bulldozed the cafe in 1989 to make room for a shopping center, the little cafe went out in a blaze of glory with free food and drink, speeches, stories, laughter, and tears.

At the Trails Restaurant in Duarte, soup has been served from a tureen ("all you want") since opening day, August 31, 1952. The famous soup is always accompanied by toasted garlic cheese sourdough bread. This spacious yet rustic family restaurant began when Bill Rinehart and Edith (Rinehart) Brothers remodeled a small office that had been created from two dining rooms, the Crossroads and Hideaway. Both had come to California in the mid-thirties, as children of farmers during the Dust Bowl era. Their food was simple American, and their goal was to serve "courtesy, friendship, and smiles." A menu board lists the daily specials as it has since the restaurant began.

Today, Edith still works in her beloved Trails kitchen. Her daughter and son-in-law Gala and Robert Basha and their daughter Aundrea make the Trails a three-generation restaurant.

This soup is one of their premier recipes, served regularly and often requested.

THE TRAILS
RANGE BARLEY SOUP

½ POUND ONIONS
I LARGE STALK CELERY, WITH LEAVES
½ SMALL GREEN PEPPER WITH SEEDS
2 LARGE GARLIC CLOVES
I TABLESPOON SALT
I ½ TEASPOONS PAPRIKA
DASH OF OREGANO
DASH OF ROSEMARY
8 CUPS WATER
I⅛ POUNDS LEAN GROUND BEEF
I CUP CANNED CRUSHED OR DICED TOMATOES
2 TABLESPOONS WORCESTERSHIRE SAUCE
I ½ TEASPOONS SUGAR
½ POUND THICK-SLICED CARROTS
I CUP PEARL BARLEY

COARSELY GRIND ONIONS, CELERY, GREEN PEPPER, and garlic in blender or food processor; do not puree. Add salt, paprika, oregano, and rosemary and let stand overnight in refrigerator.

When ready to make soup, add 8 cups of water and bring vegetable mixture to rolling boil. Add ground beef, tomatoes, Worcestershire sauce, and sugar to the boiling vegetables and return to boil. Add carrots and barley and return to a boil.
Cover container and reduce heat to slow simmer. Cook soup for another 2½ hours. Stir as needed and add water if necessary. If you prefer, simmer the soup in the oven at 325°. *8 generous servings.*

La Parisienne in Monrovia is the oldest French Restaurant in Southern California and maintains a reputation for quality and excellence. Rene Mariotti began the restaurant in 1958 and the current owners purchased it on his death. A 1979 fire caused the move to their present location at 1101 East Huntington Drive. Food at La Parisienne is Classic French. Owner/chef Julien Esperiquette specializes in nouvelle cuisine and light sauces. Quality is assured through personal attention to details.

Guests are greeted warmly by one of the owners and offered the ultimate in service in a cozy atmosphere of French floral wallpaper, lace curtains, fresh flowers, and immaculately laid tables. The restaurant is only minutes from nearby Santa Anita Race Track.

LA PARISIENNE
LEEK AND POTATO SOUP

I STALK CELERY
¼ POUND LEEKS (ABOUT 3 LARGE)
½ CUP BUTTER SALT, TO TASTE
2 POUNDS POTATOES, PEELED AND DICED
I QUART WATER
I QUART CHICKEN BROTH
½ CUP HEAVY CREAM
SALT AND WHITE PEPPER, TO TASTE

FINELY CHOP CELERY AND LEEKS (INCLUDING TOPS). Melt ¼ cup butter and add chopped vegetables. Reduce heat, cover and cook for 5 minutes or until leeks "sweat." Do not fry. Add water, broth, potatoes, and salt and pepper to taste. Simmer 45 minutes or until leeks and potatoes are very soft. Put vegetable mixture through sieve and return to pot. If too thick, add more chicken broth. Just before serving, add remaining ¼ cup butter and heavy cream and heat thoroughly. *8 servings.*

LA PARISIENNE POULET AUX FRAMBOISES

2 BONELESS CHICKEN BREASTS
½ PINT WHIPPING CREAM
3 TABLESPOONS RASPBERRY WINE VINEGAR
SALT AND PEPPER TO TASTE
LEMON
16 FRESH RASPBERRIES

REMOVE THE SKIN FROM THE CHICKEN BREASTS. Sauté and cook chicken breasts slowly for 15 minutes. Remove the grease and deglaze with vinegar. Add the cream; let reduce to thicken. Adjust the seasoning with salt and pepper and a squeeze of lemon juice. Add fresh raspberries to sauce and serve over chicken. *2 servings.*

LA PARISIENNE CRÉME BRULÉE

75 FRESH RASPBERRIES
RASPBERRY COULIS
15 EGGS YOLKS
1¼ CUPS SUGAR
2 QUARTS HEAVY CREAM
VANILLA TO TASTE
POWDERED SUGAR

PREPARE 15 RAMEKINS (3 inches in diameter and 1½ inches deep) by placing 5 raspberries and 1 spoonful of raspberry coulis (jelly or preserves) in the bottom of each.

In a large bowl, mix the egg yolk and the sugar. Beat until foamy and nearly white in color. Strain. Beat in cream and vanilla.

Pour approximately ⅔ cup of mixture into each prepared ramekin. Put ramekins into a bain-marie (a large pan filled with at least one inch of water) and bake in a 350° oven for 1 hour.

Allow the ramekins to cool for approximately ½ hour before sprinkling them with powdered sugar. To brown the sugar, place the ramekins in a dish filled with ice water and put under the broiler until sugar has browned. *15 servings.*

The very earliest routing of Historic 66 was on Foothill Boulevard through Monrovia, where the one-of-a-kind Aztec Hotel should not be missed. The Aztec was designed by Robert Stacy-Judd of Hollywood and completed in 1925 to be like no other hotel in the world.

This exceptional building is thought to be the first structure built in this country in imitation of Mayan architecture. Judd called it "Mayan Revival," since it incorporated design from Southern Mexico and Central America where he had traveled extensively.

The Aztec Hotel opened with great fanfare and for a few years was the most exclusive hotel in the area. But historians say it may have been too fantastic in appearance for success. Monrovian financiers, who had put up the money to build their hotel during the boom years of the early 20s, quickly became disenchanted investors when the hotel closed. The building was sold at auction for $50,000.

Since then, the Aztec has had varying fortunes. When nearby Santa Anita Race Track opened in the 1930s, the hotel was renovated and opened to host such celebrities as Bing Crosby and Mickey Rooney.

The old hotel is on the National Register of Historic Places and still retains much of its unique charm, even though it has become a bit tired with age. The hotel is home to the Brass Elephant Restaurant and Bar, thirty-six rooms, eight apartments, a patio, and banquet room.

The original tile floor remains in perfect condition and the dome-shaped windows are original. Stained glass, well-preserved murals, lighting fixtures, a unique fireplace, and Mayan sculptures remain. Stop by to take a look at this bit of history. There are many untold stories about this unique piece of Route 66 history.

BRASS ELEPHANT CARAMEL DUMPLING PUDDING

1½ CUPS BROWN SUGAR
1½ CUPS WHITE SUGAR
4 CUPS WATER
½ CUP BUTTER
2 CUPS FLOUR
1 CUP SUGAR
1 CUP MILK
2 TEASPOONS BAKING POWDER
1 CUP CHOPPED WALNUTS
1 CUP CHOPPED DATES OR RAISINS

MAKE A SYRUP OF THE FIRST FOUR INGREDIENTS by bringing them to a boil. Pour syrup into an 8½ x 11 inch baking pan. Make a soft dough with remaining ingredients by combining flour, sugar, milk, baking powder, nuts, and fruit. Drop by spoonfuls into hot syrup. Bake at 425° for 30 minutes. *8 servings.*

In the 1930s and 1940s, Monrovia was home to the Sportsman's Tavern, located at 1452 Huntington Drive. The lovely country house, located in a beautiful setting, served wild game raised on the premises. The restaurant was also noted for steak, chicken, trout, and frog legs. The Misses Wadsworth and Baker operated the exclusive stop that catered to the wealthy.

By the mid 1940s, 'Leven Oaks Hotel had become the glamour stop in Monrovia. The hotel was noted for homemade relishes, avocado cocktails, and quality ice cream. Famous celebrities made the 'Leven Oaks a popular stop as they headed toward Hollywood.

Sierra Madre was home to the Wisteria Vine Gardens that opened in 1938. The restaurant was six miles east of Pasadena, just off a very early Route 66 alignment. The glass-enclosed pavilion looked over a garden containing the largest wisteria vine in America, covering over an acre. The vine remains, but the elegant restaurant has been gone for many years.

St. Anthony's Greek Festival in Pasadena is held near Santa Anita Race Track and Colorado Boulevard on a late September weekend each year. The festival, which began over 30 years ago, attracts over 10,000 enthusiastic participants. The festival offers an opportunity to experience Greek art, music, food, and dance.

Route 66 traveled down the length of Colorado Boulevard in Pasadena, following the path of the Rose Bowl Parade.

Several popular eating spots from the heyday of Route 66 sported unusual names to catch the tourist eye. Most are gone today but memories linger.

Pasadena's Pig 'N Whistle at 412 East Colorado Boulevard was popular with home folks and visitors alike. It was known for satisfying entrees, salads, ice cream, pastries, and good coffee. Brotherton's Family Restaurant, run for many years by Jack Brotherton, was also popular with Route 66 travelers. The Stuft Shirt at 1000 East Green Street was modeled after wayside inns that used to dot the countryside in France and England. Squab, pheasant, and guinea hen were often on the menu.

Today, the Raymond Restaurant in Pasadena offers a nostalgic trip into the past for those who remember stories of the celebrated Raymond Hotel 100 years ago. The restaurant is located in the turn-of-the-century hotel caretaker's cottage and features fairy tale craftsmanship complete with hardwood floors, secluded booths, leaded glass, and candlelit patios, all in a wooded setting.

At the turn of the century, Walter Raymond lived in the cottage below his baronial hotel. Often called "The Royal Raymond," the dining room was considered the most sophisticated and elegant place to eat in the Pasadena area. Waitresses memorized orders and stood stiffly at attention, ready to comply with their guests' slightest whim.

In 1895 the elaborate hotel burned. Undaunted, Raymond built an even grander hotel with 300 rooms. The new establishment opened in December of

1901. He built the present Raymond Restaurant bungalow at the same time, living there and sometimes renting it to special guests who desired both elegance and seclusion.

Unfortunately, the Great Depression felled the Raymond. A mortgaging bank shut down the hotel in 1931, although Raymond and his wife were allowed to live in the cottage until his death in 1934.

During the following decades, apartments sprang up where acres of elegant flowers had once bloomed in the hotel gardens. "It's really a phantom hotel," Suzanne Bourg says wistfully. "I inherited a great deal."

Thankfully, the cottage remained, but by the late 1970s, the building was a shambles. When restoration specialist Roger Whipple bought the property, his careful remodeling brought back the magic. His partner, Ken Correira, opened the cottage as a restaurant in 1978. Suzanne and her husband bought the restaurant from him after falling in love with the unique ambiance.

Bourg sees to it that the service and cuisine at the Raymond Restaurant is as fine as it was in the original

hotel. The allure of the cottage today is its quality food, but customers also come back for the intimacy and elegance of bygone times.

THE RAYMOND RESTAURANT'S ROAST DUCKLING WITH APRICOT OR CRANBERRY SAUCE

DUCKLING

2 FOUR-POUND DUCKS
SALT AND PEPPER

APRICOT SAUCE

10 OUNCES DRIED APRICOTS WITH BRIGHT COLOR
GRATED PEEL AND JUICE OF 1 LEMON
1½ CUPS WATER
½ CUP SUGAR

POMEGRANATE GARNISH

1 POMEGRANATE

FOR THE ROAST DUCKLING, have butcher saw ducks in half lengthwise. Separate breast meat from rib cage. Cut wings at shoulder joints. Remove wing and breast from carcass, keeping it on one piece.

Cut thigh joints at lower back to release all meat from skeleton. Trim off wing tips, extra skin, and fat (save and roast with carcass the next day and use as the base for soup). Salt and pepper both sides of duck servings and place on large jelly roll pan, skin side up. Bake at 350° for about 2½ to 3 hours until skin is completely rendered and crisp, pouring off fat as it accumulates.

For the sauce, cook apricots and water over medium heat for 30 minutes until soft, but not mushy. Add sugar and lemon to saucepan; cook to dissolve sugar. Press mixture through strainer. Taste and adjust consistency, tartness, and intensity of flavor by adding more lemon, sugar, or boiling water. Makes approximately 1 cup sauce. Pool sauce generously under duck to serve.

For the garnish, peel pomegranate, remove seeds carefully. Scatter 2 to 3 tablespoons of the seeds over duck and sauce.

NOTE: Do not overcook the apricots or they will pass through the strainer too easily and the sauce will have a pureed texture without sufficient body. Do not pour the sauce over the duck because it will make the skin soggy. When adding extra sugar, make sure sauce is hot enough to thoroughly dissolve it.
4 servings.

CRANBERRY SAUCE (A VARIATION)

2 CUPS CRANBERRIES
½ CUP SUGAR
½ CUP RED CURRANT PRESERVES
½ TO 1 CUP WATER
1 GRATED ORANGE PEEL

Combine cranberries, sugar, preserves, and water in saucepan. Bring to boil and reduce heat, then simmer for 20 minutes. Remove from heat and stir in orange peel. Pour the sauce on service dish and spoon a small amount over each serving of duck. Serve with pureed parsnips and toasted almonds.

The Mother Goose Pantry, housed in a giant shoe, and Garmshausen's Bakery, on the north side of Mission in South Pasadena, are gone. But Gus's Restaurant and Cocktail Lounge has been serving world famous barbecue in South Pasadena since 1929. Ribs, chicken, and beef dip sandwiches are the specialties.

There were several old alignments of the highway through this area. It's best not to be a purist, just flow with the traffic and enjoy!

Barney's Beanery is located at 8447 Santa Monica Boulevard, just past the boutique and theater district. This old two-story converted Hollywood bungalow, with what looks like a near-original green roof, first opened in 1920. Barney Anthony was the early owner and made his mark with the chili and raw onions he served to the stars heading for the studio. Barney's has had a roller coaster existence. In the 1960s it was considered the ultimate hangout for the rock-and-roll crowd, then Hell's Angels discovered the retreat. More recently, newspaper reviews have referred to the old house that nestles between posh Beverly Hills and Hollywood as both a place of questionable taste and a great place to go slumming. Irwin Held has presided over the chili pot at Barney's Beanery for over twenty-four years and has recently enlarged his classic wood house. The old grape patio has given way to pool tables and naugahyde booths, and today's young patrons play video games. Over 200 brands of beer are available at the bar and the newspaper format menu is almost a collector's item. A stop at Barney's Beanery is a jolting reminder of the diversity that can be found along the old road.

Less than two miles away, Lem Quon's Formosa

Barney's Beanery

"BESTAURANT"
BAR
BAKERY
BREWERY

ur Favorite International or Domestic Brew on

Cafe has won a battle for survival against its neighbor to the west, gigantic Warner's Studio. Quon took over the reins at the Formosa Cafe back in 1945, but the tiny eatery had been a Route 66 fixture for years before that.

Quon grew up in Hong Kong, getting his first restaurant job at age thirteen. He specializes in quality Cantonese food, serving seafood and chicken dinners to an eclectic crowd.

The Formosa has been a popular stop for Warner Brothers employees since the old Samuel Goldwyn and United Artist Studio days and it would be shorter to list famous stars who have not eaten with Quon. The slightly scruffy little restaurant has a bar that almost fills one of its two rooms. The other is a 1902 Pacific Electric Railway car with low ceilings, dark wood floors, and red vinyl booths. The place is always crowded. Often called "Hollywood's last truly authentic watering hole," this smoky hideaway was a favorite stop for Elvis Presley and Marilyn Monroe. Rudee Valee once passed out at the bar after complaining that the drinks were too weak and Keenan Winn drove his motorcycle through the doors one day.

Dolores Restaurant began business in 1944 at Wilshire and La Cienega as a drive-in. Remember miniskirted waitresses sliding hamburgers onto a tray hooked to the car window? Remember long spiral Suzy Q potatoes? Remember the low prices? The Hollywood version of roller-skating waitresses disappeared with a Beverly Hills ordinance prohibiting drive-ins, so Dolores relocated at 11407 Santa Monica Boulevard.

Their food will take you back. Double-decker burgers come wrapped in burger-stand yellow paper, the chili is terrific, and the dinner rolls are huge and homemade. There are hot fudge sundaes and deep-dish apple pies ready to be topped with ice cream. It's the all-American dream of the good old days. Open twenty-four hours a day, Dolores is a place where you can close your eyes and reminisce. Dig in and enjoy.

DOLORES CHILI SEASONING

5 POUNDS CHILI POWDER
3 POUNDS PAPRIKA
1 POUND GARLIC SALT
1½ POUNDS SUGAR
1 CUP GROUND COMINO (CUMIN)
1 CUP GROUND OREGANO
½ CUP CAYENNE PEPPER
2 TEASPOONS BLACK PEPPER
½ POUND SALT
1 CUP GROUND INSTANT COFFEE

COMBINE AND STORE TO SEASON YOUR OWN CHILI. When ready to use, add to taste to chunks of your own cooked chili meat, tomato sauce, and beans.

Another giant dose of nostalgia can be found near Federal and Santa Monica Boulevard at Cafe 50s, located at a former A&W Root Beer site. Joey Rooney runs the little cafe where the walls and ceilings are plastered with great old movie posters. A vintage juke box plays oldies and blue plate specials are printed on a big blackboard next to the kitchen. The waitresses wear full circular skirts and bobby sox. Above the fountain, a sign reads, "We're only as good as the last meal we served."

Santa Monica, like Chicago, offers Route 66 travelers a wonderful array of food. There are hundreds of unique restaurants throughout this vibrant city on the Pacific Rim. Many restaurant owners mix California/light with ethnic favorites to provide creative dishes of exceptional quality. Gilliland's Cafe can be found on Main, only a few blocks from the termination of the historic route. The restaurant isn't old, but Gilliland's has Route 66 ties that make a perfect "all-American" success story.

Gerri Gilliland came to the United States from Ireland in 1975 for a three-month holiday. She traveled Historic Route 66 all the way from Chicago to Santa Monica, falling in love with our country, the bountiful Southern California produce, and the weather. She never went home.

Armed with a B.A. in home economics and a two-year degree in classical French cuisine, she knocked on the door of every cooking school in the Los Angeles area and ended up teaching, catering, and manufacturing her favorite plum pudding. The opening of Gilliland's at 2424 Main, just a few

blocks from the end of Route 66, was a dream come true.

According to Gerri, the food at Gilliland's is, "California/Southern European cuisine with a touch of the Blarney." Others call her creative style eclectic Californian with a multi-textural taste of Santa Monica. Her food is good, the style creative, and there is often a touch from home. Sunday nights are reserved for traditional Celtic harp music, lamb with mint sauce, and other Irish country favorites.

Route 66 became Gerri Gilliland's "Yellow Brick Road" to success.

GILLILAND'S SWEET POTATO TORTELLINI WITH BASIL CREAM SAUCE

FILLING

2 POUNDS SWEET POTATOES
1 CUP GOAT CHEESE
3 TABLESPOONS CHOPPED PARSLEY
2 TABLESPOONS CHOPPED PROSCIUTTO (OPTIONAL)
1 EGG YOLK
½ TEASPOON NUTMEG
½ TEASPOON SALT
2 TO 4 TABLESPOONS HEAVY CREAM
1 PACKET ROUND WONTON SKINS
CORNSTARCH

SAUCE

1 CUP BASIL LEAVES
4 CLOVES GARLIC
¼ CUP PINE NUTS
1 CUP HEAVY CREAM
SALT AND PEPPER TO TASTE

HEAT THE OVEN TO 450° AND BAKE THE SWEET POTATOES for 20 minutes. Reduce temperature to 400° and cook until fork tender. Remove; split and scoop out the pulp. Mash with a fork and add the other filling ingredients, taste for seasoning.

Place wonton skins out on a board and with your finger dampen the edges with cold water. Place a teaspoon of filling in each skin and fold into a half-moon shape. Then twist into a little hat by twisting ends together. Place on a sheet covered with cornstarch to prevent them from sticking. Do not cover with plastic wrap if you are making ahead and storing overnight.

For the sauce, puree the basil, garlic and pine nuts in food processor and add heavy cream. Season with salt and pepper and place in a small saucepan. Heat to boiling and cook for a few minutes to adjust consistency. Keep warm while cooking pasta.

Cook the wonton pasta in boiling water. When they start to rise to the top they are almost cooked. The filling should shine through the dough and become a bright orange color. Remove from water and drain well. Toss into sauce and serve at once. *6 to 8 servings.*

GILLILAND'S VIETNAMESE CHICKEN SALAD

4 WHOLE BONELESS CHICKEN BREASTS OR
8 BONELESS CHICKEN BREAST HALVES
1 POUND CHINESE NOODLES
PEANUT OIL
¼ SMALL RED CABBAGE, THINLY SLICED
½ NAPA CABBAGE, SLICED
1 BUNCH CILANTRO, CHOPPED
¼ CUP WHOLE ROASTED PEANUTS
PEANUT DRESSING

PEANUT DRESSING:

½ CUP RICE VINEGAR
2 TABLESPOONS CHOPPED GREEN ONIONS
½ CUP PEANUT BUTTER
½ TABLESPOON CHOPPED GINGER ROOT
2 TABLESPOONS SUGAR
2 TABLESPOONS SESAME OIL
½ CUP SOY SAUCE
2 TABLESPOONS CHOPPED CILANTRO

GRILL CHICKEN BREASTS UNDER BROILER 4 inches from source of heat until cooked on both sides, about 35 minutes. Remove skin and slice diagonally into thin strips.

Cook noodles according to package directions, drain and rinse in cold water. Toss with small amount of peanut oil to prevent sticking. Set aside.

Mix sliced cabbage and cilantro. Toss noodles with just enough peanut dressing to coat lightly. Place on serving plates. Top with cabbage mixture. Place chicken over cabbage. Sprinkle with peanuts. Top with more dressing or serve on side for dipping chicken. Combine all dressing ingredients. Blend well. Makes 1 ¾ cups dressing. *8 servings.*

GILLILAND'S BLARNEY CHEESE AND ONION TART

PASTRY

1¼ CUPS PASTRY FLOUR
PINCH OF SALT
6 TABLESPOONS (¾ STICK) CHILLED UNSALTED BUTTER, CUT INTO PIECES
2 TABLESPOONS SOUR CREAM

FILLING

¼ CUP (½ STICK) UNSALTED BUTTER, CUT INTO PIECES
1 POUND ONIONS, THINLY SLICED
3 OUNCES BLARNEY (AVAILABLE AT SPECIALTY FOOD STORES AND SOME SUPERMARKETS) OR FONTINA CHEESE, SHREDDED (3/4 CUP)
1 CUP WHIPPING CREAM
2 EGGS
2 EGG YOLKS
FRESH GROUND PEPPER
½ TEASPOON SALT
PINCH OF FRESHLY GRATED NUTMEG

FOR PASTRY, BLEND FLOUR AND SALT IN PROCESSOR. Cut in butter using on/off turns until mixture resembles coarse meal. Add sour cream and blend until dough just begins to come together. Gather dough into ball; flatten into disc. Wrap and refrigerate 30 minutes. Preheat oven to 350°. Roll dough out to ⅛ inch-thick round between sheets of waxed paper. Transfer dough into 9-inch round tart pan with removable bottom, discarding paper. Trim edges. Line shell with parchment or foil. Fill with dried beans or pie weights. Bake until pastry is set, about 18 minutes. Remove foil and beans. Bake until pastry is just beginning to brown, about 5 more minutes. Cool completely.

FOR FILLING, PREHEAT OVEN TO 350°. Melt butter in heavy large skillet over low heat. Add onions and cook until very soft, stirring occasionally, about 35 minutes. Sprinkle cheese over bottom of tart. Cover with onions. Blend cream, eggs, yolks, salt, nutmeg, and pepper in bowl. Pour over onions. Bake until filling is set and top is golden brown, about 40 minutes. Cool slightly. Remove pan sides. Cut tart into wedges. Serve warm or at room temperature.
6 servings.

In 1991, Gerri Gilliland and a partner opened Lula Cocina Mexicana, a few blocks away on Main Street, naming it for a famous cookery teacher in Mexico City. Gerri loves to travel in Mexico and opened Lula's to showcase traditional Mexican food and her own creations. The popular restaurant adds to the ethnic blend that makes so many satisfying choices for eating in this crown jewel at the end of the mother road.

LULA'S MAPLE BLUE CORN BUTTERMILK BISCUITS

2 CUPS COARSE BLUE CORNMEAL
2 CUPS ALL-PURPOSE FLOUR
2 TABLESPOONS BAKING POWDER
½ TEASPOON SALT
⅔ CUP MAPLE SYRUP
1⅓ CUPS BUTTERMILK
6 OUNCES BUTTER
2 EGGS, BEATEN

COMBINE CORNMEAL, FLOUR, BAKING POWDER, AND SALT in a large bowl. Mix well. Mix maple syrup with buttermilk and add beaten eggs and melted butter.

Mix into the flour bowl to a very soft dropping consistency.

Drop ¼ cupfuls of dough 2 inches apart onto a greased cookie sheet. Bake 15 minutes or until a pale golden brown. *16 biscuits.*

The premier hotel on Ocean Avenue is Loews Santa Monica Beach Hotel, just two blocks from the pier and Palisades Park. It is the only hotel located on the beach in the Los Angeles area.

The hotel's lovely centerpiece is a five-story contemporary glass atrium affording a spectacular view of the Pacific, yet including design details reminiscent of the Victorian era when Santa Monica flourished as a resort community.

Loews Santa Monica Beach Hotel is on the site of the turn-of-the-century Arcadia Hotel, one of the most luxurious in the Los Angeles area in its time. After the Arcadia was destroyed, several motels occupied the 2.7-acre site before this luxury establishment became a part of the beach skyline.

The hotel offers an innovative California-Italian menu in the Riva Restaurant and the Coast Cafe.

Chef Joe D. Cochran, Jr. oversees all the hotel's culinary endeavors. This pasta is his signature recipe.

LOEWS SANTA MONICA BEACH HOTEL PENNE PASTA IN SPICY SAUSAGE PAPRIKA SAUCE

12 OUNCES PENNE PASTA (COOKED AL DENTE IN BOILING, SALTED WATER WITH 1 TEASPOON OLIVE OIL)
1 TABLESPOON OLIVE OIL
1 TABLESPOON MINCED GARLIC
2 TEASPOONS MINCED SHALLOTS
12 OUNCES SPICY ITALIAN SAUSAGE
2 TABLESPOONS PAPRIKA
PINCH OF CAYENNE PEPPER
8 OUNCES CHICKEN STOCK, OR MORE IF NECESSARY
8 OUNCES HEAVY CREAM

¼ TEASPOON SALT
3 GREEN ONIONS, CHOPPED
6 OUNCES GRATED PARMESAN CHEESE
3 MEDIUM TOMATOES, DICED
2 TABLESPOONS FRESH CHOPPED BASIL
1 TABLESPOON FRESH CHOPPED OREGANO

G A R N I S H

4 SLIVERS SHAVED PARMESAN
4 SPRIGS OF BASIL
4 SPRIGS OF OREGANO

LIGHTLY SAUTÉ GARLIC AND SHALLOTS IN HOT OLIVE OIL. Add sausage and stir. Add paprika and cayenne and stir. Cook sausage completely. Pour off fat. Add chicken stock and reduce by half. Add cream and reduce by half. *Note: Sauce should thicken in bowl. If reduced too much, add small amount of stock (by tablespoons) while in pan.* Add hot cooked pasta and salt. Toss with green onions, grated Parmesan, diced tomato, chopped basil, and oregano. Adjust seasoning with salt and black pepper. *4 servings.*

LOEWS SANTA MONICA BEACH HOTEL ASPARAGUS WITH TOMATOES, SHALLOTS, AND PISTACHIOS

¼ CUP UNSALTED BUTTER
2 TABLESPOONS MINCED SHALLOTS
1 LARGE TOMATO, CHOPPED AND SEEDED
1 TABLESPOON FRESH PARSLEY, CHOPPED
1 TEASPOON FRESH LEMON JUICE
SALT AND FRESHLY GROUND PEPPER
1 POUND FRESH ASPARAGUS, TRIMMED
¼ CUP CHOPPED SHELLED ROASTED PISTACHIOS

MELT BUTTER IN HEAVY LARGE SKILLET OVER MEDIUM HEAT. Add shallots and sauté 2 minutes. Add tomato, parsley, and lemon juice and stir to heat through. Season with salt and pepper.

Meanwhile, cook asparagus in large pot of boiling salted water until tender-crisp, about 2 minutes. Drain well. Divide asparagus among plates. Spoon sauce over. Sprinkle with nuts. *4 servings.*

On the last block of Santa Monica Boulevard, there are at least six ethnic restaurants, all serving unique cultural specialties to hungry patrons. Ye Old King's Head Pub specializes in incredibly good fish and chips. Chinese, Thai, Greek, Italian, and French cuisines are also offered. Route 66 meets the Pacific Ocean on Santa Monica Boulevard at Ocean Avenue. On the corner, the Belle Vue Restaurant served discriminating customers from 1937 until it closed in December of 1991. The Belle Vue was a place where memories flowed easily, a place to contemplate the miles, to relive history, and to remember roads taken.

For years, the classic Belle Vue served moderately priced French bistro food at its best. The restaurant's signature dishes included poached garlic soup, chicken vol-au-vent with fennel and saffron, a classic chocolate mousse, and the "best bouillabaisse West of Paris."

A 1943 menu that was framed in the bar illustrated how times have changed. In 1943, abalone steaks were priced at $1.50. Now, abalone sells, wholesale, for over $31 a pound.

Ann and Jimmy Wallace established the Belle Vue and through the years, the restaurant had only three owners. Most recently, Stella Pilloni owned the Belle Vue with her son, Louis. The 1919 building was remodeled several times. The most recent changes brought French doors that opened to accommodate outdoor dining in the true Left Bank fashion — at a leisurely pace, with a view of the world going by.

By now, perhaps another tenant will have come along to continue the ambiance and tradition where Historic Route 66 had its California beginning and end. Louis Pilloni shares this favorite soup recipe, just as it was prepared during his years at the Belle Vue.

BELLE VUE FRENCH RESTAURANT POACHED GARLIC SOUP WITH MELTED BRIE CHEESE

90 GARLIC CLOVES
1½ QUARTS CHICKEN STOCK
BUTTER FOR SAUTÉING
18 LEEKS (WHITE PART ONLY)
12 LARGE POTATOES
SALT TO TAST
GROUND WHITE PEPPER TO TASTE
3 QUARTS CHICKEN STOCK
3 QUARTS HEAVY CREAM
DAY OLD SOURDOUGH BREAD
BRIE CHEESE SPREAD

BOIL THE GARLIC CLOVES WITH THE CHICKEN STOCK for 15 minutes. Let cool. Cut leeks ½ inch thick. Melt butter and sauté the leeks. Add potatoes, peeled and diced that have been salted and peppered to taste. Add to remaining chicken stock and simmer for 25 minutes. Add heavy cream and cook an extra 10 minutes. Add the garlic-chicken stock. Blend the soup and strain.

To serve, place hot soup into "au gratin" bowls. Top each bowl with one slice of day-old sourdough bread with brie cheese spread. Slide under broiler a few moments and serve. *6 quarts of soup.*

The closing of the Belle Vue is reminiscent of the passing of an epoch in the life of America's great lost highway. Changes occur but memories remain. Historic Route 66 can never be captured and held to one time. It remains a symbol of movement, adventure, and exhilaration, an icon of a more innocent time when a shining coast-to-coast highway first beckoned to intrepid travelers. It reminds us of a moment when a more leisurely pace encouraged long road trips rather than rapid jet travel, when people pulled up at roadside cafes from Chicago to Los Angeles to linger over steaming cups of coffee with newfound friends. It remains a living, breathing monument to the people who live along its many miles, and to everyone who ever sat behind the wheel — or in the back seat — and watched the wonderful sights roll by along the Mother Road.

BIBLIOGRAPHY

BOOKS

Deaf Smith County Historical Society, *Deaf Smith County History, Texas.* 1876-1981.

Edwards, Jim, Olephant, Mitchell, and Ottaway, Hal, *The Vanished Splendor, I, II, and III, Postcard Memories of Oklahoma City.* Oklahoma City: Abalache Book Shop Publishing, 1985.

Franks, Ray, and Ketelle, Jay, *Amarillo, Texas Postcard History, The First Hundred Years, I and II.* Amarillo, Texas: Ray Franks Publishing, 1986.

Hines, Duncan, *Adventures in Good Cooking and the Art of Carving.* Bowling Green, Kentucky, Adventures in Good Eating, Inc. 1951, 1957.

Hines, Duncan, *Adventures in Good Eating.* Bowling Green, Kentucky, Adventures in Good Eating, Inc. 1940, 1947, and 1949.

Kittel, Gerd, *Diners, People and Places.* New York: Thames and Hudson, 1990.

Kroc, Ray, with Anderson, Robert, *The Making of McDonalds.* Chicago: Henry Regnery Co., 1977.

Mayor's Office of Special Events, City of Chicago, *Taste of Chicago Cookbook.* 1990.

Mariani's Coast to Coast Dining Guide. Times Books, 1986.

Noe, Sally, *Greetings From Gallup, Six Decades of Route 66.* Gallup Downtown Development Group, 1991.

Murphy, Rosalea, *The Pink Adobe Cookbook.* New York: Dell Publishing, 1988.

Poling-Kempes, Lesley, *The Harvey Girls, Women Who Opened the West.* New York: Paragon House, 1989.

Rittenhouse, Jack D., *A Guide Book to Route 66* (a facsimile of the 1946 first edition). Albuquerque: University of New Mexico Press, 1989.

Rodrequez and Miller, *The Interstate Gourmet, Texas and the Southwest.* New York: Summit Books, 1986.

Scott, Quinta, and Susan Croce Kelly, *Route 66: The Highway and Its People.* Norman: University of Oklahoma Press, 1988.

Snyder, Tom, A. *A Route 66 Traveler's Guide: A Roadside Companion.* New York: St. Martin's Press, 1990.

Stern, Jane and Michael, *Good Food.* New York: Alfred A. Knopf, 1983.

Teague, Tom, *Searching for 66.* Springfield, Illinois: Samizdat House, 1991.

United Methodist Women, McLean, Texas, *Cruisine Down Old Route 66.* Self-published, 1990.

Wallis, Michael, *Route 66, The Mother Road.* New York: St. Martin's Press, 1990.

MAGAZINES

Baird, Robert, "The Arizona Roadhouse." Phoenix, Arizona *New Times,* February 26-March 3, 1992.

Cameron, S.M., "La Tertulia, Good Food in Good Surroundings." *New Mexico Magazine,* January, 1978, pp. 34-35.

Cravins, Gwyneth, "Our Footloose Correspondents, The M & J Sanitary Tortilla Factory." *New Yorker,* August 6, 1984.

Farrell, Robert J., "Route 66, The Melody Lingers On." *Arizona Highways,* March, 1988, pp. 34-41.

Griffiths, Therese, "Southern Elegance in New Mexico." *New Mexico Magazine,* January, 1981, p. 28.

Hillerson, K., "Roadside Attractions Give Character to 66 Towns." *New Mexico Magazine,* February, 1989, pp. 51-52.

Kennedy, Nancy, "Favorite Restaurant Recipes, the Ranch Kitchen." *Ford Times,* June, 1985, p. 44.

King, Scottie, "Bus Stop on Route 66." *New Mexico Magazine,* June 1983. pp. 16-17.

Long, John and Betty, "The Shed Restaurant." *Country Folk Art Magazine,* summer, 1989.

Phillips, Aileen Paul, "A Santa Fe Classic, The Pink Adobe." *New Mexico Magazine,* June, 1979, pp. 39-40.

RECIPE INDEX

INDEX OF NAMES AND PLACES